RELIGION, FAMILY, AND THE LIFE COURSE

RELIGION, FAMILY, AND THE LIFE COURSE

Explorations in the Social History of Early America

GERALD F. MORAN

AND

MARIS A. VINOVSKIS

Ann Arbor

THE UNIVERSITY OF MICHIGAN PRESS

1995   1994   1993   1992   4   3   2   1

Library of Congress Cataloging-in-Publication Data

Moran, Gerald F. (Gerald Francis), 1942–
    Religion, family, and the life course : explorations in the social
history of early America / Gerald F. Moran and Maris A. Vinovskis.
        p.   cm.
    Includes bibliographical references and index.
    ISBN 0-472-10312-1 (alk. paper)
    1. Family—United States—Religious life—History. 2. Sociology,
Christian—United States—History.   I. Vinovskis, Maris.
II. Title.
BV4526.2.M588   1992
261.8′3585—dc20   92-3309
                                                              CIP

for Marian and Mary,
—tennis widows—

Acknowledgments

During the course of writing the original essays, we were indebted to many different scholars who generously took the time to provide us with their thoughtful and perceptive comments. Among the individuals who assisted us on one or more of the essays were Andrew Achenbaum, Peter Amann, Timothy Breen, Georgia Bumgardner, Elaine Clark, Mary Kay Carter, John Demos, Ronald Formisano, Victoria Getis, Philip Greven, John Hagen, Tamara Hareven, John Hench, David Hollinger, Bob Ketterlinus, John King, Michael Lamb, Kenneth Lockridge, Mark Noll, Martin Pernick, John Shy, Kathryn Sklar, Alice Smuts, Bob Smuts, Leslie Tentler, Tom Tentler, James Turner, James Walsh, and John Zeugner. In addition, we would like to thank the two readers for the University of Michigan Press, John Shy and Philip Greven, for their helpful criticisms and suggestions, and also Joyce Harrison, editor of the Press, for her very able assistance.

Erik Seeman has played a very key role in this project in reformatting the footnotes, compiling the bibliography, and doing the index. He has also provided us with useful suggestions and corrections through the entire text.

The book is dedicated to our wives, Marian Moran and Mary Vinovskis, who have not only encouraged and supported our individual and collaborative scholarly work but have also usually listened good-naturedly to our incessant complaints about the futility of mastering tennis. Testimony to their good humor and patience is the longevity of our marriages, which have both just celebrated silver anniversaries.

Gerald Moran would also like to thank his mother, Shirley B. Moran, for her unstinting encouragement and his mother-in-law, Vincenza Bedetta, and his children, Erika, David, and Jennifer, for their patience. Maris Vinovskis would like to thank his mother-in-law, Elizabeth Dahlenburg, for her continued support and understanding.

Contents

Introduction

These essays, published over the last fifteen years, explore the social history of early American religion in the light of the family and the life course.[1] A belief in the efficacy of the social study of religion in past time and an interest in the relationship of religion to society in colonial America have been staples of our friendship and of our professional careers as well. Though the social history of colonial American religion has attracted the interest of a number of scholars in recent years, much work remains to be done. The present volume, while exemplary of recent work in the field, will also, we hope, point the way to the future.

Together these essays touch upon two general themes of methodological and historiographical significance to the study of religion and society in early America. The first theme, which is the focus of part 1, is the centrality of the family to the study of religion. Nearly fifty years ago, Edmund S. Morgan used the New England Puritan family to demonstrate the many close correspondences between the family and religion, showing that any change in the one sphere would resonate in the other and that the structures and images of the one domain would be mirrored in the other. This reciprocal influence of Puritanism and the family, he suggested, made it possible to speak of *a* Puritan family and *a* domestic Puritanism. Unfortunately, few historians have followed his lead. The several social studies of early American religion which have been undertaken have tended to follow H. Richard Niebuhr's influence in ascribing socioreligious patterns and changes to class, race, and/or ethnicity.[2] While these forces were certainly powerful in shaping early American religious behavior and experience, at times familial factors had an impact of equal or even greater power. The Puritans were the first Anglo-Americans to establish viable families, and this proved crucial to the survival and subsequent revitalization, in the mideighteenth century, of their religious system.[3] In addition, as American Puritanism evolved, congregational churches reconstituted themselves along lines related to family, gender, and/or age, not class, race, and/or ethnicity. In examining the social sources of colonial faiths, historians need to pay closer heed to such factors. We urge historians to adopt Morgan's agenda on the sociology and anthropology of the family and religion but also advise them to move beyond his literary techniques into methods of sociohistorical analysis, using primarily local records to supply the data.

The second broad theme focuses on the relationship of religion to society in early America in the context of life stages and through the method of the life course. Religion, family, and society intersected in past time, especially at times of developmental life transitions, when children were born, youth were passing through puberty, couples were marrying, and people were dying. Such vital moments found meaning and significance in the religious ideologies and rituals social groups employed and enacted to interpret them. Even the Puritans, who voiced a consistent opposition to icons and myths, and who strove "to return, recover, simplify, and eliminate," could not live without rituals and, in fact, relied increasingly heavily upon them to interpret childhood, adolescence, marriage, and death and dying.[4] Such events had an importance in the lives of Puritans and of other early Americans, belied by the scant scholarly attention paid to them.

To understand the historical, religious, and social meaning of such life stages, we suggest that scholars study them through the method of the life course. To study people in past time through their mutual participation in age-related events is to uncover new, significant dimensions of their group life. Consider, for example, the key event of joining the church in Puritan New England, a subject we address throughout the present study. Admission roles available for Congregational churches, when examined in conjunction with vital records, show that the event was highly sensitive to developmental passages and was surprisingly dynamic. The age at admission changed significantly for subsequent sets of cohorts at the time of the Great Awakening, dropping from the upper to lower twenties for men and from the lower twenties to high teens for women. Life course analysis, we indicate, makes it possible to link this and other changes to social, economic, and religious processes affecting not individuals alone but also groups united by birth or other vital events.[5]

2

Aside from the general themes concerning the relationship of religion to the family and the life course, the present study addresses issues that form the centerpiece of individual chapters. One such theme, introduced in chapter 1, concerns itself with Puritan tribalism. Ever since Morgan introduced the subject in *The Puritan Family,* Puritan tribalism has dominated discussions of the history of Puritanism and the family. Morgan's analysis of the Puritan family was mostly prescriptive, however, and was biased heavily toward the theme of religious declension. We propose a different approach to the study of Puritanism and the family—that of the core family—and argue that this be used to study the reality as well as the rhetoric of early New Englanders, their behavior and their ideas. Core families, composed often of the well-established, well-off clans of villages, are found in many different cultures and take care of the local church with almost a proprietary prejudice. Peripheral families, on the other hand, are often made up of transients and the less well off and are rarely found in the church, unless they choose to settle down.

The core-periphery dichotomy, we suggest, can be used to ground comparative analyses of religion and the family in all regions of North America and can also be adopted in the discussion of popular religion in early America.[6] To studies of popular religion which view lay religion as united against clerical elitism, the core-periphery approach can serve as a healthy corrective. Relationships among the laity were often as tense as those between the laity and the clergy, and politically astute ministers could use those divisions to their distinct advantage, or try to, at least, playing tribal politics to strengthen their local authority.[7] While tribalism certainly had an exclusionary effect, producing in time a large, peripheral group of the unchurched, the practice also provided a significant outlet for lay piety and an important source of popular commitment to institutional, established religion. Although historians, including Morgan, have tended to view tribalism as the clergy's creation, it more likely derived from the people, as David D. Hall has recently suggested. Laymen and -women valued the ordinances for reasons unrelated to official church doctrine and placed their own interpretation upon the sacraments. Their tendency to confuse family, church, covenant, baptism, and protection, Hall argues, "did not originate with the ministers, though they would more or less acknowledge its legitimacy. Ordinary people imposed their own needs on the church."[8]

3

The idea of the core family helps us to understand another, more specific theme, that of the organic renewal of the Puritan churches of New England, which is discussed in chapters 1 and 2. Based especially on church records, which scholars continue to ignore in their studies of Puritanism, and of other religious movements, our analysis shows that core families were responsible for generational cycles of church membership, including the Great Awakening of the 1740s. Thus, in Milford, Connecticut, the church was rejuvenated every generation by core families descended from the first settlers of the town. Each generation of church members produced another generation of church members, all from the same core families. Though ministers increasingly preached jeremiads lamenting the decline of piety, their parishes were not declining in piety at all, at least from the perspective of church membership.

Another subsidiary theme, also presented initially in chapter 1, is that of family strategies. Historians of early American religion and society have ignored the relationship of family practices and dynamics to religious change; they have also neglected the impact of conscious family strategies on such change. Only recently have social historians begun to view the family as more of an independent than a dependent variable in producing historical change. Family planning, we argue, had major consequences for the history of the New England church and should be linked, in the research of scholars, to religious and secular events, including inheritance and child rearing. We know, for example, that Puritan patriarchs began altering their goals for their children during the early eighteenth century, just when ages at admission dropped, but no one has yet tried to link the two developments, although some scholars have discussed the possibility of doing so.[9]

The core family, religious renewal, and family planning all touch upon a key issue, discussed in chapter 3: the feminization of church membership in early New England. After the 1660s the great majority of Puritans who joined the church were women. Behind the feminization of church membership, we argue, was the ritualization of religious experience.[10] The increasing association of church membership with marriage, parenthood, and other rites involving especially the women of the region, by the 1660s and the 1670s, led to the numerical preponderance of women in full communion. The impact of the feminization of church membership upon the culture was significant and included shifts in clerical rhetoric, which placed increasing emphasis

4

on the ideal of the pious and virtuous women. Another effect could be seen in the area of household education, where women shouldered increasingly the responsibility for the education of young, preschool children. By the early eighteenth century, family planning for children's religious future and the religious nurture of children had become, even in core families, the primary responsibility of women.

The subject of women and education is crucial to chapter 4, in which we examine the distinctiveness of early childhood as a separate stage of life in the Puritan lexicon of life stages. Taking their cue from Philippe Ariès, who in *Centuries of Childhood* argued that people lacked clear-cut concepts of life stages until the modern era, many scholars of early American childhood maintained that the colonists treated children as if they were "miniature adults." We take exception to that hypothesis and argue instead that in the case of one group of early Americans—the New England Puritans—well-defined stages of life, including early childhood, existed and deserve historical scrutiny.

In chapter 4, we call for careful study of the colonial history of early childhood, and suggest that it be focused in part on household education and the activities of women in producing precociously literate children. At a time when church membership was becoming feminized, church and state began aggressively promoting literacy among women, who then passed it on to their children. How or if this changed prevailing attitudes toward children, however, are questions that have not been posed. We also suggest that the study of colonial children be linked to changes in religious ideologies, especially to the rise within America of pietism and evangelicalism. While Philip J. Greven, Jr., has argued that Protestants' temperaments, including the evangelical mode, had a profound influence on child-rearing practices and subsequently religious experience, his analysis lacks periodization. To us, the Great Awakening and the accompanying influx of evangelicalism first into New England and then into other regions of British America produced widespread support among prorevival groups for an authoritarian approach to child rearing. In this sense, the Great Awakening is a turning point in the history of early American childhood; whether it held a similar significance for the history of the family is a question that historians have failed to address.[11]

Religion also played a role in the reactions of early Americans to troubled youth, a subject that we explore in chapter 5. Societal reactions to delinquent and troubled youth were strongly affected not only

5

by religion but also by other factors such as demographic and economic shifts as well as the changing adult perceptions of young people in England and America. In this chapter, we analyze the growing concern about vagrant youths in early modern England and the transmission of these worries to the American colonies. Particularly interesting is how Puritan religion affected the perception and treatment of youths in New England compared to the South. Then we trace the contemporary scholarly and societal responses to troubled youth in nineteenth-century America and close with the so-called discovery of adolescence by G. Stanley Hall and his colleagues.

The relationship of religious ideology to age-related experience in early America was often an illusive and disjunctive one, as chapter 6 suggests. Focusing on attitudes toward old age and on retirement among the New England ministry, chapter 6 shows how old age remained venerated in New England throughout the colonial period, despite the fact that succeeding generations of aged ministers became increasingly susceptible to bitter attacks from within their churches. Why? The positive image of aging, which had been created by the first generation, persisted for as long as the first generation was venerated, and that was many generations. In the meantime, the status and economic situation of subsequent generations of ministers declined, and conflict between them and their parishioners increased, in part because of structural friction in the congregational mode of hiring ministers; whether town or church had the last say in the selection of the preacher was a question that plagued Puritan communities for several generations. By the end of the colonial period, the gap between the image and the treatment of aging New England ministers was wide and growing wider. Historians who have looked to images of age as a guide to the reality have, thus, missed the point, which was, instead, the growing disharmony between ideology and experience.

Similar dissonance can be detected in the history of death and dying, which we analyze in chapter 7 and also in chapter 1. One of the significant issues that emerges in studies of death and dying is the relationship of ideology to experience. While mortality rates among English-speaking folk declined upon their resettlement in America, their preoccupation with death did not. In fact, after the 1660s, some historians have argued, the Puritan fear of death grew, as the Puritans focused more and more on their physical frailties. The Puritan obsession with death, however, was as misleading a guide to reality in New

England as it had been an accurate measure of experience in old England, where mortality rates were customarily high.

How did this conflict between the apparent and the real affect the Puritans' handling of death and dying? One possible answer to this question may be found in the history of funerary rituals, which expanded after 1660 along with the Puritans' fear of death. Ritualizing death perhaps enabled Puritans to preserve both the traditions of the first generation and those of particular families at a time of growing isolation and increasing self-centeredness; it also surely served the function of reintegrating family and kin ties at a time of the partial dissolution of the network. Whatever the functions of funerary rituals, early Americans' incessant preoccupation with death has misled previous historians into believing that high death rates were characteristic of seventeenth- and eighteenth-century America. In this and other areas of historical controversy addressed in the present work, sociohistorical analysis of local records reveals a different history.

If anthropologists are correct in asserting that the very origin and development of religion derive from mankind's fear of and concern with death, then perhaps the history of death and dying in early America can disclose new truths about colonial religion. Maybe the growing fear and subsequent ritualization of death among New Englanders contributed to the concomitant ritualization of religion, and perhaps each had a common origin: the established ministry. Surely the clergy had the most to gain from establishing rituals that served to preserve and perpetuate the collective memory of their beloved predecessors and, thus, to shore up their declining status. Yet one of the great ironies of sacerdotalizing ministries, as Max Weber argued many decades ago, is their increasing affinity with lay habits and routines. "The more a priesthood aimed to regulate the behavior pattern of the laity in accordance with the will of the god," Weber said, "the more it had to compromise with the traditional views of the laity in formulating patterns of doctrine and behavior."[12]

As in the history of death and dying, so in the history of church women, core families, and the life course, ministers were probably not leading but being led. Though the history of popular religion has attracted increasing numbers of historians, that history is still written as if the view from the pew were identical to that from the pulpit and as if that view had little influence on the pulpit.[13] In other words, it is written as if the clergy were doing all of the leading and also all of the thinking. Future studies of early American religion will have to be more sensitive not only to lay culture but also to the diverse and dynamic character of that culture. Max Weber said that, as prophecy petrified and sects became churches, ministers had to contend not only "with the enduring habits of the masses" but also with new social forces, transported by new social groups.[14] The interplay between tradition and change within increasingly diverse and differentiated colonial parishes should be central to future social histories of early American religion.[15]

While these essays originally were published elsewhere, we have carefully reviewed, revised, and updated each one of them for this book. The amount of revision varies from essay to essay. Chapter 2, for example, entitled "'Sisters' in Christ: Women and the Church in Seventeenth-Century New England," required only minor modifications, while chapter 4, "The Great Care of Godly Parents: Early Childhood in Puritan New England," has been expanded to nearly twice its original length.

We decided to revise and republish these essays in part to make them accessible to a wider audience, since the original pieces had appeared in a rather diverse set of journals and books. We also decided to undertake this effort because the essays, taken together, shed light on a crucial aspect of our religious history: the relationship of the life course and the family to personal religious experience and development. Given the complexity of the relationship, we realize that these essays represent but a first step toward understanding it fully.

Notes

1. Chapter 1, one of the three co-authored essays, appeared in the *William and Mary Quarterly,* 3d ser., 39 (1982): 29–63. Chapter 2, written by Gerald F. Moran, was published in the *William and Mary Quarterly,* 3d ser., 36 (1979): 236–54. Chapter 3, included in *Women in American Religion,* ed. Janet Wilson James (Philadelphia, 1980), 47–65, was also written by Gerald F. Moran. Chapter 4 is the second co-authored piece and appeared in *History and Research in Child Development,* Monographs of the Society for Research in Child Development, ed. Alice Boardman Smuts and John W. Hagen (Chicago, 1986), 24–37. Chapter

5 was co-authored and is a revised version of an essay that appears in *Adolescent Problem and Risk-Taking Behavior,* ed. Robert Ketterlinus and Michael Lamb (Hillsdale, N.J., 1992). Chapter 6, published in *From Birth to Death: Social-Temporal Perspectives,* ed. Matilda W. Riley and Ronald P. Ables, vol. 2 (Boulder, Colo., 1982), 105–37, was written by Maris A. Vinovskis, as was chapter 7, which appeared in the *American Antiquarian Society Proceedings* 86 (1976): 273–302.

2. H. Richard Niebuhr, *The Social Sources of Denominationalism* (1929; reprint, New York, 1968). For a recent analysis of the social sources of denominationalism, see Anne C. Rose, "Social Sources of Denominationalism Reconsidered: Post-Revolutionary Boston as a Case Study," *American Quarterly* 38 (1986): 243–64.

3. The seventeenth-century South had much more difficulty creating viable families, and the religious system was weak. But, as recent studies have demonstrated, southern settlers did manage in time to create cohesive kin networks and, in addition, viable churches. Though the people lacked public support for churches and ministers, they developed religious communities, which provided a source of personal identity, emotional support, and shared rituals. Once the population became denser, however, and society more diverse, churches served to differentiate people rather than unite them. See Lois Green Carr, Philip D. Morgan, and Jean B. Russo, *Colonial Chesapeake Society* (Chapel Hill, N.C., 1988), 22–26; James R. Perry, *The Formation of a Society on Virginia's Eastern Shore, 1615–1655* (Chapel Hill, N.C., 1990). The boundary-maintenance functions of colonial faiths remain unexplored scholarly terrain.

4. Theodore Dwight Bozeman, *To Live Ancient Lives: The Primitivist Dimension in Puritanism* (Chapel Hill, N.C., 1988), 139. Charles E. Hambrick-Stowe discusses the "reritualization" of religious experience by the Puritans in early New England in *The Practice of Piety: Puritan Devotional Disciplines in Seventeenth-Century New England* (Chapel Hill, N.C., 1982), 51, 101–3.

5. For a recent, sophisticated analysis of age at admission in Puritan New England, see Stephen R. Grossbart, "Seeking the Divine Favor: Conversion and Admission in Eastern Connecticut, 1711–1832," *William and Mary Quarterly,* 3d ser., 46 (1989): 696–740.

6. For a recent analysis of core families in early America, see Joyce D. Goodfriend, "The Social Dimensions of Congregational Life in New York City," *William and Mary Quarterly,* 3d ser., 46 (1989): 252–78. As Goodfriend says, Dutch housewives remained loyal to the Reformed church of their birth, despite their marriage to English men, "joining the church in large numbers and early in their life course" (276).

7. For a prime example of this, note the behavior of the Reverend Samuel Parris during the opening phases of the Salem Village witchcraft episode, as described in Paul Boyer and Stephen Nissenbaum, *Salem Possessed: The Social Origins of Witchcraft* (Cambridge, Mass., 1974). For a more recent biography of Parris, see Larry Gragg, *A Quest for Security: The Life of Samuel Parris, 1653–1720* (Westport, Conn., 1990).

8. David D. Hall, "Toward a History of Popular Religion in Early New England," *William and Mary Quarterly*, 3d ser., 41 (1984): 54.

9. For a recent analysis of family planning as practiced among English and American Quakers and of the consequences and often ironic ramifications of strict conformity to earlier but subsequently outmoded strategies, see Barry Levy, *Quakers and the American Family: British Settlement in the Delaware Valley* (New York, 1988).

10. For the rapid spread of sacramental and devotional rituals among the early New England Puritans, see Hambrick-Stowe, *Practice of Piety.*

11. Historians need to explore the possible relationship of the feminization of church membership and the domestication of Puritan piety to the rise of evangelicalism, the Great Awakening, and changing child-rearing practices and attitudes.

12. Max Weber, *The Sociology of Religion,* ed. Talcott Parsons (Boston, 1963), 77.

13. For a recent analysis of Puritan "religious culture" as seen exclusively through the eyes of the ministry and its sermons, see Harry S. Stout, *The New England Soul: Religious Culture in Colonial New England* (New York, 1986).

14. Weber, *Sociology of Religion,* 79.

15. One possible line of inquiry is the relationship of the eighteenth-century transition to capitalism to new social forces, evangelical revivalism, and subsequent changes in lay and clerical culture.

CHAPTER I

The Puritan Family and Religion: A Critical Reappraisal

Over three decades ago, Bernard Bailyn challenged historians to re-think interpretations of early American life in the light of local institutions, especially the community and the family.[1] At the time, few historians considered such topics worthy of study. But during the mid-1960s, a new generation of scholars began working piecemeal at reconstituting the early American past "from the bottom up," and, in 1970, a major breakthrough occurred in the "new social history." That year saw the publication of four now classic studies of New England towns and families. John Demos's *A Little Commonwealth* explored the familial sources of Puritan "aggression"; Philip J. Greven, Jr.'s *Four Generations* scrutinized Puritan patriarchalism; Kenneth A. Lockridge's *A New England Town* studied the corporate nature of village life; and Michael Zuckerman's *Peaceable Kingdoms* examined consensual town democracy.[2] As the 1960s gave way to the 1970s, historians of colonial New England legitimized the study of community and family and also laid the groundwork for a reexamination of all facets of early American life.

But the original promise of the new social history and particularly of family studies has not been fully realized, in part because social historians have engaged in what they criticized others for doing—writing "tunnel" history. While much excellent work has been done on such topics as household size and structure and the demographic patterns of family life, including fertility, nuptiality, and mortality, few studies have attempted to integrate the life of the family with other aspects of everyday life.[3] The family has been studied in and of itself but rarely in the context of other activities and experiences. In 1971, Tamara K. Hareven warned historians against wearing blinders when investigating the family and called for "an integrated analysis of all aspects of the family and its interaction within society."[4] Unfortunately, her proposal has fallen mainly on deaf ears.

One of the most promising areas for achieving an integrated view of the family in history is that of religion, since the life of the family and the life of the spirit have intersected at numerous points. A particularly promising region for such an analysis is New England. We recognize that some historians have bemoaned their colleagues' excessive preoccupation with the Puritan colonies, and we sympathize with their complaint about the dearth of comparative histories of American societies. But we do not agree that we should disregard New England altogether.[5] New England remains the region with the most abundant resources for the reconstitution of everyday experience, and for no other region have religious historians achieved the level of sophistication of Puritan studies. For these and other reasons, New England still seems best suited for detailed investigations of family and religion in British America.

This essay will explore several dimensions of interaction between the New England family and religion: Puritan tribalism and the core family, family strategies and the life course, and death and dying. In sections 1 and 2, we use concepts such as tribalism and the life course to explore connections between the family and religion and also to reexamine certain traditional themes in Puritan historiography such as declension. In section 3, we discuss a subject, death and dying, that has received scant attention from historians but holds great promise for furthering our understanding of Puritan life.

To be sure, these areas do not exhaust the list of research topics. It would be pertinent, for example, to include legal studies in this essay and to explore conflict resolution, child rearing and education, modes of inheritance, and divorce litigation in the light of religion.[6] We believe, nevertheless, that the subjects we have chosen show how the family shaped the course of religious life and how religion in turn influenced the life of the family. Though we focus on the New England family and Puritan, we will speculate at times on the implications of our analysis for other regions of colonial America.

Church, Community, and Clan:
Puritan Tribalism and the Core Family

The point of departure for any consideration of the New England family and religion is Edmund Morgan's *The Puritan Family*. When it was published in 1944, only a handful of scholars, most notably Arthur W. Calhoun, Alice Morse Earle, and Sanford Fleming, had approached family life by way of Puritan piety, but their studies never achieved the interpretive depth of *The Puritan Family*, nor have most recent ones.[7] *The Puritan Family* uncovered surprising points of contact between the family and Puritanism by showing some of the channels through which religion flowed into the family and the family into religion. Morgan skillfully demonstrated this reciprocity as well as the interconnections among the family, society, and values. He thus opened the way for both an anthropology and a sociology of the family and religion in early America.[8]

Consider, for example, Morgan's discussion of Puritan theology and the family. The domestic ideals of conjugal love and fidelity, he suggested, influenced Puritan doctrine. At the same time, Puritan faith and belief permeated domestic life. When, for instance, divines explained the elements of Christian piety, they often used domestic themes as expositional props, employing most frequently the analogue between fidelity to spouse and devotion to Christ. Just as husband and wife covenanted with each other at marriage, so the faithful became wedded to Christ and he to them at the moment of conversion. This and other analogues, Morgan indicated, "dominated Puritan thought so completely as to suggest that the Puritans' religious experiences in some way duplicated their domestic experiences."[9] But the metaphorical street also ran in the opposite direction—from faith to domus. Puritans not only clothed piety with ideas taken from household experience but also invested family life with religious values. Each sphere supplied codes for interpreting acts played out in the other sphere. Morgan thus set out an anthropology of the Puritan family and faith that historians would do well to emulate.

The Puritan Family, especially the sections devoted to "puritan tribalism," also created a framework for the sociology of the family and religion. Morgan maintained that, during the seventeenth century,

New England churches turned inward upon themselves, recruiting members largely from the ranks of old church families and retreating from society at large. As churches became increasingly inbred, membership continued to decline. At the same time, second- and third-generation preachers, believing that the children of the elect provided the most fertile ground for the implantation of saving grace, devoted an inordinate amount of attention to church families, often at the expense of the religious needs of the unchurched. In this religious tribalism, Morgan found the key to understanding the nature of religious change in early New England. "To be sure," he concluded at the end of the book, "other forces than tribalism had also betrayed them: they had grown prosperous and comfortable, and prosperity had proved as always an enemy to zeal. But other failings only compounded the sin of insubordination to a God for whom their fathers had defied prelacy and privilege. When theology became the handmaiden of genealogy, Puritanism no longer deserved its name."[10]

Puritan tribalism was one of Morgan's most important discoveries, but he failed to push it to its conceptual and descriptive limits. Instead, he chose to read religious inbreeding as declension, thus treating the trend as a symptom of a disease rather than as a historical process with some explanatory value. Where Morgan seeks to interpret tribalism, *The Puritan Family* ceases to instruct. First, his interpretation of tribalism implies that the phenomenon was exclusive to the Puritans, when in fact other communities in America exhibited religious inbreeding. Second, it uses declension as the inclusive explanatory concept, when in truth the concept is unilinear and one-dimensional, and not very useful for understanding changes in religion and the family. Third, it suggests failure on the part of families to revitalize religion, when in fact many proved highly successful in producing successive generations of church members.

When a comparative perspective is applied to New England society and religion, we discover that the Puritans were not unusually loyal to the families of the church but were acting out ideals common to communities in other areas of America. Morgan himself, in *Virginians at Home,* showed how Anglicans tended toward tribalism, though he failed to pursue the implications of this finding when he revised *The Puritan Family* in 1966.[11] Frederick B. Tolles revealed how Pennsylvania Quakers, after a period of accommodation to the "outward Plantation," turned in upon themselves during the 1750s, renewing their original commitment to the "inner plantation." After nearly disappearing, "Quaker tribalism," according to Tolles, "returned with renewed strength, and Philadelphia Friends came at length to resemble their co-religionists in Ireland, Great Britain, and the rural districts of the Middle Colonies in their extreme group-consciousness with its social corollaries of cohesiveness and exclusivism."[12] Moreover, J. William Frost argued that "friends became even more tribalists than Puritans, for the Quaker child who grew into an adult member was not required to make a declaration as to what he believed or whether he had experienced the light. Membership became a privilege of birth."[13] That not all religious communities followed the same tribal pattern is indicated by Gillian Lindt Gollin's *Moravians in Two Worlds.* In the Moravian settlement of Bethlehem, Pennsylvania, Count Nickolas von Zinzendorf's insistence on endogamy gradually lost favor so that "after 1776 the number of non-Moravians brought into the community through marriage increased rapidly, and their presence accelerated the demise of religious exclusivism."[14] These and other studies point the way to a comparative analysis of tribalism in religious communities throughout British America.[15]

Tribalism in religion has also been found operating in other cultures at other times. In *Person and God in a Spanish Valley,* for example, William A. Christian, Jr., shows that in peasant areas of modern northern Spain, certain families participate more frequently in Catholic services and devotional exercises than other families, thus forming a tribe of religiously active householders to whom the parish priest is especially loyal. According to Christian, "at least one family, but usually a small set of families, look after the religion with an almost proprietary air." These families are more literate than the peripheral families; "the church is the center of culture," and "the core families are closer to the church than most"; the fathers of these families are likely to be devout and prosperous.[16]

To ethnographers like Christian, the village church is both the locus of religious activity and the focal point of the culture, the institution through which communal ideals and values achieve their fullest expression. Moreover, the guardians of the church and the caretakers of the culture usually belong to the same core families. Those who are most absorbed in the culture tend toward its center, the church, and the church, especially its sacraments and liturgy, is the object of loyalty for families who participate most fully in the institutional life of the village and express in their daily activities the forms of the local culture. By contrast, the piety of culturally peripheral families is not directed at the church but is more private and less structured, and participation in Catholic rituals does not reaffirm their religious and cultural identity as it does for members of core families.

To view tribalism as a common cultural process, not a pathological one, is to open up a new perspective on the family and religion in colonial America. In New England we discover that important connections existed among church, culture, and family. The local Congregational church, for example, was the center of religious and civic life in the village, the focal point of public piety and the guardian of the community's values. It performed the major rituals of local life, including baptism, the Lord's Supper, the admission of members, and covenant renewals, and it did so in front of the entire community assembled in the meetinghouse on the Sabbath. The church was also the caretaker of the covenant containing the ideals of the founding fathers. Moreover, its minister was the spokesman for the culture, the resident intellectual who on Sabbaths and lecture days delivered sermons that reminded villagers of their common values and aspirations. In these and other ways, the New England church was the nucleus of the culture, and participation in its activities brought people into harmony with the life of the community.

At the same time, participation in the church and its rituals reflected an individual's closeness to the culture, for the rules governing access to the church and its sacraments, and the people enforcing them, required conformity from prospective members to certain local norms and values. Desiring a well-ordered and harmonious church, the brethren examined candidates not only for grace and knowledge of doctrine but also for morality and ability to live up to the covenantal principles of charity, love, and fraternity. In other words, they tested a person's social and cultural fitness for membership, and the period of "propounding" through which all incoming members passed gave churches ample opportunity to uncover deviant thought and behavior. Every admission trial, in fact, saw the brethren reidentify the village's social boundaries, much as on Rogation Days European peasants reaffirmed territorial boundaries. To the church, the communal profile of a candidate was as important as his or her doctrinal rectitude.

In another way, the admission trial possessed a social and cultural character. It has been said that everyday experience informs a community's ethos and ideas and norms express social reality.[17] Accordingly, even that part of the trial that was supposed to center exclusively on piety touched on areas of everyday experience. In other words, attitudes the brethren acquired in their daily contacts with neighbors colored the test of religious conversion. Moreover, it is entirely possible that candidates approached admission knowing that the outcome would be a favorable one: they felt sufficiently acquainted with the requirements and the people who enforced them to be confident of their acceptability as members. By contrast, people who felt unsure of their position or ignorant of doctrine held back from the trial, lest they suffer the public humiliation of rejection. Such considerations help to explain why so few prospective members were judged unworthy of communion during admission itself. In fact, the bulk of the evidence on rebuffed candidacies comes from the 1630s and 1640s, when churches were working out standards of membership and an elaborated script of the trial was not yet available.

Among the social factors governing the judgments made at admission, family background and connections may have been the most crucial. When Increase Mather said that "God hath seen meet to cast the line of election so, as that generally elect Children are cast upon elect Parents," he was expressing an assumption that was common among the New England ministry, namely, that saintly children almost always sprang from the loins of saintly parents.[18] Tribal attitudes among the Puritans suggest that churches considered descent and heredity important criteria for admission, but whether expectations accorded with reality is an unexplored question. This is an unnecessary oversight, for documents alluding to the family profile of incoming members are abundant for both New England and other regions of colonial America.

Besides parish records and admission lists, there exist records of births, marriages, and deaths as well as town meeting records, all of which can be used to reconstitute the history of churches and parishes in the context of the history of their families. These documents should enable us to answer several key questions. Did Puritan tribalism exist at the level of experience and practice? What relationship did new church families have to old church families? Did New England parishes possess core and peripheral families, and, if so, did worship and piety differ between churched and unchurched families?

Jon Butler has called for the study of "noninstitutional, popular religion" that existed outside the established Christian community; such study could be undertaken along lines suggested by the core-periphery dichotomy.[19] Did there exist in New England a structured piety, mediated by core families and churches, and an unstructured, informal worship among less established families with less involvement in the local culture? Moreover, did membership in the church influence behavior in secular areas of life? Did it affect the extent and nature of participation in communal networks? These questions seem particularly well suited to the study of the New England family and religion.

Historians have demonstrated the consequences of one important aspect of family life—geographic mobility—for participation in the church and other village institutions. In several seventeenth-century Connecticut towns, church membership centered on well-established families, especially those of the founders and their descendants. Conversely, less stable families and transients either tended to stay away from the church or joined it only after a lengthy waiting period. The same holds true for their involvement in other areas of the community, including landholding and office holding. People who moved frequently did not enjoy the institutional life of people who stayed put.[20]

Churches demanded that candidates be educated in the ways of the local religion—that they have some "backstage knowledge" of village mores—and transients simply did not possess this kind of familiarity with local life.[21] As towns and churches aged, however, a person's social profile and conformity to community values influenced membership even more. Paul R. Lucas has shown that, during the late seventeenth century, the brethren gained control over the keys to the church, at the same time shifting the central criterion of membership from piety to morality. Intent on healing the wounds caused by several decades of ecclesiastical strife, reform-minded members sought "to create a program to ensure peace in the congregation and morality in the community." To this end, they revised church covenants to reflect the newly won power of the fraternity and the necessity of subjection to its standards on the part of new members, and they also rigidified the admission trial. As Lucas writes, "Those found worthy of the principles of the church covenant—whether halfway members or new-comers to the town—were admitted only after a serious and often lengthy public and private examination of past behavior."[22]

With increasing emphasis being placed on congregational consensus and discipline, late seventeenth-century churches treated strangers with considerable circumspection, denying even newcomers with church affiliation elsewhere immediate entry into communion. In Middletown, Connecticut, for example, persons transferring from other churches were pushed into halfway status and were not granted full membership until they had proven their worth to the lay saints. "The brethren," writes Lucas, "trusted no one's judgment but their own. The emigrant church member followed the same circuitous path as the emigrant nonmember, justifying his character to gain half-way status, then justifying it again to keep it."[23]

To the growing power of the brethren was added the increasing influence of certain well-established families, a development that further promoted the parochialism of congregations and the uneasiness of communicants with outsiders. In Milford, Connecticut, for example, during the period 1660–99, just twenty-three kin groups with common surnames contributed 77 percent of the male members, even though they accounted for only 57 percent of the town's inhabitants in 1686; women from only twenty kin groups, eleven of them common to the males, made up 63 percent of the female members whose families of origin are known. Moreover, three out of every four male and female members alike were descendants of people who had entered the church at settlement in 1639–44. Under such conditions, newcomers or townspeople without local ties or kin among the brethren perhaps avoided membership, not because they lacked piety but because they felt alienated from powerful families who stood guard at the church doors.[24]

During the period of settlement, churches served an organizing function, knitting strangers together by a purposeful covenant, and they continued to perform that service on the expanding frontier.[25] But, in aging towns, churches became the preserve of kin groups that expressed through religious activities their aspirations for their families and communities. Just as in late medieval and early modern England, kin relationships were "the constituent elements of the Christian community as a whole," so in late seventeenth-century New England, the church was the established kin group writ large.[26]

Given the abundance of New England's local records, it would be possible to examine even more thoroughly the kin networks that dominated the church and formed the context for religious experience. If we used vital records to reconstitute family genealogies and then linked such data to church admission lists, we could trace the ties among church families and also explore the church's penetration within the community and its clans. We could, for example, determine affinity between membership and choice of spouse. If we added other records to our store of evidence—including deeds, wills, and diaries—we could search for the concentricity of church ties within certain patterns of interpersonal relationships as manifested in such activities as land and labor exchanges, loan granting and receiving, and the putting-out of children. We could thus apply the methods of Alan Macfarlane's *The Family Life of Ralph Josselin* to the study of the Puritan church, community, and clan.[27] And if we added accounts of conversion to our pool of evidence, we could reconstruct the roles people played when a family member underwent religious conversion or joined the church. In these and other ways, family records open a window on the life of the spirit, and church records, a window on the life of the community and kin group.

Family Strategies and the Life Course

For Morgan, Puritan tribalism signified the failure of "the Puritan system." Because the Puritans restricted communion to the converted and baptism to the children of saints, the church became "an exclusive society for the saints and their children" and "the means of perpetuating the gospel among a hereditary aristocracy." But even though the descendants of the elect received membership privileges and the special attention of the clergy, "the children did not get converted, either before they came of age or after." According to Morgan,

The number of full members in the church gradually shrank until the ecclesiastical structure could no longer hold together. The Half-Way Covenant of 1662 enabled the unconverted children of church members to retain their incomplete membership after becoming adults, but it did not increase the number of full communicants. Before the end of the century the Puritan system was tottering. . . . Though Increase Mather was still mumbling his phrases about the loins of godly parents in 1721, it was long since clear, to anyone with eyes to see, that grace was not hereditary.[28]

But in *Visible Saints,* published in 1963, three years before the revision of *The Puritan Family,* Morgan expressed much greater sympathy for the Puritans and much less support for the theme of declension. In *Visible Saints,* he argued that, although the 1640s and 1650s witnessed far fewer conversions than the fathers had expected, "this was not a sign of decline in piety." Because the fathers entered the church before the creation of the test of conversion, the second generation was the first to confront the new admissions system, and a lower rate of admission was the result. As for the Half-Way Covenant, it "was neither a sign of decline in piety nor a betrayal of the standards of the founding fathers, but an honest attempt to rescue the concept of visible saints from the tangle of problems created in time by human reproduction."[29] In addition, as Morgan argued elsewhere, "the very fact that the Half-Way Covenant was needed may be testimony, not to the decline of religion, but to the rise of an extraordinary religious scrupulosity, which still existed in the eighteenth century." The children, he continued, "may have become so sophisticated in the morphology of conversion that they rejected, as inconclusive, religious experiences that would have driven their parents unhesitatingly into church membership."[30] On second glance, then, Morgan found that grace was indeed hereditary and that religious scrupulosity was somehow transmitted across generations.

In *The Puritan Family,* Morgan perpetuated the tradition of viewing changes in New England Puritanism in terms of the deterioration of piety. Although such a view, whose most able proponent was Perry Miller, has received much criticism from historians, it still crops up in the recent literature.[31] Even the new social history often reads as it were just another rendition of declension. In *A New England Town,* for example, Lockridge described a village coming apart at its consensual seams as overpopulation led to diversity. Under such conditions, Lockridge maintained, one could not expect the first generation's collective outlook to have remained intact or the ideals of the covenant to have survived. In a chapter entitled "Decline," he concluded that "in Dedham, when the saints dwindled and died away, the rule of love dwindled and died with it. In this sense, . . . the New England preachers of the 1670s and 80s could take some satisfaction in being right. Their famous laments over the decline of the spirit of the founders were justified by events in Dedham."[32]

But other social histories, such as Greven's *Four Generations* and Zuckerman's *Peaceable Kingdoms,* presented a sharply contrasting picture of traditions being renewed and revitalized across generations. As

James A. Henretta recognized some time ago, these works gave strong hints of "organic growth and rebirth in the society of colonial New England" so that "it is time we begin to write its history in the positive terms that its substance demands." Zuckerman's account of "the peaceable kingdoms," Henretta argued, "does not correspond to the image of declension and disintegration." In the Massachusetts towns of the eighteenth century, "the substance of community had changed, but not the value of its existence in the minds of men." And in Andover, "the decline in Community was paralleled and to some extent offset by the rise of the family." Even though "patriarchy had given way to parental solicitude and aid by the eighteenth century," he maintained, "the ties of family and kinship remained as smooth, organic, and positive factors in the lives of the colonists, smoothing the passage from one generation and one community to the next."[33]

A similar case could be made for organic growth and rebirth in the churches of New England. Some of the strongest arguments against declension come from historians who have reconstituted the membership of particular churches. Until Robert G. Pope published *The Half-Way Covenant* in 1969, no historian had undertaken a systematic study of admissions during the latter half of the seventeenth century. Exploring membership in four Massachusetts churches for the period from 1650 to 1690, Pope discovered several surprising patterns. "Admissions to full communion," he found, "reached their lowest ebb, not in 1690, but in the middle of the century, when Congregationalism was most secure." During the 1670s and 1680s, "personal piety and the need for religious ties increased as Massachusetts society became less secure. The increase in full communicants, the implementation of the half-way covenant, the mass covenant renewals, and the inclusion of formerly unchurched inhabitants in the church covenant are signs of an awakening, not a decline." Echoing the ideas Morgan had put forward in *Visible Saints* and "New England Puritanism: Another Approach," Pope concluded that "the recurrent themes of reluctance and scrupulosity suggest that the third generation of New Englanders was no less religious than the first and that its conception of true religion corresponded remarkably with that of its forebears. Only the forms had changed."[34]

A more recent study of membership discloses the presence of long-range admission cycles in the First Church of Milford, Connecticut, where a commitment to the test of conversion was maintained for many generations. Admissions to this church shot upward during the late 1660s, the late 1690s, the early 1710s, and the late 1730s, giving the church enough new members to more than offset losses from death or emigration. These periodic increases extended the embrace of the church in every generation to between 40 and 50 percent of all male inhabitants.[35]

Aside from other membership studies, recent research on New England's "middle period" also points not to declension but to the creative revitalization of Puritan religion over time. Scholars such as Emory Elliott, David D. Hall, E. Brooks Holifield, Charles E. Hambrick-Stowe, David Levin, Richard F. Lovelace, Paul Lucas, Robert Middlekauff, and Harry S. Stout have shown the deep piety that existed among second- and third-generation New Englanders and, by so doing, have demonstrated a need for a conceptual model of religious change in Puritan America that takes into account organic rebirth and renewal.[36] We also need to study those mechanisms by which faith and membership were revitalized across generations, the most important of them being familial.

Only recently have historians begun to explore intergenerational patterns of church membership. One of the churches for which we now have data is the First Church of Milford, where, with each successive generation, the children of certain well-established church families tended to become communicants at adulthood and were most responsible for revitalizing membership at cyclical intervals. The family in Milford was responsible for the growth and vitality of the church. During the period 1660–83, for example, households with at least one parent in communion supplied 68 percent of new members, while families with both parents in fellowship contributed 54 percent. During the period 1686–99, families with one or both parents in membership provided, respectively, 79 and 44 percent of incoming members. Moreover, the religious lineage of persons admitted during the period 1660–99 often stretched back to the origins of the church, with one-half of the communicants coming from families whose founders had become visible saints before 1645. These same families were the major source of additional increases in admissions up to and through the Great Awakening.[37]

On the basis of this and other evidence on church membership and piety, we can propose a new view of the Puritan family and religion.[38] In the past, historians have indicted Puritan parents for loss of faith and failure to educate children in grace, a charge also leveled by the clerical jeremiads of the seventeenth century. But it seems that, among many New England families, just the reverse was true—that Puritan mothers and fathers managed to pass on to their children piety and an interest in the church. Put another way, the family served a positive religious function in New England, preserving and perpetuating Puritan values and culture across generations. It was a purposeful and resourceful instrument of religious renewal.

This view comports with recent findings on the family in past time. As family studies have matured and grown in sophistication, historians have come to believe that families were more resilient and creative in the face of change than originally depicted. They were less the object of demographic, economic, or social forces than they were the institutions through which people adjusted to alterations in the world around them. As Hareven has recently observed, "Rather than continuing to view the family as a passive agent, historical studies have revealed that the role of the family was in fact that of an active agent, fostering social change and facilitating the adaptation of its members to new social and economic conditions."[39]

A concept that underscores the creative activities of the family is that of family planning or strategies. One of the few historians who have used this concept is Natalie Zemon Davis. In "Ghosts, Kin, and Progeny," she invites scholars to consider the importance of "family planning" in history and to explore the strategies families used to shape the future of the line. For many sixteenth- and seventeenth-century families a central concern was "to plan for a family future during and beyond the lifetimes of the current parents." With an eye to enhancing the family's "store and reputation," many French families manipulated land, dwellings, occupations, careers, and marriages. And, as Davis proposes, family planning had important consequences for thought and feeling in three areas: "a new sense of the relations between the living and the dead"; a keener awareness "of the boundary around the immediate family as a privileged locus for identity and gratification, and reward"; and "a clearer sense of the right ordering of the planning family, with wife and children ideally in accord, but with sovereignty vested in the father." The strategic actions of French families, she concludes, furnish examples "of men and women in small groups deciding how they are going to conduct themselves."[40]

If the notion of family strategy is used cautiously, with the understanding that it applies only under special conditions, it can direct attention to hitherto untouched areas of early New England life. Among the few histories of the family which stress the institution's conscious and strategic functions, as opposed to its susceptibility to demographic, economic, and social forces, is Greven's *Four Generations*. In Andover, many families manipulated their resources to achieve control over such matters as inheritance and the marriages of children. Greven finds that Andover fathers wielded enormous power over their children and also shows the impact of patriarchalism on several crucial facets of experience, including the ages at which sons married and achieved autonomy. Desiring, among other things, to preserve economic security through old age, fathers planned their patrimony in such a way as to ensure until death their dominion over their sons. By retaining title to their lands throughout their lifetimes, the patriarchs prevented sons from attaining early economic independence and also contributed to delayed marriages, to the prolongation of that phase of the family life cycle in which older children lived under the same roof with their parents, and to the postponement of the day when one generation succeeded another in power. Moreover, by controlling land and dowries, Andover fathers inhibited freedom of choice in marriage.[41]

Among recent studies of the Puritan family, the one that comes closest to approaching religion in terms of family strategies is Greven's *The Protestant Temperament*, although similar concerns appear in Demos's *A Little Commonwealth*. Greven argues that three kinds of temperament and piety existed in early America—the evangelical, the moderate, and the genteel—and he explores these temperaments with reference to child rearing and other family activities. "By discovering how differently people of different temperaments reared their children, by seeing how they chose to feed, to clothe, to discipline, and to educate their children, by recognizing the issues that seemed to many parents to be of decisive importance for the development of character and the fostering of piety, we can begin to perceive the recurrent patterns of early life experiences associated with each of these three distinctive patterns of adult temperament and piety."[42]

Greven also suggests the importance of family choice, planning, control, and decision making in structuring piety and the temperaments. Within evangelical households, for example, parents were highly conscious of their religious heritage and deeply concerned with the religious future of the line. "Evangelicals usually recalled being raised by pious parents who had sought consciously to bring their children up in the ways of the Lord, with a proper sense of love and fear for Him." Imbued with a deep awareness of their religious heritage, evangelicals attempted, by manipulating those experiences and resources at their disposal, to thrust this heritage into the future. Thus, according to Greven, "what one ate, how much one ate, how one dressed and how one behaved mattered profoundly to evangelical parents, who sought to govern the outer lives of their children according to the values which dominated their inner lives as well."[43]

Although some reviewers have criticized *The Protestant Temperament* for being ahistorical and too dependent on neo-Freudian psychology, its insights into the religious strategies and goals of families are extremely suggestive. Historians should pursue these insights not only for what they reveal about the way certain experiences were transmitted over time but also for what they tell us about "the least understood aspect of family behavior—the process of decision making within the family."[44] The choices people make, including those of a religious nature, often depend on the strategies and goals of the family. Those choices, as Hareven indicates, also depend on timing with respect to the developmental life cycle, to transitions within the family, and to prevailing social conditions.

The question of when decisions are made is a crucial one, for the timing of decisions "can reveal the important area in which the major changes in family behavior have taken place." To understand these changes, we must look at three interrelated "time patterns": individual time, family time, and historical time. Family time, for example, includes "the timing of events such as marriage, birth of a child, leaving home, and the transition of individuals into different roles as the family moves through its life course." Timing can create discord in families because family time and individual time are not always in agreement. Thus "the decision to leave home, to marry, or to form one's own family could not in the past be timed strictly in accordance with individual preferences, depending instead on the decisions and needs of the family as a collective unit and on institutional supports." As Hareven concludes, "research has only just begun to sketch some of the basic patterns of the timing of family transitions and to link them with 'historical time'—that is, with changing social conditions."[45]

The concept of "time patterns" can be applied to the study of the most important religious decision made by New England men and women—the decision to enter the church. Many families desired communion for their children and reared them with that goal in mind. What sort of person joined the church was often contingent, moreover, on the expectations of the brethren and the minister and their attitudes toward a candidate. But the decision was also made within a particular context—during certain transitions in the life of the individual and the family—so that, in order to understand why people made the decisions when they did, we need to know the timing of those transitions.

Historians have begun to explore one aspect of the timing of admission—age—especially for the period of the Great Awakening. They have found that, during the revival, an abrupt change took place in the ages at which people experienced conversion and joined the church. Before the awakening, most men did not become communicants until their late twenties or early thirties, while most women did not do so until their middle or late twenties. During the early 1740s, with the onset of the awakening, a marked decline in ages at conversion among both men and women occurred, so much so that many converts were in their teenage years or early twenties. After the revival subsided, the ages of new members rose to previous levels, remaining there through the period of the Revolution until the beginning of the second Great Awakening, when youthful conversions again became common.[46]

What explains these changes in religious experience? This question has been answered in several ways. According to Greven, rapidly declining ages at conversion reflected a fundamental change in the life cycle of Andover's youths, a rapid acceleration in the attainment of maturity,[47] while J. M. Bumsted finds for Norton, Massachusetts, that economic frustrations arising from overpopulation led young people to "turn to the one factor in their experience which did not depend upon success in the world—religion." "Responding to the Awakening," in Bumsted's view, "was not an action of the primarily disinherited but of the temporarily frustrated." It was mainly a question of timing, a matter of young people who would eventually achieve material success being denied it for the moment. Bumsted concludes that "high admissions tend to occur in communities which, like Norton, had a large number of young men coming of age and offered only limited opportunities for their full acceptance into adult society."[48]

Similarly, Christine Leigh Heyrman argues that the awakening in Gloucester, Massachusetts, attracted youth who were most sensitive to the economic and military uncertainties of the times.[49]

These studies suggest that changes in the timing of conversions were linked to fundamental shifts in the family and society, but no historian has undertaken a rigorous analysis of the awakening with respect to familial and historical time.[50] To accomplish this, we need to look at admission in the light of the life course of the individual, a concept found in family studies. As the concept's most able proponent, Glen H. Elder, Jr., explains it, "The life course refers to pathways through the age-differentiated life span, to social patterns in timing, duration, spacing, and order of events. . . . Age differentiation is manifested in expectations and options that impinge on decision processes and the course of events that give shape to life stages, transitions, and turning points."[51]

If we were to use local records to reconstruct the life courses of people who joined the church before and during the awakening, we would better understand the conditions under which changes in the timing of admission took place. The same could be accomplished through diaries and other literary sources. We would want to discover especially when people experienced conversion or joined the church in conjunction with other events such as betrothal, marriage, the birth of a child, and the acquisition of land. With such information in hand, we could then supply answers to several interesting questions. For example, was there a common sequence of turning points before the awakening? Did people tend to join the church at betrothal or at marriage or at the birth of the first child or near any other transition? If so, what impact did declining ages at admission have on the usual schedule? Did other changes in the timing of events take place simultaneously? Did, for instance, ages at marriage and ages at admission change synchronically? That is, did people who joined the church at an early age during the awakening tend to marry earlier than their contemporaries or people before them, as Greven's theory of accelerated autonomy suggests?

Since abrupt changes in the life of the family could affect the timing of transitions, we also need to know whether admission may have coincided with the death of a parent, spouse, or child, or whether these variables had any important impact on ages at admission. Did people tend to enter the church in the aftermath of a family member's death?

Were ages at admission lower for men and women with recently deceased parents? As Daniel Scott Smith has demonstrated, ages at marriage among men whose fathers had died tended to be lower than among those with living fathers; perhaps the same association prevailed for ages at admission.[52] If, indeed, sons avoided the church until their fathers were no longer around to test their piety, as John Murrin suggested some time ago, then perhaps, through examination of church and vital records, we might discover a prevalent correlation between the death of patriarchs and their sons' attainment of membership.[53] Such factors as the birth order of men and women could also have had a direct bearing on ages at admission and even the achievement of admission.[54]

To achieve the best possible perspective, historians should organize the data on the life course into decadal cohorts by date of birth. This would allow us to explore admission and other transitions in a number of ways. First, we could trace life schedules among people as they passed together through the same set of historical circumstances or the same historical time. Second, we could determine the prevalence of certain schedules among people growing up at different periods. Third, we could, if necessary, explore changes in the transitional events of life with reference to the special set of social and cultural conditions that people experienced.[55]

Recently Stephen Grossbart has applied a life course analysis to the study of New England religion and society with remarkable results. Using the most sophisticated statistical analysis of church membership to date, Grossbart finds that conversion during the eighteenth and early nineteenth centuries coincided with rites of adulthood—including marriage, parenthood, and first land acquisition—but not for all people. Ages at conversion, he demonstrates, exhibited too much variation to be ascribed to any single life course event. Rather, conversion was sensitive not only to the onset of social maturity but also to religious tribalism, the influence of a spouse, revivalism, and a church's doctrinal practices. Thus, church children tended to enter communion at significantly younger ages than those without church affiliation; pious wives exerted considerable influence over the timing of their husbands' conversions; revivals at all times, not just during the two Great Awakenings, produced youthful admissions; and the stricter doctrinal practices adopted by many churches after the Great Awakening affected men more adversely than women. Since men were more doctrinal in religious orientation than women, who were more personal about faith, men were intimidated by strict admission standards into delaying admission. In a ringing indictment of prevailing interpretations of the social sources of the great revivals, Grossbart argues that "changes in social conditions, which were seen as sparking these revivals and causing youthful conversions, probably played little if any role in explaining the revivals' occurrence and outcomes. Not only did revivals take place without regard to socio-economic conditions, but their impact was remarkably uniform throughout the eighteenth century, suggesting that a revival itself accounted for younger ages of admission."[56]

Unfortunately, firm conclusions on the social meaning and importance of the youth conversions of the first Great Awakening must await further study since Grossbart's data on the subject are exceedingly thin. One of the three churches used to canvass the period 1710 to 1745, the First Congregational Church of Canterbury, Connecticut, is nearly devoid of full admission data for the period from November 1740 to May 1743, when the Great Awakening in New England reached full force, while a second church, Canterbury Separate Church, was not established until January 1745, well after the revival had ended.[57] To make up for the deficiency of the data on pre-1745 revival converts, Grossbart adds halfway members and communicants admitted through letters of recommendation to his data base, but this only confuses the analysis, since halfway membership and admission by recommendation were distinctive rituals with distinctive internal dynamics.[58]

Since full admission roles are available for many eighteenth-century New England churches, we have plenty of opportunity to test Grossbart's theories on the life course, conversion, and revivals, using his sophisticated methodology as our guide. Such studies should be comparative and should be prepared to comment on the relationship of conversion to other devotional rituals, including baptism, covenant renewals, and Half-Way Covenant, and on the relationship of these to the social forces that shaped them. As Mary McManus Ramsbottom has recently demonstrated, the lay people of Charlestown scheduled certain religious events, such as church admission, to coincide with others, such as infant baptism, and they mediated these key devotional rituals through the life course, family traditions, and their religious experiences. The social and psychological significance of individual religious rituals, however, varied among families according to their personal histories. As Ramsbottom says, "Charlestown's godly families clearly observed many subtle distinctions in social and spiritual relations and saw to it that the church also acknowledged them by maintaining various kinds of membership, some more covenantal and family-oriented than others."[59] Was this the case in other New England churches? And did revivalism disrupt traditional lay interpretations of the social significance of religious ritual? Only future studies of the social sources of Puritan devotional life, both during and apart from times of revival, will tell.

On the basis of recent evidence, we can say that such studies should also be sensitive to the role of gender, since religious experience and the timing of conversion often varied along sexual lines. In fact, over the course of the seventeenth century, New England church membership became feminized, especially in urban areas with heavy concentrations of women. Whereas during the 1630s, in churches like Boston First, Salem First, and Charlestown First, women made up between 47 and 56 percent of the membership, by the 1690s they composed between 70 and 76 percent, and their preponderance in membership continued well into the eighteenth century.[60] More and more, then, the typical Puritan household contained a churched wife and an unchurched husband.

What did this drift mean for churches, families, and culture? We know that second- and third-generation ministers were aware of the deep piety of women and were willing to speculate on its sources, including fear of dying in childbirth and confinement to the household. We also know that some preachers extolled the piety and virtue of women.[61] But we lack information on other important areas touched by this issue of feminine piety, including the kinds of relationships existing between ministers and pious wives and mothers. What type of pastoral contacts did clergymen have with their female congregants? Did preachers cultivate the support of women as the male members grew increasingly powerful? Did women become the benefactors of clergymen and an active lay extension of the ministry?

We also need to inquire into the implications of feminine religiosity in the area of education. It is a truism that Puritans placed great emphasis on religious training in the home under the direction of the master. But, as some English scholars have pointed out, the role of the woman in educating children in grace was also considerable, especially if the patriarch neglected his duties. As Thomas Paget maintained in *Demonstration of Family Duties* (1643), "if the governor be remiss or indisposed hereunto, then his wife or some other ought to put the work forward."[62] As more and more New England households contained masters without claim to being among the elect, did primary responsibility for teaching children religion gradually shift to the mother? That the answer might be a positive one is suggested by the many expressions by men of reverence for pious mothers who had taught them the rudiments of religion.[63] Moreover, were mothers particularly influential in shaping the religious decisions of their grown children? By exploring the many ramifications of feminine piety and its pervasiveness, we can advance considerably our understanding of the ways in which families acted to sustain grace and church membership over generations.

Death and Dying

Compared to the richness of the debate on the influence of families on religion, the studies of the impact of religion on family life are not only fewer but also less analytical. Historians of the family have paid very little attention to the role of religion in the lives of individuals or their families. Investigators of premarital sexual behavior in colonial New England, for example, have not even bothered to ascertain whether the fornicators were members of a church.[64] Similarly, most analyses of marriage in colonial America have not attempted to discover whether a common religious background and orientation influenced one's choice of a spouse.[65] Indeed, historians of the family often leave the impression that religion was not a significant factor in the everyday lives of colonial Americans.

To illustrate some of the weaknesses as well as the potential of the analysis of religion and the family, we will examine death and dying. It is an appropriate topic because the anticipation of death can greatly influence the way men and women conduct their lives. Furthermore, the death of a family member affects not only the survivors but the community as well. The family must adjust to the loss, while society seeks to provide meaning and support in the face of the inevitability and terror of death. Religion plays a crucial role in relationships between death and the family or society by offering spiritual comfort and understanding for the living. Anthropologists such as Bronislaw Malinowski have theorized that the very origin and development of religion lie in a person's concern with and fear of death.[66] During the past twenty-five years, historians have paid considerable attention to death and dying in early America, though their work has been too diverse and specialized to produce a comprehensive synthesis. Particularly insufficient are investigations of the relationships between religion and death in the experiences of individuals and their families.

Most of the recent work on death in early America has been done by demographic historians. Starting with the studies published by Demos, Greven, and Lockridge in 1970, scholars have revised many of our earlier ideas about the extent and patterns of mortality in colonial America. Historians formerly assumed high levels of mortality and stressed the social instability to which they contributed. As Oscar Handlin put it in 1959, "Some of the harsh features of pioneer life disappeared with the development of settled communities. But others endured for a long time. A high death rate remained constant and throughout the seventeenth century embittered the personal relationships of the colonies."[67]

Rejecting the notion of universally high mortality, demographic historians have found that death rates in New England were generally lower than in England and that, although high in towns such as Boston or Salem, they were considerably lower in rural communities such as Andover or Hingham. Perhaps the most astounding finding has been that, while infant mortality was very high throughout New England compared to today, adult mortality rates in rural areas were far lower than previously believed, so that a person who survived to age twenty in seventeenth-century Plymouth Colony, for instance, might expect to live another forty or fifty years.[68] Recent studies of death in the Chesapeake area confirm earlier views of high mortality in the South. In seventeenth-century Andover, Massachusetts, twenty-year-old males and females could look forward to living another forty years; in seventeenth-century Middlesex County, Virginia, on the other hand, males at age twenty could expect to live another twenty-nine years and females only twenty years.[69]

Focusing on rates and patterns of mortality, demographic historians have made less effort to explore the implications of their findings for family life and religion. Daniel Scott Smith has investigated the relation of age at marriage of sons with their age at the death of their fathers in an attempt to determine the extent and nature of parental control over marriage, and Alexander Keyssar has examined the plight of widows in Woburn, Massachusetts, by correlating their economic situation with their chances of remarriage.[70] On the whole, however, historians have been content to offer a few broad generalizations—for example, that high infant and childhood mortality may have made parents hesitant to invest too much emotional energy in their young offspring—rather than using these new estimates of colonial death rates to view the impact of death on families in comparative perspective.

Many questions remain to be answered. For instance, did the fact that rural death rates in New England were markedly lower than urban ones make a difference in inheritance patterns between village communities and towns? If there was such a difference, how much of it can be attributed to variations in the wealth and occupational structures of those settings? Were the problems widows faced more difficult in urban areas than in rural communities due to the higher incidence of mortality among urban males? How much of the impression of higher death rates in New England is related to the fact that most ministers who wrote on the subject lived in towns, where mortality was comparatively high? Though overall death rates were not very high in rural areas, did the continuing experience of epidemics that could suddenly destroy a large proportion of the population, particularly those under twenty, create anxiety among New Englanders? Did the fact that levels of mortality were lower in New England than in the South have any effect on the ways in which family life was organized and perceived? These instances of unanswered and, for the most part, unexplored questions suggest exciting new research opportunities.[71]

At the same time that major advances are being made in the statistical analysis of mortality, there is a growing interest in the social and cultural aspects of death. Critics of present-day funeral practices frequently point to the Puritans for examples of how death and dying could be handled with simplicity, openness, and dignity.[72] Students of Puritan religion, on the other hand, have begun to challenge the idea that Puritans faced death with equanimity and that they had little concern for funerary ritual.[73] As a result, there is increased interest in seeing how these people dealt with mortality within the context of their family life and religious orientation.

Death was a common occurrence in colonial New England, especially among infants and young children. Though mortality rates were lower than in England or the South, at least 10 percent of newborn children died during the first year. Since most families produced five or six children, this meant that they were likely to experience the loss of an infant or young child.[74] Yet we cannot simply assume that colonial Americans reacted to the death of their children in the same way that we do today, since their views of the nature of children or the meaning of death may have been quite different from ours.

The reactions of parents to the death of a child, or a child to the death of a sibling or parent, depend in large part on assumptions about the nature of children. Are children the same throughout history? Is love between children and parents constant over time? Are reactions to death and dying among children closely tied to their developmental cycle regardless of the cultural and historical context in which they live? If children in colonial America were significantly different from children today, perhaps they did not react to death the same way our children do.

Contrary to the belief that there is little change or variation in the way young children were raised or perceived in the past, many colonial historians such as Demos and Zuckerman have adopted the views of Philippe Ariès, who maintained that young children were regarded and treated as miniature adults.[75] The Puritans assumed, for example, that children should learn to read the Holy Scriptures as soon as they could talk in order to prepare themselves for salvation in the next world.[76] Perhaps one consequence of this view of the intellectual and emotional maturity of children was that ministers did not hesitate to depict the horrors of hell for even the youngest of babes.[77] This willingness to confront young children with the harsh realities of death and dying was reinforced by the Calvinist belief that children were depraved beings who needed to be restrained and chastised.[78] While many parents today try to protect their offspring from violence on television and from discussions of death and dying—since children are regarded as innocent beings in need of love and protection—Puritan parents and ministers preached to their young about the torments of hell in store for the unrepentant and unsaved. Not only was the likelihood of dying much higher for children in colonial New England than today, but the discussions of it were more frequent and terrifying.

Such preaching is well documented. Less clear, however, is the effect it may have had on children and parents. Though Puritans accepted the idea of infant damnation in general, Peter Slater has shown that this doctrine was seldom evoked when a particular child died.[79] The harshest aspects of Puritan theology in regard to the death of young children were thus considerably mitigated by the willingness of ministers and congregations to overlook the logical implications of their doctrine in practice.

Even if the survivors of a dead child were spared the most gruesome implications of infant damnation, the emphasis on death and dying surely must have had some impact on children. To assess it, we must first consider at what ages children are capable of understanding and reacting to death. A few scholars such as Jill Barbara Menes Miller, Humberto Nagera, and Martha Wolfenstein argue that real mourning cannot occur until adulthood is reached.[80] Some, like Harriet H. Gibney, state that children under six cannot conceive of death, while Jean Piaget claims that the idea of death is not established much before puberty.[81] Others such as John Bowlby or Robert and Erna Furman counter by showing that even children aged two or three can recognize the death of a loved one and experience a deep sense of loss.[82]

There is no easy way of resolving this complex debate, but the weight of evidence appears to be on the side of those who argue that very young children can experience such a loss.[83] Accounts of Puritan children reacting to the threat or actuality of death support this position, for they were often terrified by the prospect of dying and going to hell. Perhaps part of the reason that children in our society appear to be less capable of reacting to death stems from our insistence that they should be shielded from the realities of death—often even when their own parents die. Yet, if Puritan children were capable of conceptualizing death, it still remains to be seen exactly what impact it had on them immediately or in the long run. On the one hand, they lived in a society that dealt with death more openly than we do today, so that the loss was easier to accept within the existing framework. On the other hand, the threats of the torments of hell often terrified children. The issue becomes even more complicated by the fact that we do not know what proportion of Puritan ministers or parents actually stressed the immediacy and horrors of death to children.

One might expect that adults in colonial New England coped with death and dying much better than did children. Adult mortality rates there, particularly in rural areas, were much lower than in England and the South. Yet, surprisingly, seventeenth- and eighteenth-century New Englanders believed that their immediate chances of dying were very high. This discrepancy can be explained by the emphasis on death and dying in Puritan culture. The settlers came from a country with high adult mortality. The difficulties of the early years of settlement, the uncertainty of life due to the ravages of periodic epidemics, and the frequent death of children reinforced the image of high mortality in the New World. The great religious stress on death and dying made it almost impossible for adult New Englanders to realize that large improvements in their survival rates had occurred.[84]

If adults exaggerated their immediate chances of dying, perhaps they coped better with this misinformation because of the assurances of salvation provided by their religious beliefs. Therefore, we need to consider the ways in which Puritans dealt with death as individuals, families, and communities. Unfortunately, while historians of mortality, family life, and funerary practices have published a considerable number of studies on death and dying in colonial New England, scholars investigating Puritans and religion have produced much less on this subject. A notable exception is David Stannard, whose impressive short monograph, *The Puritan Way of Death,* appeared in 1977. One of the strengths of his analysis is that it tries to relate death and dying to the life courses of individuals. Though many aspects of Stannard's work are controversial, *The Puritan Way of Death* provides a very helpful set of hypotheses for future work as well as the best synthesis of the subject to date.

Stannard's interpretation of death and childhood in early New England is similar to that of other scholars, such as Peter Gregg Slater, but his analysis of death and dying among adult Puritans remains unsubstantiated.[85] Contrary to the assumption that Puritans did not fear death because they could look forward to the rewards of heaven, Stannard argues that their doctrine provided little comfort of this kind. Since the best sign of assurance was to be unsure, even the most pious Puritans could not be confident of their eternal future. As a result, they "were gripped individually and collectively by an intense and unremitting fear of death, while *simultaneously* clinging to the traditional Christian rhetoric of viewing death as a release and relief for the earth-bound soul."[86]

As Stannard admits, it is impossible to ascertain exactly what proportion of Puritans faced their final hours with fear and trembling rather than serenity. We suspect exaggeration in the argument that feelings of assurance were believed to indicate that a man or woman was not among the saved. New Englanders, both Puritans and non-Puritans, undoubtedly feared death; certainly they devoted much energy to dealing with it. But many probably found considerable reassurance in their rituals and took comfort from their status as visible saints. Stannard underestimates, in our opinion, the ability of people to convince themselves that they are somehow exempt from the torments of hell. Though he is certainly correct that some Puritans experienced serious doubt about their salvation as they faced death, it remains to be seen whether this anxiety was very common among them.[87]

Puritans were expected to meditate daily on their human finiteness. In addition, they inherited from the Middle Ages a model of dying based on the "Ars Moriendi," or "Art of Dying Well."[88] During the fifteenth century, an explicit description and prescription of how to die well became part of Western literary tradition. Though Puritans abandoned many of the elements of the Ars Moriendi, they still maintained a deathbed ritual with implicit duties and responsibilities for both the dying person and the survivors.[89] This ritualization of death was useful in that it encouraged individuals to think about dying well before they were likely to experience it themselves. It was also helpful in generating for the dying person, as well as family and friends, a pattern of mutually supportive behavior that could provide comfort for everyone involved.

Though the early rituals of death and dying had many positive aspects, historians have neglected to consider whether they also had some negative elements. Perhaps by prescribing how individuals should behave while dying, colonial Americans may have made it an even more troublesome and difficult experience for anyone who failed to follow the prescribed pattern. Great emphasis was placed, for example, on the composure of dying persons and on their ability to bid farewell to their family and friends. Signs of dread or panic were regretted, since the dying person was supposed to instruct survivors on the proper values for living. Individuals who failed to die correctly may have disappointed themselves as well as their family and friends. Though deathbed rituals provided comfort and support for many men and women, did they also make others less able to cope with their last-minute fears?[90]

Funerary practices provide further insight into the Puritan way of death. Funerals were initially very simple but became increasingly complex and lavish in the late seventeenth and early eighteenth centuries. The many gravestones that have withstood the ravages of time provide a solid basis for analyzing this change. Though earlier scholars pointed to the importance of studying the origins and carvers of colonial gravestones, they did not focus on their design origins or symbolic significance.[91] But, in 1966, Allan I. Ludwig published his influential analysis of New England gravestones from 1650 to 1815. Ludwig argued that, as Puritans channeled their religious practices into more tightly controlled areas of expression, their emotional need to deal with the fear of death was not adequately met by the church. As a result, they unconsciously looked for other ways of coping with that fear. Gravestone imagery provided an opportunity to express their terror of death and hope of salvation outside the narrow confines of established religious practices and beliefs. Yet, as Ludwig acknowledged, the exact relationship between religion and gravestone symbols is not very clear.[92]

When Ludwig's work was first published, it did not attract much scholarly interest among social and demographic historians. In recent years, however, his pioneering study is being reconsidered and revised. His argument that Puritans were hostile to art and his conclusion that gravestone imagery was an unconscious creation emerging from folk tradition have been questioned by Dickran and Ann Tashjian, who contend that Puritans were much more interested in art than Ludwig allows.[93] Anthropologists and archaeologists such as James Deetz and Edwin S. Dethlefsen have investigated the distribution and diffusion of three different gravestone designs—death's heads, cherubs, and urns and willows.[94] Peter Benes, using some of the same approaches as Deetz and Dethlefsen, while expanding his work to include more detailed study of individual gravestone cutters, has published an investigation of folk gravestone carvings in Plymouth Colony, Massachusetts, from 1689 to 1805.[95] Several scholars have even questioned whether or not the symbols on gravestones are really closely related to religion at all.[96] Overall, the study of early American gravestones is one of the most promising and exciting areas of research on death and dying. Not only has the field attracted an active group of scholars but also its practitioners have steadily improved their methodological and conceptual tools to deal with the complex issues raised by these inquiries. From the perspective of religion and the family in the colonies, however, there are many general problems, which have received only slight attention.

The major analytical breakthrough came with Ludwig's attempt to relate shifts in gravestone designs to changes in Puritan religion. Most subsequent work has also tried to develop the close interconnections between religious beliefs and the symbolic representations on the markers. Though such studies have improved since Ludwig, they are still rather limited. While students of gravestones have a broad knowledge of early American development, for example, some of them seem not especially well versed in Puritan religion.[97] As a result, they have found it difficult to link shifts in gravestone designs with general changes in religious beliefs and practices.

Because studies of colonial gravestones have been devoted almost exclusively to those of New England Puritans, it is difficult to distinguish the impact of Puritan religious views on the evolution of marker designs from that of more general trends in colonial culture. Allan Ludwig and David Hall, for example, argue that the sentiments and symbols expressed on eighteenth-century gravestones were continued and modified in nineteenth-century hymns.[98] An interesting comparative examination of eighteenth-century burial practices in Massachusetts by John Brooke shows that significant differences existed between Congregationalists and Baptists, with the latter making much less use of personal imagery on their gravestones. Brooke also demonstrates that Baptists were far less likely to invest in the traditional rituals and artifacts of death and dying.[99] We need more comparative analyses of colonial gravestones, not only among towns or groups in Massachusetts but also among religious groups such as Puritans, Anglicans, and Catholics in other colonies.[100]

Another major shortcoming of some of the work is that it focuses too narrowly on the markers and does not place the evolution of the use and type of gravestones within the framework of Puritan burial practices. To be sure, scholars such as Ludwig and Benes have speculated on other aspects of the burial rituals of Puritans, but they have been handicapped by a lack of readily available information. Before we develop much further our interpretation of colonial attitudes toward death and dying on the basis of these gravestones, we need to ascertain the importance of these artifacts relative to other parts of the funeral ritual. We also need to consider whether the images of death portrayed on the markers were also present on other funerary items, such as mourning rings or pictures, with a similar evolution of designs.[101] How closely did the sermons preached at funerals, and often published, reflect such images? More fundamentally, we need to refocus the study of gravestones by analyzing the ways in which early Americans buried their dead. It might be useful, for example, to find out whether expenditures for funerals, either in absolute figures or as a percentage of family wealth, increased or decreased as images on gravestones depicted death in a less terrifying manner. Similarly, one might investigate for changes in the proportion of funerary expenses devoted to gravestones.[102]

One promising area for research is the spatial patterns of cemeteries and burial plots.[103] The Puritans initially did not bury their dead in common grounds, but, well before the end of the seventeenth century, they began to create cemeteries near the meetinghouse in the center of their towns. Graveyards became a focal point of community and religious identity, perhaps an expression of core family culture. As a result, such dissenters as the Baptists felt it necessary to establish their own cemeteries on the periphery of settlement. Thus the location of the graveyards became closely linked with the religious orientation of their clientele.[104] We also need to investigate the pattern of burials within cemeteries to see if family members were clustered together as they were, for instance, at Mount Auburn in the nineteenth century.[105] Did groupings of family members include only husbands and wives, parents and children, or perhaps other kin as well? Were efforts made to reassemble members of an extended family after death, even if they had died in different communities? Were remarried widows buried alongside their first husbands or their current spouses? Where were the children of such marriages buried?

Finally, scholars should try to relate Puritan funeral practices to the life course of individuals, even though this may be a very difficult task, given the fragmentary nature of surviving household information. How, for instance, did funeral services and memorials vary by the age, wealth, or status of the deceased? Were the deaths of children and young adults or of wealthier individuals mourned more than those of the elderly or poor? Were there major differences in dealing with death and dying as the result of the deceased having a large network of immediate kin in the area? And how did the religious orientations of immediate survivors interact with these characteristics of the deceased to affect the nature of the funeral and the type of gravestone erected? As historians of gravestones expand their analyses to address such questions, it will be necessary to consider the impact of religious and family factors on the ways in which the Puritans buried and memorialized their dead.

While considerable efforts have been made to discover how individuals and families in early New England handled death and dying, very little attention has been paid to how such experience may have changed over time. This is somewhat surprising in view of the recent emphasis on a life course approach that argues for the necessity of placing the experiences of each individual within their historical contexts. Though, for example, Stannard's discussion of young children and adults is sensitive to the interaction of cultural and familial factors in shaping the ways in which individuals faced death, it fails to consider elements of change over time. While he portrays the fear of death among Puritan adults as comparatively constant in the seventeenth century, others have identified some major shifts. Charles Allen Shively, for one, argues that the first generation of Puritans was rather unconcerned with and unafraid of death but that, after 1660, their descendants increasingly began to fear death as they focused more and more on their physical frailties. "Faltering hopes required physical reassurances, and these were found in a multitude of physical tokens—funerals, gravestones, elegies and sermons—tokens not of heaven but of death."[106] The later chapters of Stannard's book acknowledge alterations in Puritan funerary practices after 1660 but emphasize more, as do the Tashjians, the reactions of New Englanders to the material aspects of their lives.[107] Despite the general similarities between Shively and Stannard on change in funeral rituals after the 1660s, Stannard's discussion of the fears of Puritan adults does not reflect the apparent growing fear of death among the Puritans after the 1660s.

Why was there such a marked expansion of funeral rituals after about 1660? Scattered evidence on funeral practices in the middle or southern colonies suggests that New England was exceptional in this regard.[108] Stannard accounts for the appearance of more elaborate and expensive funerals in New England as a reaction to the frustrations and setbacks that caused Puritans in the second half of the seventeenth century to become more self-centered and self-righteous.[109] This plausible explanation reinforces similar interpretations by such scholars as the Tashjians.[110] Yet the major evidence for it is the mere coincidence of factors chronologically and geographically. It needs to be substantiated by efforts to determine which elements of New England society actually led the way in the use of more elaborate funerals. Were the earliest gravestones purchased by the most devout Puritans who sensed the failing of their "errand in the wilderness"? Or was the use of gravestones and high expenditures on funerals more common, for instance, among the newer merchants, who were less disturbed by late seventeenth-century developments than were the more religiously active colonists? Did the ministers who lamented the waning of Puritanism take the lead in pushing for more elaborate rituals, or did they merely try to reassert the religious aspects of these civil funerals, which were becoming increasingly secular and expensive? Until such questions are pursued, it is impossible either to reject or to accept Stannard's interesting hypothesis.

Though Stannard examines the role of the family in socializing children about death and in consoling the dying, most of his attention, like that of other scholars, is given to the effects of Puritan religion and New England social developments on death and dying. As a result, it is still not clear exactly what role family and kin played in changing attitudes and practices in the disposal of the dead.

Both Stannard and the Tashjians stress the reactions of individuals to the decline of Puritanism in the later seventeenth century as the explanation for the increase in funeral rituals and expenditures. Yet there are some reasons, as indicated earlier, to question the causal inferences that have been drawn from the limited available evidence. In fact, though Plymouth County did not regard impurity and declension as so threatening as did the rest of Massachusetts, it surpassed most other areas of New England in making and decorating grave markers.[111] Discussions of the use of gravestones must therefore take into consideration not only Puritan reactions to their difficulties in the New World but also the broader functions of these funeral memorials.

It may be fruitful to view the growth of more elaborate funerals and the use of gravestones from the perspective of the family. While many of the original settlers of the Massachusetts Bay Colony anticipated returning to England, by the 1660s it was clear that those who remained could no longer expect a change in English religious practices sufficient to warrant repatriation. At the same time, the first generation, which was by then growing old, became increasingly concerned about its members' own deaths and their children's future. Farmers in Andover, Massachusetts, for example, were anxious to provide land for their children so that they could settle nearby.[112] New England was becoming increasingly self-centered and isolated from events abroad, and many people sought to preserve not only the cultural and religious heritage of the first settlers but also that of their particular families.[113]

Could it be that some of the emphasis on grave markers reflected efforts to perpetuate the memory of one's own family? In fact, the earliest markers gave only the name of the deceased and did not convey spiritual messages to the survivors.[114] Perhaps the same impetus that led some wealthy individuals to establish family tombs in Boston also persuaded the less affluent to remind themselves of their family heritage by the use of gravestones and family plots.[115] The transition from simple burials to more elaborate funerals also needs to be considered from the perspective of family reactions. The older members of the Puritan community in the second half of the seventeenth century had grown up during the 1630s and 1640s, when lavish displays at funerals or in cemeteries were frowned upon. Yet, as they were about to face death themselves or to bury their spouses or close friends, funeral practices were drastically changing. How did successive generations react to these changes? Was the elaboration brought about by the first settlers, by their children, or by recent immigrants?

Did the new practices represent a way of bringing together the survivors, not only for the sake of the community as a whole but also to meet the needs of immediate family and kin? Was the practice of distributing mourning rings at funerals, for example, a means of reintegrating family and kin ties in the face of the partial dissolution of the network?[116] In other words, to what extent were the rise of elaborate funerals and the use of gravestones the results of the effort of families in New England to establish a more lasting heritage for themselves and their descendants, and how was this process guided or shaped by the needs of the larger community? How much of the strong negative reactions against the new rituals came from older members of the community, who may have been horrified by widespread departures from the traditional Puritan ways of burying the dead? Perhaps the older generation had the most difficulty in coping with these changes because they may have lived in a period of increasing fear and concern about death without being comforted by innovations that many of them must have regarded as strange or blasphemous.

Conclusion

This chapter has examined many of the recent works dealing with the relationship between the Puritan family and religion in early America.

We have evaluated these studies in order to identify promising lines of inquiry by looking at three subjects: Puritan tribalism and the core family, family strategies and the life course, and death and dying. These are among the most attractive areas for research but are by no means the only ones that beckon scholars. The entire field calls for extensive exploration, building on and revising the work done in the 1960s, 1970s, and 1980s. The conceptual and methodological ideas used in New England studies should be applied elsewhere in order to develop comparative analyses for other regions of early America. At the same time, we believe that New England is a particularly suitable region in which to initiate deeper and more systematic investigation of religion and the family because of the richness of its sources and the scholarly advances that have been made in exploiting them.

The literature discussed in this essay not only testifies to the productivity and freshness of the field but also points out directions for future studies. Historians of the household or the kin group must consider how its development and functioning may have been shaped by the life of the church and spirit. Conversely, historians who seek to understand the life of the spirit must do so in terms of the family. Families often behaved with religious strategies and goals in mind, while the church grew because of the initiatives of successive generations of pious householders. Moreover, communal life was played out along networks that often centered in the church, and people dealt with dying in ways established and conditioned by religion. In several respects, as this chapter has shown, the inquiry into the relationship of family and religion offers opportunities to employ or test unconventional methods of research—a fact that should make the undertaking all the more attractive and challenging to scholars who are seriously concerned about recovering these fundamentals of human experience in past time.

Notes

1. Bernard Bailyn, *Education in the Forming of American Society: Needs and Opportunities for Study* (Chapel Hill, N.C., 1960), esp. 75–78.
2. John Demos, *A Little Commonwealth: Family Life in Plymouth Colony* (New York, 1970); Philip J. Greven, Jr., *Four Generations: Population, Land, and Family in Colonial Andover, Massachusetts* (Ithaca, N.Y., 1970); Kenneth A. Lockridge, *A New England Town, The First Hundred*

Years: Dedham, Massachusetts, 1636–1736 (New York, 1970); Michael Zuckerman, *Peaceable Kingdoms: New England Towns in the Eighteenth Century* (New York, 1970).

Among the essays that review all four books and also the historiographical ramifications of the new social history, see especially Jack P. Greene, "Autonomy and Stability: New England and the British Colonial Experience in Early Modern America," *Journal of Social History* 7 (1974): 171–93; James A. Henretta, "The Morphology of New England Society in the Colonial Period," *Journal of Interdisciplinary History* 2 (1971): 379–98; and John Murrin, "Review Essay," *History and Theory* 11 (1972): 226–75.

3. For a summary of recent demographic studies, see Maris A. Vinovskis, "Recent Trends in American Historical Demography: Some Methodological and Conceptual Considerations," *Annual Review of Sociology* 4 (1978): 603–27.

4. Tamara K. Hareven, "The History of the Family as an Interdisciplinary Field," *Journal of Interdisciplinary History* 2 (1971): 412–13. For a recent overview of developments in American family history, see Tamara K. Hareven, "The History of the Family and the Complexity of Social Change," *American Historical Review* 96 (1991): 95–124.

5. In 1972, in a rejoinder to David Grayson Allen's critique of *Peaceable Kingdoms,* Michael Zuckerman advised historians "to become anthropologists, social psychologists, and comparative historians of the colonies, for we are beginning to know enough about them to make the comparison with other cultures worth our while. And at the same time, we are beginning to know enough about New England to make it not merely worthwhile but also quite necessary to canvass such comparisons: we have got to get out of New England or we will never know the significance of what we know." "Rejoinder," *William and Mary Quarterly,* 3d ser., 29 (1972): 467–68. Several years later, in 1974, Greene argued "that interest in New England has run so deep that the importance of its study has come to be taken for granted. The result has been that no one any longer bothers to ask the questions of why New England should be studied, why its investigation should be given priority over that of other areas of the British-American colonial world, or what it might tell us about that world that the experiences of other colonies would not." "Autonomy and Stability," 173. In contrast, we call for both comparative, interdisciplinary studies of all colonial societies *and* further investigation into New England towns, churches, and families.

6. See chapter 4 for a discussion of Puritan religion and education.

7. Edmund S. Morgan, *The Puritan Family: Religion and Domestic Relations in Seventeenth-Century New England,* rev. ed. (New York, 1966).

For earlier studies that touch on Puritanism and the family, see Arthur W. Calhoun, *A Social History of the American Family from Colonial Times to the Present,* 3 vols. (Cleveland, Ohio, 1917–19); Alice M. Earle, *Child Life in Colonial Days* (New York, 1899); *Home Life in Colonial Days* (New York, 1898); and Stanford Fleming, *Children and Puritanism: The Place of Children in the Life and Thought of the New England Churches, 1620–1847* (New Haven, Conn., 1933).

8. For an examination of Morgan's historical explanations, see David Mark Trousdale, "Society and Culture, Order and Change in Early America: The Sociology of Edmund S. Morgan" (Ph.D. diss., Case Western Reserve, 1976).

9. Morgan, *Puritan Family,* 166.

10. Morgan, *Puritan Family,* 186.

11. Edmund S. Morgan, *Virginians at Home: Family Life in the Eighteenth Century* (Williamsburg, Va., 1952).

12. Frederick B. Tolles, *Meeting House and Counting House: The Quaker Merchants of Colonial Philadelphia, 1682–1763* (Chapel Hill, N.C., 1948), 230. See also Barry Levy, *Quakers and the American Family: British Settlement in the Delaware Valley* (New York, 1988).

13. J. William Frost, *The Quaker Family in Colonial America: A Portrait of the Society of Friends* (New York, 1973), 68. See also Susan S. Forbes, "Quaker Tribalism," in *Friends and Neighbors: Group Life in America's First Plural Society,* ed. Michael Zuckerman (Philadelphia, 1982), 145–73.

14. Gillian L. Gollin, *Moravians in Two Worlds: A Study of Changing Communities* (New York, 1967), 120.

15. See, for example, James A. Henretta, "Families and Farms: *Mentalité* in Pre-Industrial America," *William and Mary Quarterly,* 3d ser., 35 (1978): 3–32; Gerald F. Moran, "Conditions of Religious Conversion in the First Society of Norwich, Connecticut, 1718–1744," *Journal of Social History* 5 (1972): 331–43; Timothy L. Smith, "Religion and Ethnicity in America," *American Historical Review* 83 (1978): 1155–85; and James Walsh, "The Great Awakening in the First Congregational Church of Woodbury, Connecticut," *William and Mary Quarterly,* ser. 3, 28 (1971): 543–62.

16. William A. Christian, *Person and God in a Spanish Valley* (New York, 1972), 144.

17. See, for example, Peter L. Berger and Thomas Luckmann, *The Social Construction of Reality: A Treatise in the Sociology of Knowledge* (New

York, 1966), esp. chap. 1, "The Foundations of Knowledge in Everyday Life." Using the testimonies delivered in Thomas Shepard's Cambridge, Massachusetts, church during the 1630s and 1640s, Charles Lloyd Cohen has recreated the sociocultural context of church admission in *God's Caress: The Psychology of Puritan Religious Experience* (New York, 1986), chap. 5. For an analysis of the "three-sided" character of the admission process—one involving speaker, audience, and church—see Patricia Caldwell, *The Puritan Conversion Narrative: The Beginnings of American Expression* (New York, 1983), chap. 1.

18. Increase Mather, *A Call from Heaven* (Boston, 1679), 7.

19. Jon Butler, "Magic, Astrology, and the Early American Religious Heritage, 1660–1760," *American Historical Review* 84 (1979): 317–46; see also *Awash in a Sea of Faith: Christianizing the American People* (Cambridge, Mass., 1990); and "The People's Faith, in Europe and America: Four Centuries in Review," *Journal of Social History* 12 (1978): 159–67.

20. Linda Auwers Bissell, "From One Generation to Another: Mobility in Seventeenth-Century Windsor, Connecticut," *William and Mary Quarterly,* 3d ser., 31 (1974): 79–110; see also chapter 2.

21. For the concept of backstage, intimate knowledge of a group's values, see Erving Goffman, *The Presentation of Self in Everyday Life* (Edinburgh, 1956), esp. chap. 3.

22. Paul R. Lucas, *Valley of Discord: Church and Society along the Connecticut River, 1636–1725* (Hanover, N.H., 1976), 106–7.

23. Lucas, *Valley of Discord,* 138.

24. See chapter 2.

25. For religion as an organizing process, see Donald G. Mathews, "The Second Great Awakening as an Organizing Process, 1780–1830: An Hypothesis," *American Quarterly* 21 (1969): 23–43; and Timothy L. Smith, "Congregation, State, and Denomination: The Forming of the American Religious Structure," *William and Mary Quarterly,* 3d ser., 25 (1968): 155–76.

26. John Bossy, "Blood and Baptism: Kinship, Community and Christianity in Western Europe from the Fourteenth to the Seventeenth Centuries," *Studies in Church History* 10 (1973): 130–31. On the "instinctive tribalism" of the early New England laity, see David D. Hall, *Worlds of Wonder, Days of Judgment: Popular Religious Belief in Early New England* (New York, 1989), 152–56.

27. Alan Macfarlane, *The Family Life of Ralph Josselin: A Seventeenth-Century Clergyman* (Cambridge, Eng., 1970). The diaries that seem best suited to the study of society and religion include those of Jonathan Edwards,

Joshua Hempstead, John Hull, Cotton Mather, Thomas Minor, Ebenezer Parkman, Samuel Sewall, Thomas Shepard, and Stephen Williams.

Network theory might also be used to study religion and interpersonal relationships. See Darrett B. Rutman, "Community Study," *Historical Methods* 13 (1980): 29–41.

28. Morgan, *Puritan Family*, 174, 185.

29. Edmund S. Morgan, *Visible Saints: The History of a Puritan Idea* (New York, 1963), 137.

30. Edmund S. Morgan, "New England Puritanism: Another Approach," *William and Mary Quarterly*, 3d ser., 18 (1961): 241–42.

31. Robert G. Pope traces the historiography of declension in "New England versus the New England Mind: The Myth of Declension," *Journal of Social History* 3 (1969): 95–99, and Philip J. Greven, Jr., examines Miller's usage of declension and his critics in *The Protestant Temperament: Patterns of Child-Rearing, Religious Experience, and the Self in Early America* (New York, 1977), 5–12. Michael McGiffert surveys writings of Miller's critics but also warns historians against reading declension too readily into Miller's corpus. "American Puritan Studies in the 1960s," *William and Mary Quarterly*, 3d ser., 27 (1970): 36–67.

Surely, it is high time to omit declension from the lexicon of Puritan studies; it has ceased to be a useful concept. But what concepts do we replace it with? Unfortunately, what McGiffert noted in 1970 is just as true today: "At present Puritan and New England historiography is remarkable more for vitality than for coherence. This may signify an impending change of paradigm, yet, as Kuhn points out, paradigm revolutions cannot occur unless and until an alternative paradigm is available to replace the old outworn one—and that is very far from the present case in Puritan studies" (67). Recently, though, David D. Hall has made a convincing case for the coherence around several central themes of Puritan studies, including the multifacetedness of American Puritanism, in which preachers and lay people responded to multiple influences, and the new confidence in language as a guide to behavior. "On Common Ground: The Coherence of American Puritan Studies," *William and Mary Quarterly*, 3d ser., 44 (1987): 193–229.

32. Lockridge, *New England Town*, 90. As Greene observed, *New England Town* "is the classic story of New England declension, much refined and retold at the community level in terms of not merely the religious but also the broad social, political and economic experiences of the residents of the town." Greene, "Autonomy and Stability," 173.

33. James A. Henretta, "The Morphology of New England Society in the Colonial Period," *Journal of Interdisciplinary History* 1 (1971): 396–98.

34. Robert G. Pope, *The Half-Way Covenant: Church Membership in Puritan New England* (Princeton, N.J., 1969), 273, 238.

35. See chapter 2. Recently, a convincing case has been made for studying noncommunicant adherents, including halfway members, pew holders, and irregular attenders. See Patricia U. Bonomi, *Under the Cope of Heaven: Religion, Society, and Politics in Colonial America* (New York, 1986), 87–92; and Patricia U. Bonomi and Peter R. Eisenstadt, "Church Adherence in the Eighteenth-Century British American Colonies," *William and Mary Quarterly*, 3d ser., 39 (1982): 245–86. Given what we now know about the devotional richness and variability of American Puritanism, future statistical studies of the church will need to include evidence on baptisms, Half-Way Covenants, and other covenantal rites. In this respect, the work of Mary MacManus Ramsbottom is groundbreaking. "Religious Society and the Family in Charlestown, Massachusetts, 1630–1740" (Ph.D. diss., Yale University, 1987).

36. Emory Elliott, *Power and the Pulpit in Puritan New England* (Princeton, N.J., 1975); E. Brooks Holifield, *The Covenant Sealed: The Development of Puritan Sacramental Theology in Old and New England* (New Haven, Conn., 1974); David D. Hall, *The Faithful Shepherd: A History of the New England Ministry in the Seventeenth Century* (Chapel Hill, N.C., 1972); David Levin, *Cotton Mather: The Young Life of the Lord's Remembrancer, 1663–1703* (Cambridge, Mass., 1978); Charles E. Hambrick-Stowe, *The Practice of Piety: Puritan Devotional Disciplines in Seventeenth-Century New England* (Chapel Hill, N.C., 1982); Harry S. Stout, *The New England Soul: Preaching and Religious Culture in Colonial New England* (New York, 1986); Richard F. Lovelace, *The American Pietism of Cotton Mather: Origins of American Evangelicalism* (Grand Rapids, Mich., 1979); Lucas, *Valley of Discord*; Robert Middlekauff, *The Mathers: Three Generations of Puritan Intellectuals, 1596–1728* (New York, 1971).

37. See chapter 2. For another recent analysis of cyclical, intergenerational patterns of local religious activity, see Ramsbottom, "Religious Society." Ramsbottom's significant study is distinctive for its statistical treatment of baptismal membership as well as halfway and full membership.

38. See Gerald F. Moran, "The Puritan Saint: Religious Experience, Church Membership, and Piety in Connecticut, 1636–1776" (Ph.D. diss., Rutgers University, 1974), chaps. 5, 9. Walsh also sees tribal propensities existing among church families. "Great Awakening," 551, 561–62.

39. Tamara K. Hareven, "Family Time and Historical Time," *Daedalus* 106 (1977): 58.

40. Natalie Zemon Davis, "Ghosts, Kin, and Progeny: Some Features of Family Life in Early Modern France," *Daedalus* 106 (1977): 87, 92, 108.

41. Greven, *Four Generations,* esp. chap. 4. Greven's analysis of parental power inadequately relates the economic dependence of children on their fathers to demographic factors such as their ages at marriage. Unfortunately, his work does not actually establish statistically the link between the retention of farm titles by the fathers and the postponement of the ages at marriage of the sons. Rather, it cites as evidence a weak correlation between age at marriage and birth order for the second generation without properly subdividing the families by the type of land transmission. Furthermore, though some fathers apparently tried to extend the same type of control to the third generation, any possible correlation between birth order and age at marriage is never established. Accordingly, as historians begin to pursue such interesting hypotheses, it is imperative that they devise appropriate statistical tests to validate them. Greven's data need reanalysis before historians can fully accept his interpretations of them. On these issues, see Maris A. Vinovskis, "American Historical Demography: A Review Essay," *Historical Methods Newsletter* 4 (1971): 141–48.

42. Greven, *Protestant Temperament,* 16.

43. Greven, *Protestant Temperament,* 22, 43.

44. Hareven, "Family Time," 59.

45. Hareven, "Family Time."

46. See, for example, J. M. Bumsted, "Religion, Finance, and Democracy in Massachusetts: The Town of Norton as a Case Study," *Journal of American History* 57 (1971): 817–31; Philip J. Greven, Jr., "Youth, Maturity, and Religious Conversion: A Note on the Ages of Converts in Andover, Massachusetts, 1711–1749," *Essex Institute Historical Collections* 108 (1972): 119–34; Moran, "Conditions of Religious Conversion"; Patricia J. Tracy, *Jonathan Edwards, Pastor: Religion and Society in Eighteenth-Century Northampton* (New York, 1980), esp. chaps. 4–5; Walsh, "Great Awakening"; William F. Willingham, "Religious Conversion in the Second Society of Windham, Connecticut, 1723–1743: A Case Study," *Societas* 6 (1976): 109–19.

47. Greven, "Youth, Maturity, and Religious Conversion," 129–30.

48. Bumsted, "Religion, Finance, and Democracy," 828–30.

49. Christine Leigh Heyrman, *Commerce and Culture: The Maritime Communities of Colonial Massachusetts, 1690–1750* (New York, 1984), 193–95.

50. A recent important exception is Stephen R. Grossbart, "Seeking the Divine Favor: Conversion and Church Admission in Eastern Connecticut, 1711–1832," *William and Mary Quarterly,* 3d ser., 46 (1989): 696–740, which we examine at some length below.

51. Glen H. Elder, Jr., "Family History and the Life Course," in *Transitions: The Family and the Life Course in Historical Perspective,* ed. Tamara K. Hareven (New York, 1978), 17–64. On the life course approach, see also Tamara K. Hareven, "Cycles, Courses and Cohorts: Reflections on Theoretical and Methodological Approaches to the Historical Study of Family Development," *Journal of Social History* 12 (1978): 97–109; and Maris A. Vinovskis, "From Household Size to the Life Course: Some Observations on Recent Trends in Family History," *American Behavioral Scientist* 21 (1977): 263–87.

52. Daniel Scott Smith, "Parental Power and Marriage Patterns: An Analysis of Historical Trends in Hingham, Massachusetts," *Journal of Marriage and the Family* 35 (1973): 422–24.

53. John Murrin, "Review Essay," *History and Theory* 11 (1972): 236–39.

54. The relationship between religious experience and birth order is examined in Richard T. Vann, *The Social Development of English Quakerism, 1655–1755* (Cambridge, Mass., 1969).

55. For the concepts of "spread" and "prevalence" in the timing of personal events, see John Modell et al., "Social Change and Transitions to Adulthood in Historical Perspective," in *The American Family in Socio-Historical Perspective,* ed. Michael Gordon, 2d ed. (New York, 1978), 198–201.

56. Grossbart, "Seeking the Divine Favor," 739.

57. In the Canterbury First, only one full member, Esther Jackson, appears on the admission roles for the entire period November 1740 to May 1743, while ten others appear admitted by recommendation from other churches. Alan C. Bates, ed., *Records of the Congregational Church in Canterbury, Connecticut, 1711–1844* (Hartford, Conn., 1932), 46–47.

58. Thus, Grossbart's sample of first-time communicants who joined churches during the Great Awakening is exceedingly small, consisting only of the thirty-seven new members who entered New Concord First, Connecticut, in the period 1741–42.

But Grossbart is not alone in downplaying the social significance of the youthful conversions of the Great Awakening. As Harry Stout has argued, variations in socioreligious data on the great revival "point to the limitations of social variables as final explanations for the impact of revivals in New England." *New England Soul,* 359 n. 36. Yet Peter S. Onuf has argued that youth as well as poverty played a highly conspicuous role in revival separatism. As he explains it, "The large number of teenagers among the separatists reflected the New Light tendency to dissociate the new-birth conversion experience from worldly considerations." "New Lights in New London: A Group Portrait of the Separatists," *William and Mary Quarterly,* 3d ser., 37

(1980): 627–43. That the social meaning of the Great Awakening will continue to occupy historians for years to come is a judgment that finds final confirmation in the controversy surrounding Jon Butler's recent valiant but misguided effort to purge the phrase entirely from the lexicon of early American history. See Jon Butler, "Enthusiasm Described and Decried: The Great Awakening as Interpretative Fiction," *Journal of American History* 69 (1982): 302–25.

59. Ramsbottom, "Religious Society," 271.

60. Mary Maples Dunn, "Saints and Sisters: Congregational and Quaker Women in the Early Colonial Period," in *Women in American Religion,* ed. Janet Wilson James (Philadelphia, 1980), 27–46; see chapter 3.

61. Margaret W. Masson, "The Typology of the Female as a Model for the Regenerate: Puritan Preaching, 1690–1730," *Signs: Journal of Women in Culture and Society* 2 (1976): 304–15; Laurel Thatcher Ulrich, "Vertuous Women Found: New England Ministerial Literature, 1668–1735," *American Quarterly* 28 (1976): 20–40.

62. Quoted in R. C. Richardson, *Puritanism in North-west England: A Regional Study of the Diocese of Chester to 1642* (Manchester, Eng., 1972), 106.

63. See, for example, David Ferris, *Memoirs of the Life of David Ferris, an Approved Minister of the Society of Friends . . . Written by Himself* (1825; reprint, Philadelphia, 1855) 16, and Michael G. Hall, ed., "The Autobiography of Increase Mather," American Antiquarian Society *Proceedings* 71 (1961): 278. We explore these issues in greater detail in chapters 3 and 4.

64. Daniel Scott Smith and Michael S. Hindus, "Premarital Pregnancy in America, 1640–1971: An Overview and Interpretation," *Journal of Interdisciplinary History* 5 (1975): 537–70; Robert V. Wells, "Illegitimacy and Bridal Pregnancy in Colonial America," in *Bastardy and Its Comparative History,* ed. Peter Laslett et al. (Cambridge, Mass., 1980), 349–61.

65. Smith, "Parental Power and Marriage Patterns."

66. Bronislaw Malinowski, *Magic, Science and Religion, and Other Essays* (Garden City, N.Y., 1948).

67. Oscar Handlin, "The Significance of the Seventeenth Century," in *Seventeenth-Century America: Essays in Colonial History,* ed. James Morton Smith (Chapel Hill, N.C., 1959), 8.

68. For a critical review of mortality estimates in early America, see Maris A. Vinovskis, "Mortality Rates and Trends in Massachusetts before 1860," *Journal of Economic History* 32 (1972): 184–213; and "Recent Trends in American Historical Demography," *Annual Review of Sociology* 4 (1978). Many of the articles dealing with early American mortality

have been reprinted in Maris A. Vinovskis, ed., *Studies in American Historical Demography* (New York, 1979).

69. Darrett B. Rutman and Anita H. Rutman, "Of Agues and Fevers: Malaria in the Early Chesapeake," *William and Mary Quarterly*, 3d ser., 33 (1976): 31–60; *A Place in Time: Middlesex County, Virginia, 1650–1750* (New York, 1984); Carville V. Earle, "Environment, Disease, and Mortality in Early Virginia," in *The Chesapeake in the Seventeenth Century: Essays on Anglo-American Society,* ed. Thad W. Tate and David L. Ammerman (Chapel Hill, N.C., 1979), 96–125; Alan Kulikoff, *Tobacco and Slaves: The Development of Southern Cultures in the Chesapeake, 1680–1800* (Chapel Hill, N.C., 1986).

70. Smith, "Parental Power and Marriage Patterns"; Alexander Keyssar, "Widowhood in Eighteenth-Century Massachusetts: A Problem in the History of the Family," *Perspectives in American History* 8 (1974): 83–119.

71. While analysts of colonial New England have not done much to study the impact of death on the family, those of the colonial South have become much more concerned about this issue, in large part due to the high adult death rates in that society. See Darrett B. Rutman and Anita H. Rutman, "'Now-Wives and Sons-in-Law': Parental Death in a Seventeenth-Century Virginia County," in Tate and Ammerman, *Chesapeake Essays,* 153–82; Daniel Blake Smith, *Inside the Great House: Planter Family Life in Eighteenth-Century Chesapeake Society* (Ithaca, N.Y., 1980); and Lorena S. Walsh, "'Till Death Us Do Part': Marriage and Family in Seventeenth-Century Maryland," in Tate and Ammerman, *Chesapeake Essays,* 126–52.

72. Jessica Mitford, *The American Way of Death* (New York, 1963).

73. David E. Stannard, *The Puritan Way of Death: A Study in Religion, Culture, and Social Change* (New York, 1977).

74. Maris A. Vinovskis, "Death and Family Life in the Past," *Human Nature* 1 (1990): 109–22.

75. See, for example, Carl N. Degler, *At Odds: Women and the Family in America from the Revolution to the Present* (New York, 1980), 69; John Demos, "The American Family in Past Time," *American Scholar* 43 (1974): 428; Fleming, *Children and Puritanism,* 60–61, 67; and Zuckerman, *Peaceable Kingdoms,* 73.

76. For critiques of the idea that young children in early America were seen as miniature adults, see Ross W. Beales, Jr., "In Search of the Historical Child: Miniature Adulthood and Youth in Colonial New England," *American Quarterly* 27 (1975): 379–98; Gusti Wisenfeld Frankel, "Between Parent and Child in Colonial New England: An Analysis of the Religious Child-oriented Literature and Selected Children's Work"

(Ph.D. diss., University of Minnesota, 1976), 14–16; Carl F. Kaestle and Maris A. Vinovskis, "From Apron Strings to ABCs: Parents, Children, and Schooling in Nineteenth-Century Massachusetts," in *Turning Points: Historical and Sociological Essays on the Family,* ed. John Demos and Sarane Spence Boocock (Chicago, 1978), S539–S580; and David E. Stannard, "Death and the Puritan Child," in *Death in America,* ed. David Stannard (Philadelphia, 1975), 9–29.

77. See chapter 7.

78. Greven, *Protestant Temperament;* Peter Gregg Slater, *Children in the New England Mind: In Death and Life* (Hamden, Conn., 1977); Stannard, "Death and the Puritan Child."

79. Slater, *Children in the New England Mind.*

80. Jill Barbara Menes Miller, "Reactions to the Death of a Parent: A Review of the Psychoanalytic Literature," *Journal of the American Psychoanalytic Association* 19 (1971): 697–719; Humberto Nagera, "Children's Reactions to the Death of Important Objects: A Developmental Approach," *Psychoanalytic Study of the Child* 25 (1970): 360–400; Martha Wolfenstein, "How Is Mourning Possible?", *Psychoanalytic Study of the Child* 21 (1960): 93–123.

81. Harriet H. Gibney, "What Death Means to Children," *Parents' Magazine* 40 (1965): 64. For an analysis of the views of Piaget, see Sylvia Anthony, *The Discovery of Death in Childhood and After* (New York, 1972).

82. John Bowlby, *Loss: Sadness and Depression* (New York, 1980); Erna Furman, *A Child's Parent Dies: Studies in Childhood Bereavement* (New Haven, Conn., 1974); Robert A. Furman, "The Child's Reaction to Death in the Family," in *Loss and Grief: Psychological Management in Medical Practice,* ed. Bernard Schoenberg et al. (New York, 1970), 70–86.

83. For a useful summary of the current theories of the experiences of young children and death, see Marian Osterweis, Frederic Solomon, and Morris Green, eds., *Bereavement: Reactions, Consequences, and Care* (Washington, D.C., 1984), 99–141.

84. See chapter 7.

85. Slater, *Children in the New England Mind;* Stannard, *Puritan Way of Death,* 44–71.

86. Stannard, *Puritan Way of Death,* 79.

87. Gordon E. Geddes even questions Stannard's analysis of the role of "assurance" for prominent Puritans such as Michael Wigglesworth and Increase Mather, in *Welcome Joy: Death in Puritan New England, 1630–1730* (Ann Arbor, Mich., 1981), 210.

88. On the medieval background of the "Ars Morendi," see Philippe Ariès,

Western Attitudes toward Death: From the Middle Ages to the Present, trans. Patricia Ranum (Baltimore, 1974); T. S. R. Boase, *Death in the Middle Ages: Mortality, Judgment, and Remembrance* (New York, 1972); Johan Huizinga, *The Waning of the Middle Ages* (New York, 1964); and Mary Catharine O'Connor, *The Art of Dying Well: The Development of the Ars Moriendi* (New York, 1942).

Ariès divides the evolution of Western attitudes and behavior toward death into five roughly sequential, though overlapping, stages: (1) tame death, (2) the death of the self, (3) remote and imminent death, (4) the death of the other, and (5) invisible death. Philippe Ariès, *The Hour of Our Death,* trans. Helen Weaver (New York, 1981). Though his work is very interesting and useful, his stages are not convincing. For critiques, see Lawrence Stone, *The Past and the Present* (London, 1981), 242–59, and Maris A. Vinovskis, review of *The Hour of Our Death,* in *Journal of Social History* 16 (1982–83): 129–31.

89. On deathbed rituals among Puritans, see Geddes, *Welcome Joy,* 58–81. These rituals seem to have become even more widespread in the nineteenth century. Discussions of death and dying in nineteenth-century America can be found in James J. Farrell, *Inventing the American Way of Death, 1830–1920* (Philadelphia, 1980); Barbara G. Rosenkrantz and Maris A. Vinovskis, "'Sustaining the Flickering Flame of Life': Accountability and Culpability for Death in Ante-Bellum Massachusetts Asylums," in *Health Care in America: Essays in Social History,* ed. Susan Reverby and David Rosner (Philadelphia, 1979), 155–82; and Stannard, *Death in America.*

90. An interesting twentieth-century counterpart to this problem is the work of Elisabeth Kübler-Ross on the five stages of death and dying, which seems to be developing a new myth about the proper way of dying. For a critique of her work and a detailed discussion of this point, see Maris A. Vinovskis, "Kübler-Ross and the Five Stages of Dying: Some Methodological and Conceptual Reservations," *Proceedings of the World Conference on Records* 3 (1981), ser. 328, 1–20.

91. Harriette Merrifield Forbes, *Gravestones of Early New England and the Men Who Made Them, 1653–1800* (Boston, 1927).

92. Alan I. Ludwig, *Graven Images: New England Stonecarving and Its Symbols, 1650–1815* (Middletown, Conn., 1966).

93. Dickran Tashjian and Ann Tashjian, *Memorials for Children of Change: The Art of Early New England Stonecarving* (Middletown, Conn., 1974).

94. Edwin S. Dethlefsen and James Deetz, "Death's Heads, Cherubs, and Willow Trees: Experimental Archaeology in Colonial Cemeteries," *American Antiquity* 31 (1966): 502–10.

95. Peter Benes, *The Masks of Orthodoxy: Folk Gravestone Carving in Plymouth County, Massachusetts, 1689–1805* (Amherst, Mass., 1977).

96. David D. Hall, "The Gravestone Image as a Puritan Cultural Code," *Annual Proceedings of the Dublin Seminar for New England Folklife* (1976): Puritan Gravestone Art, 1:23–32; Lance R. Mayer, "An Alternative to Panofskyism: New England Grave Stones and the European Folk Art Tradition," *Annual Proceedings of the Dublin Seminar for New England Folklife (1978): Puritan Gravestone Art*, 2:5–17. For a useful discussion of the relationship between the religious and civil aspects of Puritan gravestone designs and imagery, see Dickran Tashjian, "Puritan Attitudes toward Iconoclasm," *Annual Proceedings of the Dublin Seminar for New England Folklife (1978): Puritan Gravestone Art*, 2:37–45.

97. For a good critique of the early work on gravestones from a religious perspective, see Hall, "The Gravestone Image."

98. Allan I. Ludwig and David D. Hall, "Aspects of Music, Poetry, Stone-carving, and Death in Early New England," *Annual Proceedings of the Dublin Seminar for New England Folklife (1978): Puritan Gravestone Art*, 2:18–24.

99. John Brooke, "The Earth and the Water: Human Geography, Ritual Practice, and Personal Life Cycle in Orthodox and Dissenting Communities on the Near Frontier" (Paper presented at the 41st Conference in Early American History, Millersville, Pa., May 1981).

100. For discussions of cemeteries and gravestones outside of New England, see Diana Williams Comb, *Early Gravestone Art in Georgia and South Carolina* (Athens, Ga., 1986); Richard Welch, "Colonial and Federal New York and New Jersey Gravestones," *Journal of Long Island History* 17 (1981): 23–34.

101. For an attempt to compare images of death on gravestones and mourning pictures, see Faye Joanne Baker, "Toward Memory and Mourning: A Study of Changing Attitudes toward Death between 1750 and 1850 as Revealed by Gravestones of the New Hampshire Merrimack River Valley Mourning Pictures, and Representative Writings" (Ph.D. diss., George Washington University, 1977). The most detailed analysis of the Puritan funeral is in Geddes, *Welcome Joy*. His analysis is more complete and accurate than that provided by Robert W. Habenstein and William M. Lamers, *The History of American Funeral Directing*, rev. ed. (Milwaukee, Wis., 1962), 195–224.

102. For interesting data on the amount of money spent on funerals, see Benes, *Masks of Orthodoxy*, 36–37. It would be very useful to study funeral costs by adding such information to the extensive collection of probate records for all of the colonies in 1774 gathered by Alice Hanson

Jones. These data are computerized and available from the Inter-University Consortium for Political and Social Research at the University of Michigan. *Wealth of a Nation to Be: The American Colonies on the Eve of the Revolution* (New York, 1980); and *American Colonial Wealth: Documents and Methods,* 2d ed. (New York, 1977). For detailed critiques of this important work, see Linda Auwers, "History from the Mean—Up, Down, and Around: A Review Essay," *Historical Methods* 12 (1979): 39–45; and Maris A. Vinovskis, "Estimating the Wealth of Americans on the Eve of the Revolution," *Journal of Economic History* 16 (1981): 415–20.

103. For a recent summary of the evolution of American cemeteries, see David Charles Sloane, *The Last Great Necessity: Cemeteries in American History* (Baltimore, 1991).

104. Brooke, "Earth and Water."

105. Stanley French, "The Cemetery as Cultural Institution: The Establishment of Mount Auburn and the 'Rural Cemetery' Movement," in Stannard, *Death in America,* 69–71; Blanche Linden-Ward, *Silent City on a Hill: Landscapes of Memory and Boston's Mount Auburn Cemetery* (Columbus, Ohio, 1989).

106. Charles Allen Shively, "A History of the Conception of Death in America, 1650–1860" (Ph.D. diss., Harvard University, 1969), 1:33.

107. Stannard, *Puritan Way of Death;* Tashjian and Tashjian, *Memorials for Children.*

108. Stannard, *Puritan Way of Death,* 128–29.

109. Stannard, *Puritan Way of Death,* 129.

110. Tashjian and Tashjian, *Memorials for Children,* 37–48.

111. Benes, *Masks of Orthodoxy,* 36–37.

112. Greven, *Four Generations.*

113. Hall, *Faithful Shepherd.*

114. Ludwig, *Graven Images,* 283–87.

115. Ludwig, *Graven Images,* 232–34.

116. Very little has been written on funeral rings other than general descriptions of them. See, for example, Martha F. Fales, "The Early American Way of Death," *Essex Institute Historical Collections* 100 (1964): 75– 84; and A. C. Needham, "Random Notes on Funeral Rings," *Old Time New England* 39 (1949): 93–97.

CHAPTER 2

Religious Renewal, Puritan Tribalism, and the Family in Seventeenth-Century Milford, Connecticut

Over thirty years ago, Edmund Morgan wrote that, if historians were to examine the colonial New England past "by localities, town by town and church by church," they "could discover a great deal not only about the diversity of Puritanism but also about its range and penetration within society." Such an undertaking—a new approach to New England Puritanism—could, Morgan suggested, draw upon a variety of local records, including tax lists, vital statistics, and lists of admissions to church communion, and would raise certain questions that might put "current assumptions" about colonial religious history to the test. Many of these questions would necessarily be directed at the seventeenth century. Did church membership decline after early settlement? What kind of local response did the Half-Way Covenant or Stoddardeanism elicit? What sorts of people joined the church? Were church members drawn predominantly from any one age, sex, or social grouping? How self-contained or exclusive was church membership? Did the church restrict itself to the children of members, to the descendants of the elect? Our ability to supply answers to some of these questions, Morgan warned, might be impeded by inadequate evidence, but he went on to demonstrate that even a sampling of the available records could generate a wide range of information.[1]

Since Morgan's essay, historians have slowly begun to fully exploit the church records available for the study of local lay religious activity.[2] Seventeenth-century Connecticut and New Haven, however, continue to be ignored, in part because church records and especially admission lists for the towns that were settled before 1670 are extremely rare.[3]

Yet there does exist a remarkably complete record of baptisms and admissions to communion for the First Church of Milford, Connecticut, extending from its founding in 1639 to the end of the colonial period and beyond. Town records survive as well, including vital statistics, deeds, property assessments, land distribution lists, and town meeting records. Thus, the kinds of evidence we need to pursue Morgan's questions, among others, and to reconstruct the local context of seventeenth-century Puritanism are fortunately available for this one Connecticut community.[4]

This case study of the Milford church, while adding more detail to our picture of local religious history, also offers further commentary on the once compelling model of a declining, monolithic, and exclusive early American Puritanism. Most of Milford's earliest settlers joined the church soon after arrival in town and thus quickly established a collective religious tradition fixed to the ideal of the pure church of visible saints. This ideal remained intact well into the eighteenth century but was transmitted alongside new patterns of religious experience arising out of the changing context of communal life. Declining admissions after early settlement were followed by two successive peaks, spaced twenty-five to thirty years apart, as successive generations came to maturity. Fewer men and young people entered the church toward the end of the century, although the church managed to maintain a large number of adherents, many of whom were the children of communicants and the offspring of certain religiously active families. Because the family in Milford proved to be so powerful a source of religious renewal, the descendants of the elect—the Puritan tribe, as Morgan called it—were actually responsible for sustaining the vitality of First Church through the seventeenth century and beyond. Puritan tribalism here served ironically to revitalize the collective religious tradition of the community over generations.[5]

A number of families only recently removed from communities in England and New England gathered at New Haven in August 1639 to form the first Church of Milford, just weeks before they set out to settle the town itself. Some had come with Peter Prudden from Hertfordshire to Boston in the spring of 1637 and had traveled with him and John Davenport to New Haven a year later. Others from such communities as Dorchester and Roxbury, Massachusetts, and Wethersfield, Connecticut, had moved to New Haven and there joined the

Hertfordshire subsettlement after they had been exposed to Prudden's apparently inspired preaching.[6] About a year before the day of the gathering, the men from these families had begun to hold "private meetings" for "their mutual ediffication," meetings that would eventually produce the nucleus of a new church and also imparted cohesion to strangers brought together only by their devotion to Prudden's ministry.[7] Out of these sessions, wherein individuals described "Gods gracious worke upon them," came the names of seven men, including Prudden, who, on the day of the gathering, formally united in covenant as the church's first members, its "pillars."[8]

This public subscription to a written covenant bound the pillars and future members to certain guiding principles. The "company of poor miserable wretches," whom the Lord had called "out of the world unto fellowship with himself in Jesus Christ," whom He had avouched "to be his people," and whose "hearts" He had "undertaken to circumcise," promised "to deny ourselves and all ungodliness and worldly lusts, and all corruptions and pollutions wherein in any sort we have walked." The Milford saints pledged to give themselves "wholly to the Lord Jesus Christ," who would teach and govern them "in all relations, conditions and conversations in this world." They were also "to walk before him, in all professed subjection to all his holy ordinances, according to the rule of the gospel," and "to walk together with his church and the members thereof, in all brotherly love and holy watchfulness, to the mutual building up one another in Faythe and Love." All such promises the Lord would help them keep "through his rich grace in Christ according to his covenant."[9]

Because the pillars decided to restrict membership to the professedly regenerate—to those who could demonstrate through oral testimony experience as well as knowledge of faith—the Milford church began as a "rigid Congregationalist system."[10] But this structural restrictiveness proved no insurmountable barrier to admission for Milford's first settlers; membership flourished at the outset, as it had in other churches organized before the adoption of the pure church in New England during the late 1630s.[11] The church admitted three men and women in 1639 and another twenty-four in 1640. By the end of 1644, it had added seventy-three new members, who, with the original seven, composed 82 percent of the men receiving land by November 1643 and 77 percent of the inhabitants' wives. A full 95 percent of all families now had at least one spouse in communion; 63 percent had both. Since the number of baptisms performed by the church was unusually high, with 67 recorded for the first five years and another 155 until Prudden's death in 1656, most of the children born to the founders of the town were likewise brought under the discipline of the covenant.[12]

Lacking diaries, sermons, and other such evidence, we can only imagine what kind of religious activities and experiences accompanied this remarkable surge in admissions and baptisms. Obviously, baptisms were administered frequently throughout the year, at solemn celebrations held on the Lord's Day, and the spectacle of children or adults being baptized provided public evidence of continuous spiritual renewal. Admission ceremonies also were very common before 1645 so that open confessions of faith and relations of conversion were witnessed nearly every month by the community assembled in meetinghouse on the Sabbath. While these ceremonies represented the final, and uniquely public, expression of spiritual rebirth, most were probably preceded by long periods of personal introspection and mutual reinforcement of a candidate's faith by family and neighbors. When combined with the monthly celebrations of the Lord's Supper and the regular spoken commitments to the covenant, the round of religious exercises produced a period of heightened religiosity in Milford, where individual experience and communal ceremony reflected and reinforced the piety of the settlers in the formation of a collective religious tradition.[13]

After 1644, when sixteen people entered the church, the community participated less frequently in certain religious rites and was exposed less often to public testimonies of individual piety. In 1645, for the first time in the church's short history, a year passed without the addition of a new member. Through the remainder of Prudden's ministry and beyond, admissions continued well below the level attained in 1639–44 (see table 2.1). Between 1645 and 1656, the year of the minister's death, the church averaged slightly under three new members per year (with a high of ten communicants added in 1654), as contrasted with just over twelve per year for the previous six years. In 1657–59, years when the pulpit was vacant, neither an admission nor a baptism was recorded.

Because few of the community's earliest inhabitants had failed to join the church, some immediate decline in admissions after 1644 was to be expected. Moreover, few of the settlers' children were old enough at that time to be considered candidates for communion. But the persistence of decline through the late 1640s and early 1650s stemmed not from the short supply of unchurched adults but, rather, from the failure of many of the newcomers who arrived in town after 1643 to take an active interest in the church. In 1644–54 an estimated forty-six men entered Milford, one more than had come before then, but only 54 percent of these ended up joining the church, as contrasted with 87 percent of the original inhabitants. Each successive wave of immigrants contained fewer potential church members: 77 percent of the men settling in 1644–46 became communicants, but only 44 percent of those arriving in 1647–49 and 33 percent of those entering in 1650–54 did.[14]

For Milford's newcomers, who tended to be more mobile than the town's initial settlers, length of stay was directly related to their rate of religious participation. None of the five transients whose names appear only once or twice on the town records became members, while 43 percent of the twenty-one men who stayed longer before moving joined in communion.[15] Of the twenty remaining permanently in Milford, 80 percent eventually became communicants, nearly duplicating the proportion set by the first settlers. New arrivals, however, took longer to be admitted to the church. The time between date of settlement and admission increased from an average of two years for church members who had entered the town before 1644 to six, twelve, and seven mean years, respectively, for members arriving in 1644–46, 1647–49, and 1650–54.[16]

TABLE 2.1.   Average Annual Number of New Communicants, 1639–1744

Years	Number	Years	Number
1639–44	12.2	1695–99	12.6
1645–49	3.4	1700–1704	10.6
1650–54	3.4	1705–9	5.0
1655–59	.2	1710–14	15.0
1660–64	2.0	1715–19	6.8
1665–69	11.4	1720–24	9.4
1670–74	8.4	1725–29	12.2
1675–79	5.0	1730–34	12.4
1680–84	3.8	1735–39	20.8
1685–89	4.8	1740–44	16.2
1690–94	5.2		

Note: This table excludes communicants admitted by transfer from other churches. (*Source:* Milford Church Records, 1:1–40.)

Newcomers who sought to enter the religious life of the community met with new frustrations arising from changes in the church and in the context of religious experience. The creation of the administrative offices of elder and deacon by the church in 1645–47 reflected the institutional needs of a considerably enlarged body of saints, whose size alone presented a barrier to any new arrival wishing to join it. It required courage to face nearly the entire community of adult males and present testimony consonant with the high standards set by their collective spiritual experience. In preparing for this encounter, new settlers could not rely upon the communal support that had originated in the "private meetings" at New Haven and had been reinforced by the intense religiosity that attended the town's birth. Only after gradual exposure to church tradition and expectation would newcomers gain access to communion.

As admissions ebbed in Milford, the church slowly grew isolated from the community at large. With Prudden's death came a four-year interruption in the normal operation of First Church and an intermission in the influx of new members. Admissions then resumed after the ordination of Roger Newton, former pastor at Farmington, Connecticut, and Thomas Hooker's son-in-law. But a total of only sixteen communicants was added by the church from 1660 through 1666, and only forty-one baptisms were performed at that very time when the second generation was entering the adult population, beginning to marry, establish independent households, and bear children.[17] Meanwhile, the admission of newcomers and the children of members failed to equal the number of communicants who were lost to the church either through death or emigration. When Newton became minister, the church had already lost 36 percent of the men admitted under Prudden. By the end of 1644, the percentage had reached forty-three, and, by the end of 1666, had swelled to 60 percent. Newton found himself ministering to an increasingly exclusive church and to a town with a growing proportion of unchurched inhabitants.

Faced with this widening gap between church and town, and with a considerably weakened church discipline, Newton, like other New England clergymen, may have supported or even actively sought a more comprehensive ecclesiastical polity. His predecessor had advocated such a step as early as 1651, when he had written to Richard Mather that perhaps baptism should not be denied the children of unchurched parents who were yet the sons and daughters of members.[18]

Within a year of Newton's ordination in 1660, it seemed inevitable that some change in the traditional relationship between church and town in Milford would occur, for the town was facing considerable outside pressure to join the Connecticut Colony and thus relinquish its association with the New Haven Colony. To do so would mean the end of a franchise restricted to church members. It might also mean an end to the pure church system, since the Connecticut General Court not only endorsed the Half-Way Covenant in 1664 but also asked the church elders whether it could enforce its resolution by ordering "the Churches to practice according to the premises, if they doe not practice without such an order."[19] The town resisted merger until it became futile to do so any longer. After three years of opposition, apparently accompanied by some internal dissension, Milford finally voted for consolidation in November 1664, just two months before the town of New Haven took similar action.[20]

The merger with Connecticut was partly responsible for the exodus in 1666 of at least sixteen Milford families to the new settlement of Newark, New Jersey, where they and others from several towns in the New Haven Colony adopted "fundamental agreements" that reflected their devotion to traditional Congregational practice.[21] Except for the franchise, however, little changed in Milford as the First Church persisted in opposing any further innovations. By the mid-1670s the town had acquired a reputation for "being of that perswasion wee call antisynodalianer," a reputation that held fast until 1730, when the church finally adopted the Half-Way Covenant.[22] After having gone so long without such an alternative to full membership, however, very few parishioners felt compelled to use it.[23]

Although the First Church thus stubbornly resisted changes in polity, even when it found itself becoming increasingly exclusive, it was able eventually to recapture much of its original vitality within a traditional system. Admissions turned upward after the mid-1660s, reaching several high levels during the last decades of the seventeenth century. Five new members were added in 1667, the year after the exodus to Newark, and then an impressive forty-six in 1669, a total unsurpassed in any other single year in the church's thirty-year history. From 1670 until Roger Newton's death in 1683, as table 2.1 shows, the number of new communicants remained above the number recorded for the period 1645–64, even though each consecutive five-year interval witnessed a gradual decline in admissions. Thirteen people were admitted in 1681 and then only one other until 1683, when Newton died and the pulpit was left unoccupied for two years.

With the ordination of Samuel Andrew in November 1685 came another, but more gradual, buildup in admissions, succeeded by a sharp upsurge. Twenty-four people entered the church during 1686–89 and twenty-six in 1690–94, numbers comparable to those attained during 1675–79. Admissions then increased very significantly through the last five years of the century, when sixty-three men and women joined the church, more than had joined in any previous five-year period since the early 1640s.

Such late-century increases in new membership also occurred in other New England churches, regardless of polity.[24] Local church records reveal not a linear but a cyclical history of religious participation, a history that needs to be examined comparatively, town by town and church by church, over the long range. As figure 2.1 indicates, admissions in Milford passed through several cycles from the beginning of Prudden's ministry through all of Newton's to Andrew's first fifteen years as pastor and beyond to the mideighteenth century. New membership peaked in the early 1640s, some twenty-five years afterward in 1665–69, and again thirty years later, in 1695–99. Other peaks would follow up to and through the Great Awakening.[25]

Cycles in admissions, coupled with generational turnover, led to sizable variations in the ratio of church membership to town population. In 1643, 78 percent of Milford's male inhabitants belonged to the church and, in 1660, a slightly lower 73 percent. Nine years later, just before the upswing in admissions took place, the church contained proportionately fewer inhabitants than at any other time during the seventeenth century, with only an estimated 36 percent of the adult males in communion. By 1678, after a decade of growth in new membership, 47 percent of the inhabitants were communicants and, by 1687, 46 percent. The percentage of church members to townsmen hovered around these figures well into the eighteenth century.[26]

The revivals in admissions touched some groups more than others, and the church drew upon people who tended to be of a particular sex, marital status, age, and family. When we reconstruct the social profile of the new member from the vital statistics of the town, among other local records, we find that one group—the women of the community—was especially active religiously and came more and more to predominate numerically in the church. The ratio of males to females in com-

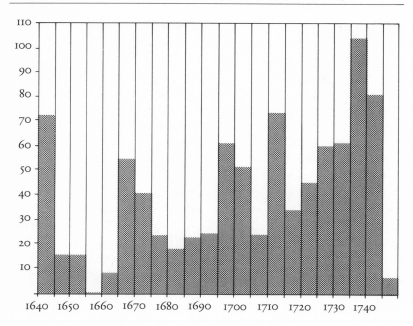

FIG. 2.1. Admissions at consecutive five-year intervals, 1640 to 1749

munion was evenly balanced during the first years of Prudden's ministry, with 51 percent of those admitted during 1639–49 being women. After that decade the percentage increased. From 56 percent in the 1650s and 57 percent in the 1660s, it jumped to 66 percent the following decade, fell to 56 percent during the 1680s, but then leaped to 67 percent in the 1690s, the largest imbalance of the seventeenth century. This feminization of new membership in Milford, with its accompanying consequences for the religious life of the family, repeated trends prevailing in many other New England parishes during the last decades of the century.[27]

Those who joined the church were also likely to be married, living in their own households, and raising children. Rarely were fewer than two of every three new members married, although, with each successive decade from 1639, more and more single males and females were admitted (table 2.2). Married men tended to outnumber married women, but usually the difference was negligible—a less than ten percentile differential in every decade other than the 1690s. Furthermore, men and women alike very often became members at three to four mean years after marriage, and three of every four were the parents of at least one child.[28]

Religious conversion and admission to the church were experiences of the adult stage of life.[29] The gap in years between the mid-year in each of the three admission peaks of 1643, 1668, and 1698 hints at what the vital statistics more clearly show about the relatively high ages at admission (table 2.3). The combined mean age never fell below twenty-four years. Rather, it continued to climb above this age with each succeeding decade after 1649.[30] While women tended to enter the church at an earlier age than men—slightly more than four years earlier overall—their mean age at admission drifted upward from the 1650s to the 1690s. Moreover, the modal age at admission for men increased, shifting from twenty-five to twenty-nine years in the 1660s and 1670s to thirty to thirty-four years in the 1680s and 1690s, with only 18 percent of the men obtaining membership over age thirty in the 1660s and 17 percent in the 1670s but 59 percent the following decade and 52 percent in the 1690s. At the same time, the modal age at admission among women rose from under twenty years in the 1670s to twenty-four years in the 1680s and 1690s; by the last decade of the century, 56 percent of new female communicants were over the age of twenty-four as contrasted with 33 percent in the 1660s and 1670s and 38 percent in the 1680s.[31]

The delayed timing of admission in Milford was in part a reflection of widely held expectations concerning the proper attributes of church

TABLE 2.2.   Marital Status of New Members, 1639–99

Years	Married		Unmarried		Unknown		Percentage Married	
	Female	Male	Female	Male	Female	Male	Female	Male
1639–49	37	39	3	6	4	1	92.5	86.6
1650–59	6	8	1	2	1	0	85.7	80.0
1660–69	20	27	7	7	2	4	74.1	79.4
1670–79	15	27	4	12	4	5	78.9	69.2
1680–89	10	14	6	10	3	0	62.5	58.3
1690–99	15	45	9	8	5	7	62.5	84.9
Total	103	160	30	45	19	17	77.4	78.0

Note: Percentage married based only on those whose marital status is known.

candidates. John Davenport stated at the gathering of the New Haven church in 1639 that the Lord's Supper should be received by "all of the Church that are of yeers"; nine years later, the Cambridge Platform advised that church candidates ought to be "grown up into years of discretion."[32] Puritans expected new members to have attained a certain level of maturity, to be able to speak for themselves or to "be accounted adult."[33] Thomas Hooker believed that "those whom God doth call it is most commonly in their middle age before they come to their old age." The "middle age," according to Hooker, "hath better Materials . . . wherein, or whereupon the frame of Conversion may be erected, or imprinted by the stamp of the Spirit."[34] Some understanding, some maturity, some discretion were required before an individual could begin to comprehend doctrine or discern the operation of God's grace in the soul. Therefore, children were unlikely to be recipients of saving faith. "Children not being usually able to examine themselves, nor discern the Lord's body," wrote Thomas Shepard, "hence they are not to be admitted to the use of this privilege."[35] But in the middle years, Hooker believed, "a man is able to conceive and partake of the things of grace, and fa(th)om them, and the power of his understanding comes on whereby he is able to embrace them."[36]

Such expectations meshed with key experiences in shaping the social circumstances of admission into the church. Because of the imprecision of middle age or other life-stage definitions in New England, and because of the lack of rituals signaling transitions in the developmental life cycle, the events of betrothal, marriage, and parenthood acted as vital signposts to the maturity expected of new members. That the

TABLE 2.3.   Mean Age at Admission, 1639–99

Years	Ages			Number	
	Male	Female	All	Male	Female
1639–49	29.8	22.4	27.4	12	6
1650–59	38.3	20.0	24.5	1	3
1660–69	26.5	22.5	24.3	17	21
1670–79	27.6	24.5	25.6	12	21
1680–89	30.4	24.8	27.7	17	16
1690–99	28.5	27.8	28.2	23	18
Total	28.7	24.5	26.5	82	85
S.D.	6.5	7.9	7.5		

people who presented themselves to the Milford church, and gained admission, happened to be new husbands and wives, fathers and mothers, meant that they had just passed beyond youth into middle age, had begun to assume responsibility for guiding a new generation, and could now be considered adults. Not only did they thus meet the church's expectations, but they were also beginning to confront new experiences that were apt to heighten interest in salvation and the church. Adult men and women had children to be baptized, and this required membership in a church without optional routes to baptism provided elsewhere by the Half-Way Covenant. Upon marriage, adult women, in particular, became exposed to one life crisis after another and to the ever-present fear that, if they were to die in childbirth before conversion and admission into the church, their souls would be eternally damned. They also chanced losing one or more children through death, incidents that may well have encouraged identification with that central passageway of conversion—humiliation, or submission to Christ.[37] Marriage, parenthood, and their accompanying crises provided the most conducive setting for conversion and admission into the church.

Those adults who sought membership in the Milford church did so within a particular familial and socioreligious context, very often coming from religiously active families with permanent and well-established ties to the community. The town's earliest settlers, followed by successive waves of newcomers, had sustained the flow of communicants until Prudden's death in 1656. Beginning with the 1660s, the major source of new members changed from immigrants to the sons and daughters of Milford's churched fathers and mothers and to the children and grandchildren of the first-generation elect. To cite one early example of this emerging trend toward religious inbreeding, in 1669, the peak year in admissions, four of every five new members whose families can be traced had been brought up in households with at least one parent in communion, while three of every five came from families with both parents in membership.[38] Overall, between 1660 and 1683, when Newton was pastor, 68 percent of the people who became members had at least one parent in communion, and 54 percent had both.

Some of the new communicants had parents who had entered the church under Roger Newton. Newton himself, together with his wife, who had been admitted in 1660, saw five of their children become members between 1669 and 1681. Fifty-six percent of the new members, however, were the children of people added by Prudden, some very early in his ministry. All five children of Thomas and Hannah Buckingham, for example, one of whom had been a pillar and the other a communicant by 1640, grew up to become church members, with a daughter doing so in 1647 and three sons and a daughter doing so during the mid-1660s. Similarly, five of the children of John and Mary Baldwin, both of whom had been admitted soon after arriving in town in 1646, entered the church, as did the four children of Henry and Elizabeth Botsford, whom the church had added by 1644. Moreover, the Milford elect included in 1660–83 no fewer than three children each from such families as those of Richard Baldwin, Timothy Baldwin, Nicholas Camp, Benjamin Fenn, Jasper Gunn, Peter Prudden, Thomas Sanford, and Thomas Tibbal—families with membership ties to the pre-1645 church.

Men and women with a special religious lineage continued to provide new members at the start of Samuel Andrew's ministry. Seventy-nine percent of the people admitted in 1686–99 had at least one parent in communion (contrasted with 68 percent in 1660–83), and 44 percent had both parents in membership (contrasted to 54 percent in 1660–83). Among these were to be found the sons and daughters of members added before 1660. Two of the people admitted by Andrew in his very first year as pastor were daughters of one of the church pillars, Thomas Welch, whose wife also belonged to the church. All told, this second generation accounted for 41 percent of admissions in 1686–99.

Those children of the church who sought admission under Andrew also included individuals from the third generation—the grandchildren of members added before 1660. The first to do so—in 1686—was Sarah Baldwin, the granddaughter of John and Mary, both church members, and the daughter of John, Jr., who had become a communicant in 1662. Her name appears in the records just before that of Joseph Fenn, the grandson of Benjamin and Sarah, both members of the church as early as 1640. But the third generation supplied only a slim percentage of the new membership until 1695–99, when, for the first time, it surpassed the parents in religious participation. During this five-year period, it contributed 44 percent of the new communicants as contrasted with only 23 percent in 1686–94. The maturation and accompanying religious activism of still another generation were partly responsible for the late 1690s peak in admissions and for a succeeding one in 1710–14 as well.[39]

The major and most important source of new members after the 1650s was thus the Puritan tribe of Milford—the descendants of the elect and the children and grandchildren of first-generation saints—although the church continued to add some people who had not been brought up under the eyes of the community's fathers and mothers. Supplying the church with an outside source of new members, one supplanting male immigrants in prominence, were female newcomers to town who usually entered Milford to marry, then settled down, and later became communicants. Seventeen percent of the people admitted by Newton belonged to this group, as did at least 9 percent of the members added by Andrew.[40] These women thus differed from most other members in their isolation from parents and kin but perhaps not in their ability to lay claim to the Puritan tribe and a religious ancestry. Most female immigrants before admission had entered the tribe through right of marriage to a son of the church, if not a member himself.[41] Most also, like their Milford counterparts, may have had a religious upbringing, since decisions to marry in Milford were often dictated by religious considerations, and the sons as well as the daughters of church members commonly espoused the offspring of saints.[42] We know for sure that several of these women, whose families of origin and parents' religious statuses can be traced, had been raised by church families and were connected by blood to the Puritan tribe.[43]

Did the Milford church and its ministry intend to be tribal, extending special privileges to the brethren's children or deliberately restricting themselves to the conversion of the elect's descendants? The way to communion was not eased for the church's children in Milford, as it was in another Connecticut church.[44] Nor, without sermons, can we say that either Roger Newton or Samuel Andrew encouraged with special force the regeneration of their members' offspring. Some New England ministers might, and others might not, have wanted to maintain a tribal church, and while, at the end of the century, Increase and Cotton Mather indicated that election often ran in the loins of the elect, their statements may have been guided by experience and not by deliberation.[45]

The extant evidence for Milford does suggest that socioreligious circumstances combined with the actions of the family to produce a tribal spirit and an inbred membership. The high rates of religious participation among the town's founders, coupled with the ebbing of male immigration after 1664, meant that many of the people whom Newton and Andrew could expect to admit had been reared within church families and had grown up under the discipline of the Milford church, since they had been baptized as infants by its minister. The call to be saved in seventeenth-century New England was limited to the parish or town, and, by the last quarter of that century, the town of Milford, whose social profile was partly reflected by its church, contained the saints' descendants in abundance.[46] The revival of the early 1640s and the persistence in town of the second and third generations ensured a community of potential church candidates who very often could boast a religious heritage.

This is not to say that the church simply mirrored the socioreligious composition of the town. Personal initiative lay behind each admission, along with a more salient element: the family. A tribal spirit stemmed largely from the actions of the family and its members, of people who were in a position to influence powerfully the religious behavior of spouses, siblings, and children. Milford's records contain no references to the covenant renewals, catechistic exercises, or other such evangelical aids to pastor and family found elsewhere in New England. Rather, the family proved increasingly important to the religious life in Milford as the community became less and less involved collectively in the church. During early settlement, decisions to enter the church were often made mutually, within the nuclear family, as spouses frequently joined in membership on the same day, or one soon after the other. These companionate arrangements at admission persisted to the end of the century, and joint admissions of siblings also became common especially during the 1650s, 1660s, and 1670s, when the second generation was coming to maturity.[47] That many parents survived to the time when their children sought membership added still another dimension to the familial context of admission.[48]

Parental initiative, extended across generations through the lineal family, was a crucial religious factor for Milford families that maintained enduring connections with the church. Pious parents, seeking to perpetuate the religious vitality of the line, could do so by nurturing their children in grace through infancy, childhood, and youth, and, if they happened to be alive when their children reached the years of discretion expected of new members, could prod them to close with the church. In 1660–99, the male members of just twenty-three kin groups with common surnames accounted for 77 percent of the men entering the church, although they represented only 57 percent of the families listed as inhabitants in 1686. Moreover, females born to only twenty kin groups, eleven of which were common to the males, made up 63 percent of the total new membership whose families of origin are known.[49] Religious ties stretching back to the early history of the community were common among both groups, for three out of every four males and females were descended from people who had entered the church before 1645. Parental desires to promote the religious traditions of the family were reflected by the actions of the firstborn, the esteemed son or daughter, who joined the church more frequently in 1660–99 than other children.[50] There is additional evidence that certain families continued to maintain close connections with the church up to and through the Great Awakening.[51]

In Milford, Puritan tribalism was the product of family nurture and the source of church renewal and revitalization. It was not the agent of declension but the instrument of cyclical upswings in church membership and religious participation. Herein lies its conceptual usefulness in promoting a better understanding of continuity and change in early American Puritanism. Pious families, and especially church mothers, proved capable of transmitting church traditions to their sons and daughters, who subscribed to the covenant and became members of the pure church of Milford usually when they attained adulthood.[52] Such families were able to exert a strong religious influence over their members, to shape the religious behavior of the line, and to sustain interest in the church. The Puritan family was an effective religious institution.[53]

Several questions arise from this examination. What was the substance of the belief expressed at admission? What ideas and values informed the experiences of Milford's church families? What modes of piety were passed on from one generation to the next until the eruption of the Great Awakening in the early 1740s, when the revivalists excited religious impulses that had been sustained over generations? Unfortunately, the wealth of local records for Milford is not balanced by an equally impressive array of information usually under the jurisdiction of the historian of ideas, and answers to these questions therefore cannot be supplied. To admit this is to confirm the accuracy of another of Edmund Morgan's caveats: that "the study of local records will never be a substitute for the history of ideas." Nevertheless, as he went on to say, "the intellectual history of Puritanism might be enriched by the information that can be gleaned from such untapped sources."[54] By adopting and expanding upon the approach to New England Puritanism proposed by Morgan some years ago, we may better understand the fit between intellectual and local history and the subtle interplay between ideas, values, and experience in the religious lives of American Puritans.

Notes

1. "New England Puritanism: Another Approach," *William and Mary Quarterly*, 3d ser., 18 (1961): 236–42.
2. Studies of the seventeenth-century New England churches include Ross W. Beales, Jr., "The Half-Way Covenant and Religious Scrupulosity: The First Church of Dorchester, Massachusetts, as a Test Case," *William and Mary Quarterly*, 3d ser., 31 (1974): 465–80; Kenneth A. Lockridge, "The History of a Puritan Church, 1637–1736," *New England Quarterly* 40 (1967): 399–424; Robert G. Pope, *The Half-Way Covenant: Church Membership in Puritan New England* (Princeton, N.J., 1969); Mary MacManus Ramsbottom, "Religious Society and the Family in Charlestown, Massachusetts, 1630–1740" (Ph.D. diss., Yale University, 1987); and Darrett B. Rutman, "God's Bridge Falling Down: 'Another Approach' to New England Puritanism Assayed," *William and Mary Quarterly*, ser. 3, 19 (1962): 408–21.
3. Membership records exist for Windsor, as recorded by Matthew Grant in the 1670s; Farmington, from 1652–61 and then resuming in 1680; Middletown, beginning in 1668; and Hartford's Second Church, starting in 1669. Admissions in New Haven's First Church from 1639 to 1685, when the actual records begin, are reconstructed by Franklin Dexter on the basis of baptismal, town, and other documents, in *Historical Catalogue of the Members of the First Church of Christ in New Haven, Connecticut (Center Church) A.D., 1639–1914* (New Haven, Conn., 1914). See the comprehensive "List of Church Records in the Connecticut State Library" (Hartford, Conn.), June 1976, MSS.
4. More precisely, the evidence available for Milford, all of which is in the Connecticut State Library at Hartford, includes the Milford First Congregational Church records, vol. 1 (hereafter cited as Milford Church Recs.); Milford Births Marriages Deaths (photostats), Barbour Collection of Connecticut Records; indices to vital statistics as recorded in Bibles, newspapers, church and town records, and on gravestones; and numerous genealogical sources. Milford's town records and deeds are on microfilm.

5. Morgan sees Puritan tribalism, or tribal spirit, as wedded to a declining Puritanism, and he quotes such men as Increase and Cotton Mather in proposing that second- and third-generation ministers believed that "'God hath seen meet to cast the line of Election . . . through the loyns of godly parents.'" Edmund S. Morgan, *The Puritan Family: Religious and Domestic Relations in Seventeenth-Century New England,* rev. ed. (New York, 1966), 182–83, see esp. chap. 7.

6. The movement of families to the Hertfordshire section of New Haven is recounted in Federal Writers' Project, *History of Milford, Connecticut, 1639–1939* (Bridgeport, Conn., 1939), 2–3. Little is known of Peter Prudden, but see Lillian E. Prudden, *Peter Prudden: A Story of His Life at New Haven and Milford, Connecticut* (New Haven, Conn., 1901). Cotton Mather cites Prudden as "an example of piety, gravity, and *boiling zeal,* against the growing evils of the times." *Magnalia Christi Americana,* (Hartford, Conn., 1820), 1:357.

7. Kenneth Lockridge calls these sessions "get-acquainted meetings," in "History of a Puritan Church," 403.

8. No record remains of the events preceding the formation of the Milford church, but in all likelihood they were nearly identical to the preparations of the settlers' coresidents, as recorded in Charles J. Hoadley, ed., *Records of the Colony and Plantation of New Haven, from 1616 to 1649* (Hartford, Conn., 1857), 15–17. See also Isabel MacBeath Calder, *The New Haven Colony,* Yale Historical Publications Miscellany, 28 (New Haven, Conn., 1934), chaps. 1–2; and Federal Writers' Project, *History of Milford,* 2–9.

9. Milford Church Recs., 1:1.

10. Paul R. Lucas, in *Valley of Discord: Church and Society along the Connecticut River, 1636–1725* (Hanover, N.H., 1976), 31–32, 42, places Peter Prudden among the rigid Congregationalists of New England—those who favored a public narration of conversion, lay control over the admission of new members, and strict purity—as opposed to the evangelicals, such as Thomas Hooker, and the moderates, such as Samuel Stone, Hooker's colleague at Hartford.

11. Edmund S. Morgan, in *Visible Saints: The History of a Puritan Idea* (New York, 1963), 137, argues that the rate of conversions declined after the 1630s because people now had to confront a more rigorous religious test before admission. The second generation, he contends, was the first to encounter the new system, and, thus, the decline in visible piety preceding the adoption of the Half-Way Covenant was perhaps only a reflection of the stricter standards of the post-1640 period. Moreover, David Kobrin suggests that, after 1640, new communicants were young people without "long religious experience in England." "The Expansion of the

Visible Church in New England: 1629–1650," *Church History* 36 (1967): 204. Yet the Milford church was able to recruit a substantial number of new members who had migrated from England even after the introduction of the pure church system. Note also that, by 1648 in Dedham, Massachusetts, where the church incorporated strict admission standards at its founding in late 1638, about 70 percent of the community's taxpayers were church members. Lockridge, "History of a Puritan Church," 409.

New England churches admitted comparatively large numbers of new members during the 1630s and early 1640s. See Gerald F. Moran, "The Puritan Saint: Religious Experience, Church Membership, and Piety in Connecticut, 1636–1776" (Ph.D. diss., Rutgers University, 1974), chap. 4.

12. For Milford's inhabitants in 1643, see "The number of acres of upland and meadow laid out to each inhabitant and house lots also," recorded in November 1643 and contained in "A Transcript of the Long Narrow Book of Records appointed by the town to be Transcribed by Rich[ar]d Bryan, December the 23d:1700," Milford, Connecticut, Register of Deeds, 1639–1707, microfilm 1:4–5, Connecticut State Library.

13. On the solemnity of New England baptismal and eucharistic ceremonies, see Charles E. Hambrick-Stowe, *The Practice of Piety: Puritan Devotional Disciplines in Seventeenth-Century New England* (Chapel Hill, N.C., 1982), 123–24; and E. Brooks Holifield, *The Covenant Sealed: The Development of Puritan Sacramental Theology in Old and New England, 1570–1720* (New Haven, Conn., 1974), 143, 159–60.

14. Information on newcomers was obtained from the town meeting, land, and vital records and from genealogies.

15. Fifty-seven percent of the forty-six newcomers eventually moved from town; only 24 percent of the forty-five pre-1644 inhabitants had done so. It was more difficult to gain access to Milford's institutions after 1643. By the end of that year, the town had been brought under the New Haven Colony's jurisdiction, which meant that the franchise would be extended only to church members. Moreover, Milford had just completed its fourth distribution of meadow, upland, and house lots in as many years, and, although another was to be undertaken in 1646, that was to be the last until 1660. Acquiring a sufficient amount of the community's wealth after 1643 was further complicated by the town's continuation of its rule of "Estates and Persons" in land distributions, a rule that in the beginning had been responsible for six of the seven church pillars receiving the largest house lots and was likewise responsible for their being given the largest allotments of new land in 1660.

16. Nontransient newcomers who ended up moving from Milford stayed

twelve mean years as compared to thirteen years for emigrants among the first settlers. Persistence, in turn, may have been partly a function of membership in the church. Of the newcomers who eventually left Milford, church members remained fifteen mean years, while nonmembers stayed only seven mean years. Religious participation, in combination with economic ties, family membership, and political roles, influenced the persistence of individuals in Windsor. See Linda Auwers Bissell, "From One Generation to Another: Mobility in Seventeenth-Century Windsor, Connecticut," *William and Mary Quarterly*, 3d ser., 31 (1974): 81 and passim.

17. At consecutive five-year intervals from 1640 through 1699, the number of recorded baptisms in Milford was 67, 72, 63, 20, 21, 6, 122, 111, 70, 105, 94, 212.

18. Prudden, *Peter Prudden*, 37. Increase Mather published Prudden's letter in *The First Principles of New England concerning the subject of Baptisme and Communion of Churches* (Cambridge, Mass., 1675), 25.

19. J. H. Trumbull, ed., *The Public Records of the Colony of Connecticut* (Hartford, Conn., 1850), 1:438.

20. Record of the vote can be found in Charles J. Hoadley, ed., *Records of the Colony or Jurisdiction of New Haven, from May, 1658, to the Union* (Hartford, Conn., 1858), 550. Charles M. Andrews reconstructs the events leading to the merger in *The Colonial Period of American History* (New Haven, Conn., 1936), 2:184–94.

21. The first of two articles in the "agreements" stipulated "that none shall be admitted freemen or free Burgesses within our Town . . . but such Planters as are members of some or other of the Congregational Churches"; the second, that "we shall with Care and Diligence provide for the maintenance of the purity of Religion professed in the Congregational Churches." To ensure that the original agreements would continue in force, the settlers resolved to exclude from inhabitation any who "willingly or wilfully disturb us in our Peace and Settlements, and especially that would subvert us from the true Religion and worship of God." "Records of Newark," New Jersey Historical Society, *Collections* 6 (1864): 2, 4. Information on the first inhabitants of Newark is contained in William H. Shaw, *History of Essex and Hudson Counties, New Jersey* (Philadelphia, 1884) 1:358–68.

22. Samuel Mather to Increase Mather, November 4, 1678, in "Mather Papers," Massachusetts Historical Society, *Collections*, 4th ser., 8 (1868): 381.

23. The Half-Way Covenant was formally adopted by First Church in 1730, according to *Proceedings at the Celebration of the Two Hundred and Fiftieth Anniversary of the First Church of Christ, in Milford, Ct., August 25th,*

    1889 (Ansonia, Conn., 1890), 162, but I have not found anyone being admitted on a halfway basis until February 1768, when Ezra Botsford and his wife "owned the Covenant." Milford Church Recs., 1:42.

24. Admissions increased substantially in Farmington, Stonington, and Middletown during the early 1690s, in Hartford Second during the late 1670s and late 1690s, and in New London during the early 1670s and early 1690s. Moran, "Puritan Saint," 127. Note also the existence of admission cycles in four Massachusetts churches as described by Pope, *Half-Way Covenant,* chap. 8 and appendix.

25. There are in print no full-scale comparative studies of eighteenth-century membership patterns; only local case studies have been undertaken. See, for example, J. M. Bumsted, "Religion, Finance, and Democracy in Massachusetts: The Town of Norton as a Case Study," *Journal of American History* 57 (1971): 817–31; Philip J. Greven, Jr., "Youth, Maturity, and Religious Conversion: A Note on the Ages of Converts in Andover, Massachusetts, 1711–1749," *Essex Institute Historical Collections* 108 (1972): 119–34; Brooks B. Hull and Gerald F. Moran, "A Preliminary Time Series Analysis of Church Activity in Colonial Woodbury, Connecticut," *Journal of the Scientific Study of Religion* 28 (1989): 478–92; Gerald F. Moran, "Conditions of Religious Conversion in the First Society of Norwich, Connecticut, 1718–1744," *Journal of Social History* 5 (1972): 331–43; and James Walsh, "The Great Awakening in the First Congregational Church of Woodbury, Connecticut," *William and Mary Quarterly,* 3d ser., 27 (1971): 543–62. A recent exception is Stephen R. Grossbart, "Seeking the Divine Favor: Conversion and Church Admission in Eastern Connecticut, 1711–1832," *William and Mary Quarterly,* 3d ser., 46 (1989): 696–740.

26. The percentages are calculated by collating the names of living male members with lists of inhabitants appearing in the following documents: "The Number of Acres that are to be laid out to each Inhabitant," March 1660, Register of Deeds, 1:54; a list of persons receiving land in January 1677, Register of Deeds (1676–1741), 9:17–18; and "The List allowed for 1686," Register of Deeds (1714–1718), 5:78–79. The 1669 figure is based on a reconstruction of the adult males likely to have been living in town in that year.

    Of course, the ratio of church membership to population never remained static as changes in the adult population, abrupt or otherwise, probably failed to coincide with changes in adult membership. But, in 1712, 42 percent of the town's inhabitants belonged to the church, a proportion strikingly comparable to the 1687 figure. "The List allowed for the year 1712," Register of Deeds, 5:80–82.

27. See chapter 3.

28. At consecutive decades between 1660 and 1700, the years from marriage to admission averaged three, three, nine, and four for men, and five, three, four, and seven for women.

29. Thus, there may be some reason to doubt the accuracy of John Demos's statement that "many Puritan conversions seem to have occurred well before puberty. Perhaps, indeed, a religious 'crisis' can more reasonably be connected with the whole matrix of changes customary for children at the age of about six to eight." A Little Commonwealth: Family Life in Plymouth Colony (New York, 1970), 146.

30. The comparatively high ages of Milford's first male settlers—an average of 30.5 years in 1640—may help to explain why ages at admission for men in table 2.2 tend to be higher for 1639–59 than for 1660–99.

31. Church members tended to be older than inhabitants outside the church: Male members on the 1686 list of inhabitants averaged forth-three years of age in contrast to thirty-four years for nonmembers. Church members were also apt to be wealthier than nonmembers. Fifty-six church members on the 1686 list held L97 in property, in contrast to L58 for seventy-two nonmembers, while 63 percent of the members were among the wealthiest 40 percent in town, in contrast to only 24 percent of the men outside the church. Moreover, 73 percent of the inhabitants in the top quintile belonged to the church, along with 62 percent in the second quintile, but only twenty-five of them were to be found in the bottom quintile in wealth. About 25 percent of the variations in wealth on the 1686 list can be attributed to age, with the Pearson coefficient obtained by correlating these two variable being a significant .47.

32. "John Davenport's Profession of Faith . . . ," in Letters of John Davenport: Puritan Divine, ed. Isabel MacBeath Calder (New Haven, Conn., 1937), 73; Williston Walker, The Creeds and Platforms of Congregationalism, 2d ed. (1893; reprint, Boston, 1969), 224.

33. See Ross W. Beales, Jr., "Cares for the Rising Generation: Youth and Religion in Colonial New England" (Ph.D. diss., University of California, Davis, 1971), chap. 2; and "In Search of the Historical Child: Miniature Adulthood and Youth in Colonial New England," American Quarterly 27 (1975): 385–87.

34. Thomas Hooker, The Unbeleevers Preparing for Christ (London, 1638), 198; and The Application of Redemption by the Effectual Work of the Word and Spirit of Christ (London, 1656), 268, both quoted in Beales, "In Search of the Historical Child," 386.

35. Thomas Shepard, The Church Membership of Children . . . , in The Works of Thomas Shepard, ed. John A. Albro (1853; reprint, New York, 1967), 3:531.

36. Quoted in Beales, "In Search of the Historical Child," 387.

37. Data on mortality rates among seventeenth-century New England children are surveyed in David E. Stannard, *The Puritan Way of Death: A Study in Religion, Culture, and Social Change* (New York, 1977), 54–56. Barbara Welter, in a study of early nineteenth-century American women, maintains that "in the diaries and letters of women who lived during this period the death of a child seemed consistently to be the hardest thing for them to bear and to occasion more anguish and rebellion, as well as eventual submission, than any other event in their lives." "The Cult of True Womanhood: 1820–1860," *American Quarterly* 18 (1966):161 n. 53. On humiliation and submission in conversion, see Charles Lloyd Cohen, *God's Caress: The Psychology of Puritan Religious Experience* (New York, 1986), esp. chap. 3; James W. Jones, *The Shattered Synthesis: New England Puritanism before the Great Awakening* (New Haven, Conn., 1973), 10, 36–37; Moran, "Puritan Saint," 31–33, 36–38; and Morgan, *Visible Saints*, 68–69.

38. These and other references to family membership include only those communicants with known parentage. Fourteen percent of the people admitted under Roger Newton were women whose surnames before marriage could not be traced, as were 31 of those added by Samuel Andrew. It is especially difficult to identify the maiden names of females marrying in 1685–1700 because there are no vital records for that period of Milford's history.

39. The percentage of second-generation men and women among total admissions continued to dwindle from twenty-five in 1695–99 to zero in 1710–14, while the number of members supplied by the third generation peaked in 1710–14, equaling over one-half of all recorded admissions. By 1735–44, the fourth generation had come to exceed the third in total new membership.

40. If more data on the women marrying from 1685 to 1700 were available, it is likely that the proportion of female newcomers admitted by Andrew would be higher than this 9 percent. The number of men entering town at successive five-year periods went from twenty-three, twelve, twelve, and fifteen in 1645–64 to two, six, six, and five in 1665–84, while male newcomers accounted for only 8 percent of the new members brought in by Newton and only 5 percent of the people admitted by Andrew.

41. Ninety percent of female migrants had married before becoming members, and 78 percent of these had spouses with at least one parent in communion, while 35 percent were married to church members.

42. Fifty-eight of the sons and daughters of church families married the children of similar families in the marriages recorded for the period 1660–85 in contrast to five who married people whose parents were

outside the church, although another twenty-three, the majority of them being males, married people who did not reside in Milford.

43. One was the daughter of Benjamin Wilmot, Jr., who had joined the New Haven church in 1648; another, the offspring of the Reverend Robert Lenthall of Newport, Rhode Island; and a third, the daughter of the Reverend John Whiting of Stratford, Connecticut.

44. In New London's First Church in 1687–1726, as indicated by Lucas, *Valley of Discord*, 129–30.

45. To what extent those tribal attitudes described by Morgan prevailed in New England is a question that still requires close examination. As the present study and others like it make clear, however, a tribal spirit, if widespread, did not result in a long-range decline of visible piety, as Morgan believed. *Puritan Family*, esp. 185–86. Recently George Selement has argued that early New England ministers were evangelists more than they were tribalists. *Keepers of the Vineyard: The Puritan Ministry and Collective Culture in Colonial New England* (Lanham, Md., 1984). But he ignores the important issue of lay tribalism, which certainly influenced clerical behavior. Parishional tribalism was a critical ingredient of lay religiosity, as David D. Hall has recently argued. *Worlds of Wonder, Days of Judgment: Popular Religious Belief in Early New England* (New York, 1989), 152–56; "Toward a History of Popular Religion in Early New England," *William and Mary Quarterly*, 3d ser., 41 (1984): 49–55.

46. At least 53 percent of the inhabitants on the 1686 list, for example, were the descendants of settlers who had entered the church before 1645, or the settlers themselves. Post-1664 newcomers represented only 9 percent of the inhabitants on the 1686 list.

47. At ten-year intervals from 1639 to 1700, the percentage of married persons becoming communicants within one year of their spouses was 66, 0, 34, 38, 33, and 30, while the percentage of new members with tracable families admitted within a year of a sibling was 6, 33, 32, 24, 10, and 7.

48. Thus, for example, forty-four of seventy-four people who were admitted in 1660–86 had fathers who were still alive, although it may be of some consequence that the number of males who waited until after their fathers' deaths before joining the church equaled the number who did not. For the suggestion that second-generation males were unable to undergo conversion before their fathers' death, see John M. Murrin, "Review Essay," *History and Theory* 11 (1972): 236.

49. At consecutive decades from 1660 to 1700, the two kin groups combined accounted for 76 percent, 56 percent, 72 percent, and 75 percent of the members added by the church.

50. Of fifty-nine male members with known order of birth, 41 percent were firstborn sons, 20 percent secondborn, and 20 percent thirdborn. Of fifty females, 36 percent were eldest daughters, 24 percent were born second in line, and 18 percent were third.

51. Note that, from 1639 to 1750, the percentage of new family surnames appearing on the admission list at successive decades are as follows: 100, 56, 38, 27, 12, 19, 17, 5, 10, 10, and 7.

52. Ages at admission declined abruptly, however, during the 1740s. At consecutive ten-year intervals between 1700 and 1750, mean ages at admission for men were 32.2, 29.5, 27.8, 33.7, and 25.8 years, and for women they were 28.2, 27.2, 27.3, 26.2, and 22.8 years.

53. This conclusion finds recent confirmation in Ramsbottom's work. As she says, "the essential agency of transmission for the covenantal promises was not the church but the family." Ramsbottom, "Religious Society," 271.

54. Edmund S. Morgan, "New England Puritanism: Another Approach," *William and Mary Quarterly*, 3d ser., 18 (1961): 236–42.

CHAPTER 3

"Sisters" in Christ: Women and the Church in Seventeenth-Century New England

Few subjects in the history of American Protestantism have attracted as much scholarly interest in recent years as that of religion and gender.[1] As a result, historians can now appreciate the vital role played by gender in the development of Protestant churches. Even as the first reformed churches established in British North America took root in New England, their membership displayed a striking sensitivity to gender, drifting increasingly toward female preponderance over the course of the seventeenth century. Thus, the process of "feminization," which shows up repeatedly in the history of American denominations, had its gestation in early New England. How and why this happened are the questions this chapter seeks to answer.

Evidence obtained from the records of eighteen New England churches reveals that for the seventeenth century, Massachusetts and Connecticut churches admitted substantial proportions of women. As the last column of table 3.1 shows, women made up roughly two-thirds of members added by the churches of Beverly, Boston Third, Rowley, and Salem, Massachusetts; and Hartford Second, Middletown, and New London, Connecticut. They made up about three-fifths of admissions in Boston First and Charlestown, Massachusetts; and Milford, Windsor, and Woodbury, Connecticut. Lower percentages prevailed elsewhere but no lower than the 54 percent recorded by Farmington, Connecticut. Five other churches ranged between 55 and 57 percent: Dedham, Dorchester, and Roxbury, Massachusetts; and New Haven and Stonington, Connecticut.[2]

The sex ratio of admissions changed considerably over time. Before

TABLE 3.1. Women Entering New England Churches, Percentage of All Entrants with Average Annual Increments of New Members per Decade, 1630–99

Church	Date Organized	Percentages (with increments in parentheses)							
		1630–39	1640–49	1650–59	1660–69	1670–79	1680–89	1690–99	Total
Salem	1629	52 (40)	54 (17)	74 (5)	65 (8)	67 (6)	70 (15)	76 (11)	64 (12)
Boston First	1630	47 (45)	59 (30)	62 (8)	66 (15)	65 (18)	68 (13)	75 (22)	60 (21)
Dorchester	1630	58 (40)	49 (7)	43 (4)	64 (4)	57 (7)	54 (5)	63 (6)	56 (8)
Roxbury	1631	50 (20)	59 (8)	50 (4)	65 (4)	67 (5)	54 (9)	66 (8)	57 (8)
Charlestown	1632	56 (20)	57 (11)	67 (7)	68 (7)	71 (9)	65 (8)	70 (7)	63 (10)
Windsor	1636		53 (2)	64 (1)	56 (3)	53 (2)	63 (7)	57 (4)	59 (3)
Dedham	1638		54 (12)	64 (3)	58 (3)				56 (6)
Milford	1639		51 (8)	56 (2)	57 (7)	66 (7)	56 (4)	67 (9)	59 (6)
New Haven	1639		37 (17)	46 (3)	84 (4)		65 (14)	61 (15)	55 (11)
Rowley	1639				71 (4)	64 (3)	57 (5)	69 (9)	65 (5)
New London	1646					72 (3)	50 (1)	66 (8)	66 (4)
Farmington	1652			50 (4)			59 (4)	55 (6)	54 (5)
Beverly	1667				54 (8)	58 (2)	73 (6)	67 (12)	67 (7)
Middletown	1668					63 (4)	50 (1)	68 (8)	64 (5)
Boston Third	1669					79 (19)	63 (12)	64 (17)	70 (16)
Hartford Second	1669					68 (4)	75 (2)	59 (5)	65 (3)
Woodbury	1669					55 (1)	58 (2)	59 (3)	58 (2)
Stonington	1674					58 (4)	65 (2)	50 (5)	56 (4)

1660, membership in some churches was less skewed along sexual lines or was even tipped in favor of men. Thus, fewer than one-half of the people entering Dorchester and New Haven in 1640–59 were women, as were fewer than one-half in Boston in 1630–39. A rough sexual balance existed at Roxbury during the 1630s, Milford and Windsor during the 1640s, and Farmington during the 1650s. Only Charlestown started admitting a higher percentage of women than men at the beginning of settlement and continued to add to the proportion subsequently.

From the 1660s to the end of the century, no first-generation church, including Farmington and New London, admitted more men than women in any one decade. In Boston First, Charlestown, and Salem, a nearly step-by-step increase in female communicants took place from the 1630s through the 1690s, so much so that, by the latter decade, each church had about seven women joining for every three men. Sex ratios changed more erratically in other churches, but larger proportions of women were admitted per decade in 1660–99 than in 1630–59, as table 3.2 reveals. For over half of the decades before 1660, less than 55 percent of those entering the church were women, while, in well over half of the decades after 1660, more than 64 percent of new communicants were women. In 90 percent of the post-1660 decades, more than 54 percent were women.

This history can be clarified by combining data, as in figure 3.1. The preponderance of women at admission increased substantially from 1640 to 1670, then leveled off and even dipped slightly during the 1670s and 1680s, although no fewer than three out of every five people becoming members were women. Farmington and New London together saw the sex ratio plummet during the 1680s, but they, along with other first-generation churches, underwent increases in the admission of women in the last decade of the century. These changes in the sexual composition of membership, with women acquiring more and more visibility at admission after mid-century, have escaped historians, who have failed to consider long-range trends or the evidence open to statistical analysis.

Second-generation churches established after 1660 accepted more women than men from the very start, while several were even founded upon a surplus of them, contrary to the traditional practice of gathering a church around male pillars. The Beverly church embraced twenty-seven women and twenty-four men at its founding in 1667, and Hartford Second had eighteen "sisters in full communion" consent to the new covenant along with fifteen male "brethren" shortly after its separation from Hartford First in 1669.[3] Each continued to bring in high percentages of women during the last three decades of the century, as did other second-generation churches. Only two churches, each in a different decade, added an equal number of men and women. Nearly two-fifths of all decades in 1660–99 saw over 64 percent women admitted, and more than four-fifths over 54 percent. Moreover, as figure 3.1 shows, these churches together maintained a very high, though slightly dwindling, proportion of women among new members during the 1680s and 1690s.

The combination of a late-century upsurge in membership and female preponderance at admission led to an excess of women with access to the Lord's Supper. Eleven of seventeen churches for which data exist averaged more annual admissions in the 1690s than in any other decade from 1650. Of these, the admissions for six were over 65 percent female, and for ten they were over 58 percent female. Table 3.3 shows that more churches added more women than men during this same decade than at any other time during the century, while they often

TABLE 3.2. Distribution of Percentages of Women Entering New England Churches, 1630–99

| Female Entrants (Percentage) | First-Generation Churches | | | | Second-Generation Churches, 1660–99 | |
| | 1630–59 | | 1660–99 | | | |
	Number	Percentage	Number	Percentage	Number	Percentage
35–39	1	4	0	0	0	0
40–44	1	4	0	0	0	0
45–49	3	13	0	0	0	0
50–54	8	33	4	10	3	16
55–59	6	25	9	22	6	32
60–64	3	13	5	12	3	16
65–69	1	4	15	37	4	21
70–74	1	4	5	12	1	5
75–79	0	0	2	5	2	11
80–84	0	0	1	2	0	0
Total	24	100	41	100	19	101

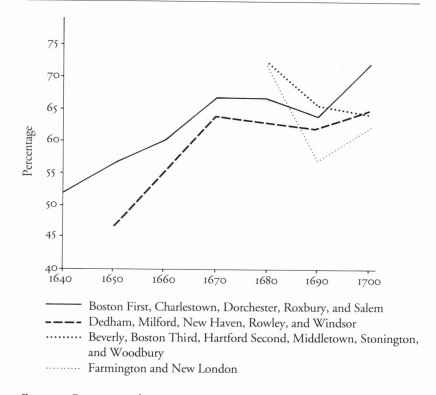

Boston First, Charlestown, Dorchester, Roxbury, and Salem
Dedham, Milford, New Haven, Rowley, and Windsor
Beverly, Boston Third, Hartford Second, Middletown, Stonington, and Woodbury
Farmington and New London

Fig. 3.1. Percentage of women entering New England churches, 1630–99

added to their surplus of female communicants with each succeeding decade from 1630.

Female-dominated admissions meant female-dominated churches, even if women were more likely than men to disappear from membership because of death or emigration. Women predominated in those churches that recorded from time to time their existing membership. Farmington had 91 communicants in 1680, 53 percent of whom were women. In New London, 54 percent of 24 members in 1670 and 65 percent of 31 members in 1691 were women; in Middletown, 58 percent of 121 communicants in 1676 were women; and in Boston First, 63 percent of 302 full members in 1688 were women.[4] By this time in Boston, nearly sixty years and two generations removed from its founding, none of the men who had entered in the 1640s remained.

As in other churches, the death or migration of first-generation males, together with the increasing visibility of women at admission, had created a church top-heavy with second- and third-generation females. By 1688, 42 percent of the membership consisted of women added in 1670–88 and 56 percent of women admitted in 1660–88, a period of rising female participation in full communion.

The late-century revival in admissions thus strengthened the trend toward female domination of church membership. Some fifty years before this time, during the 1630s and early 1640s, similar religious activity had created more sexually balanced churches. What happened between the "Great Migration" to New England and the turn of the seventeenth century to transform the gender profile of membership is a question that calls for analysis of several factors of Puritan history, including popular religious experience, clerical ideals about conversion, and ecclesiastical procedures at admission. By linking long-term changes in lay religious behavior to shifts in clerical standards and church practices regarding admission to communion, we can begin to understand why New England church membership became feminized during the seventeenth century.

TABLE 3.3.   Surpluses of Women Admitted by New England Churches, 1630–99

Churches	1630s	1640s	1650s	1660s	1670s	1680s	1690s	Total
Salem, Boston First, Dorchester, Roxbury, Charlestown	35	94	57	120	137	139	264	846
Windsor, Milford, New Haven		−43	2	42	22	66	68	157
Beverly, Middletown, Boston Third, Hartford Second, Woodbury, Stonington					134	80	133	347
Rowley, New London						20	6	60	86

In the course of Puritanism's century-long rise to prominence in England, precedents were established for the widespread and gender-balanced participation of the people in the churches of early New England. Drawing upon such venerable sources of popular piety as the fourteenth-century Lollardy movement, English Puritanism by the time of the exodus to America had become a broad-based, popular movement involving men and women in equal numbers in the struggle to purify the English church and nation through abolition of religious ritual and the Anglican hierarchy, among other efforts.[5]

In Puritan theory and practice, the laity as well as the family gained at the expense of the hierarchy. The household became the locus of the faith, and family prayer and homily key instruments of conversion. Fathers became preachers to family members, whose salvation now depended upon an effective presentation of the Word. Although this "spiritualization of the household" increased the power of the patriarch, it also improved the spiritual status of the woman. A woman became attractive for her piety rather than for her property. After marriage, she became an important religious companion to her husband, a source of spiritual support and comfort, as he was to her. At the same time, she became the special guardian of grace in children. The spiritualized household provided the energy for an aggressive English lay piety.[6]

This active English laity reasserted itself in the New World. In the course of establishing communities in Massachusetts Bay and Connecticut, laymen and -women worked with preachers in creating covenants; organizing churches; selecting ministers, deacons, and elders; devising polity; and admitting new members. Some witnesses record the presence of an intense and extensive popular piety, a popular piety expressed in outbursts of spiritual enthusiasm, lay prophesying, and voluntary testimonies of conversion before congregations. Lay piety became channeled through legally established churches, and membership increased rapidly through the 1630s and into the early 1640s. Many husbands and wives joined the church together as the family continued to serve as an instrument of spiritual companionship and reinforcement. Ultimately the established church penetrated deeply within the community.[7]

With time, admissions began to decline, partly because few unchurched inhabitants remained. By the 1660s, however, many newcomers, along with second-generation sons and daughters who were reaching maturity, were failing to join the church. In many communities, the ratio of communicants to inhabitants was slipping noticeably.[8]

Apparently the sons and daughters were having difficulty duplicating the experiences of their parents, and with reason. Most churches demanded that they testify to an experience of regeneration before gaining access to the Lord's Supper and baptism for their children; even after the introduction of the Half-Way Covenant in the 1660s, full membership was not easily attained. Many first-generation patriarchs survived through the 1660s to uphold strict admission standards and preside over the ceremony of admission, and thus the second generation had to face the scrutiny of its elders, rarely its peers. While preparing for this encounter, the sons and daughters could not anticipate receiving the kind of lay and communal support present during the 1630s, although the family and minister could, and often did, offer encouragement. They were also expected to duplicate the religious experiences of their forebears in a new set of social and cultural circumstances. Fathers and mothers might recall how their conversions had been framed by disorientation in pre–Civil War England and by the disruption accompanying resettlement in New England. In comparison to England, where Puritanism had evolved amid extreme social and religious tensions, mid seventeenth-century New England was remarkable for its stability and social cohesion.

Eventually, as table 3.1 shows, admissions turned upward; the second generation, often the children of communicants, became members with increasing frequency during the 1660s, the 1670s, and beyond, and some participated in the formation of new churches.[9] The sons and especially the daughters decided to cross the barriers to admission once they entered a new stage of life. Where previously conversion had often accompanied social disorientation, now, in late seventeenth-century New England, it became geared to crucial developmental changes in the life of the individual and the family—in particular, betrothal, marriage, and then parenthood. These changes, taken together, betokened adulthood and guided church members, who sought to admit mature and responsible individuals. As expectations concerning church candidates meshed with some of the more apparent transitions of life to relate admission to adulthood, the experiences peculiar to marriage and parenthood, among other things, led to the increasing visibility of women in church membership.

Puritan divines considered "middle age" to be the proper setting for regeneration and church candidacy. They felt that new members ought to be mature and of "years of discretion." "Children not being usually able to examine themselves, nor discern the Lord's Body," Thomas Shepard observed, "hence they are not to be admitted to the use of this privilege." Although God's mercy was free and he extended his gracious hand to all age groups, "those whom God doth call it is most commonly in their middle age," Thomas Hooker believed, "before they come to their old age." Assurance must come through reason. "Though knowledg may be without grace," John Norton explained, "yet there can be no grace without knowledg." According to Thomas Hooker, when someone reached "the ripeness of his yeares, from 20. years untill he come to be 40. or thereabouts, then the workes of reason put forth themselves, then his apprehension is quick to conceive a thing, and his memory is strong and pregnant to retaine a thing apprehended." At middle age, "a man is able to conceive and partake of the things of grace, and fa[th]om them, and the power of his understanding comes on whereby he is able to embrace them." It was "the fittest time that God should bestow his graces upon man."[10]

Thus, ministers and lay members alike were apt to depreciate youthful outbursts of piety, and, as guardians of the keys to the church, they were not willing to extend such privileges as voting at church meetings to wayward and irresponsible youths. In practice, individuals tended to become members at relatively late ages (table 3.4). Rarely in Connecticut churches during the 1660s and beyond were new members below the age of twenty; in many instances, they were in their late twenties and early thirties. Although women were very often some years younger than men when admitted (as they were at marriage), most church candidates shared the common status of matrimony.[11] In Milford, 78 percent of the women and 77 percent of the men added by the church in 1660–99 were married; in Windsor, it was 83 and 81 percent, respectively. Eighty-three percent of the women admitted to the Stonington church were married and 86 percent of the men; for the New London church, the figures were 89 and 93 percent, respectively, and, for the Woodbury church, 79 percent and 83 percent. Many individuals had also become parents before admission; 49 percent of the married women and 52 percent of the married men had one to three children, while the mode for both groups was one child.[12]

In the absence of age-specific categories of life stages, marriage and parenthood marked an individual's passage from youth to adulthood and from immaturity into the years of discretion expected of candidates for church membership. Through marriage and parenthood, a person also became more and more exposed to life crises—the birth of a son or daughter or the death of a child, spouse, or parent—events that either demanded a religious interpretation or raised interest in the church and salvation to a new level of intensity. Attitude and experience interacted at the moments of conversion and admission and were partly responsible for the timing of these important events.

Marriage and its aftermath altered the lives of women. Males were not untouched by the transition, for, among other things, they had to discard the role of obedient son for that of dominant husband and father. But women had a wider divide to cross between old and new familial arrangements, experiences, and demands as they relinquished the position of daughter for that of wife and mother. Even while courting, women perhaps faced new parental pressures to close with the church and its discipline and to submit to the brethren in preparation for submission to their husbands. Once married, they were caught up in an inexorable biological and demographic cycle. Every two years or so between marriage and menopause, they became pregnant and thus often encountered the possibility of dying in childbirth. If they survived the ordeal, they faced another possibility, the loss of an infant

TABLE 3.4. Age at Admission in Connecticut, 1660–99

Age	Male		Female	
	Number	Percentage	Number	Percentage
Under 20	9	4	34	15
20–24	30	15	69	29
25–29	52	25	58	25
30–34	57	28	30	13
35–39	24	12	18	8
40–44	15	7	8	3
45–49	7	3	13	6
50 and above	11	5	5	2
Total	205	99	235	101

Note: This table is based upon the church records of Milford, New London, Stonington, Windsor, and Woodbury, and the vital statistics of the towns as contained in the Barbour Collection of births, marriages, and deaths in the Connecticut State Library, Hartford.

or child. Anxieties about death, the afterlife of the soul, and the spiritual welfare of the child were the constant companions of women in marriage.

To say this might be to reject demographic evidence on the remarkable healthiness of early New England when weighed against contemporary England and Europe, especially if the benign disease environment of New England also made death appear less awesome. But recent studies show that Puritans were extremely fearful of death and were tormented by thoughts of hell and the prospect of eternal damnation.[13] Besides, women often did die in childbirth—they had a shorter life span than men because of its rigors—and also chanced losing, on the average, several children through death in infancy or youth.[14] Moreover, because they were more mobile than men (for example, they often moved to another town on marriage), they had to cope with familial and religious crises in greater isolation from parents, siblings, and other kin.[15]

Thus, for women in particular, passage through betrothal, marriage, and parenthood resonated beyond the secular into the religious life. An example of this, though in some ways an atypical one, is found in the autobiography of Elizabeth White. "From my Childhood," she begins her spiritual narrative, "the Lord hath inclined my Heart to seek after the best Things, and my Father's chiefest Care was to bring me up in the Nuture [*sic*] and Admonition of the Lord. My nature being some-what more Mild than the rest of my Sisters, I was ready to think my self some Body."[16]

White had parents who had joined the church and wished their children to do the same. Her father felt that a daughter, upon considering marriage, should also consider committing herself to the church: "I remember about a Month before I was married, my Father would have me receive the Sacrament of the LORD's Supper." But when she began contemplating "what was requisite to be in those which did partake thereof," she hesitated, fearing "that I had not those Things which were requisite wrought in me, as Knowledge, Faith, Love, Repentance, etc." What to do? "I was loath," she says, "to disobey my Father, and more loath to eat and drink my own damnation."

But in the end, White was unable to disappoint her father. In "this Perplexity," she wrote, "I set my Self to seek the Lord for his Grace," working through the standard preparatory stages of conversion. In time, she continued, "I began to be comforted, verily thinking, now

95

I had repented, and could believe in Christ Jesus" and had "some notional Knowledge of Things," and some hope that, "when I was married, I should have more leisure to serve God." Such proved sufficient to carry her to the minister for examination and then to the Lord's Table. After all, she believed, "I was in as good a Condition as any of the rest which did receive." This happened around the time of her marriage in 1657.

Soon, however, White began to suffer spiritual anxiety and despair. She started imagining she "had a Heart worse than the Devil," and, upon seeing a spider, a creature "most loathsome" to her, she desired to be "such a one, esteeming of it to be in a far happier Condition than I was." Fearing "to be in the Dark, lest I should meet the Devil," she doubted whether she was "Elected" and "thought if I were not Elected, is [sic] was to no Purpose to strive, for what God hath decreed must be." At one point, she "began to see mine own Vileness more than ever, and found mine Heart ran out to the Lord Jesus in Love, but doubted very much of his Love to me." For over a year, she wrote, "I had scarcely any settled Peace, now and then a good Word thrown in which would revive me for the present, but the Comfort would be soon gone."

When she became pregnant, perhaps for the first time, she started to fear that she might die in childbirth before gaining true repentance, and the prospect of suffering everlasting damnation overwhelmed her: "once when I was in great Fear least [sic] my Heart should grow dead, and when I was with Child, I was much dejected, having a Sense of my approaching Danger, and wanting an Assurance of my everlasting Happiness." But even after having "speedy Deliverance" of her child "beyond my Expectation," she still was unable to cast aside her apprehensions. One evening, while recovering from the birth and after suckling her child, she envisioned "Satan laughing at me, because I had no Sleep" and continued through the night "weak in Body, and comfortless in Mind, so that in the morning I expected nothing but Death." But these impressions suddenly became fused with other, more reassuring ones: "I have cast my self wholly upon the Lord Christ, and in him only is my Hope, and here will I Rest, and if I perish, I perish, but sure I am such shall not perish, for Christ hath promised them eternal lief [sic]." Now aware of Christ's power and mercy and "thus being assisted by the Lord, I vanquished Satan for that Time," she wrote, and being thus at peace, "quickly fell asleep" and dreamt "that I should die in Child-bed" (as she did twelve years later) and "that the Night before I died, I should have full Assurance." She then awoke, feeling an "inexpressible Joy," a sense of Christ's saving presence, "earnestly longing to be Dissolved, and to be with Christ . . . and yet willing, if the Lord pleased to suffer any Thing which might be inflicted on me."[17]

The latter phases of this spiritual journey embody a theme found time and again in sermons delivered by New England ministers: the will must submit to Christ in regeneration if true assurance is to be gained. White had gradually sensed this need as she sought spiritual comfort from the Word, her minister, and published sermons such as Shepard's *The Sincere Convert*. Humiliation formed the central passageway through conversion: only after the self had been humbled, the sinful past of youth purged, could an individual feel the joy of assurance. The unregenerate were often exhorted by those such as Shepard to "lie down under" the Lord, that "he may tread upon thee, and thereby exalt himself, as well as lift thee up and exalt thee." Because the natural soul was an unclean vessel, it had to be emptied of its impurities before it could begin to receive the benefits of God's grace. Thus, for Thomas Hooker, the self, "now being full of abominations, full of covetousnesse, full of malice, full of pride, full of love of our selves, full of hypocrisie, full of carelessenesse, and concupuscence of the flesh," is unable to receive God's saving faith. Only through humiliation—"the utter nothingness of the soul"—could the reprobate cut himself or herself off from "all high conceits and self confidence of that good which is in him."[18]

The regenerate was to God what the woman was to man after marriage. "It is a marriage-covenant that we make with God," Peter Bulkeley said, "therefore we must doe as the Spouse doth, resigne up our selves to be ruled and governed according to his will."[19] Although Puritan wives and mothers perhaps enjoyed a higher status than English and European women, New Englanders upheld the tradition of the natural subordination of the wife to the husband.[20] "The proper conduct of a wife was submission to her husband's instructions and commands. He was her superior, the head of the family, and she owed him an obedience founded on reverence."[21] All other responsibilities in marriage were mutual: husbands and wives were to cohabit, to love, honor, and respect one another, to demonstrate patience and devotion toward one another.[22] But mutual caring in marriage could be ensured by the wife's submitting willingly to the gentle yet firm rule of the husband, a belief verified by the Puritan's reading of the Pauline epistles: Thus, Cotton Mather preached that:

The *Principal Direction* for a Good Carriage in the *Married State* is that Eph. V. 24, 25. *As the Church is subject unto CHRIST, so let Wives be unto their own Husbands, in everything. Husbands, Love your Wives even as CHRIST also has loved the Church.* I do not stay upon the Observation, That the Duty of the Wife is here, as elsewhere prescribed before that of the *Husband;* Because there may be more of *Difficulty* in *Her* Duty than in *His;* And, Because His cheerful doing of *His* Duty, will very much depend upon *Her* doing of *Hers.*[23]

Partly because of striking analogies between the position of the woman in marriage and the proper role of the regenerate Christian, New England ministers often employed the metaphor of marriage to elucidate Puritan doctrine on conversion. No other image conveyed so intimately the nature of true piety. "In sermon after sermon," Edmund Morgan shows, "the ministers of New England explained to their congregations that the true believer was wedded to his God in a holy marriage." Redemption could be understood as marriage to Christ; imperfect holiness in contrast to sanctification, as betrothal versus marriage; the trinity, as the family under God paralleling the secular family under the father.[24] By resorting to such imagery from the pulpit, however, ministers only reinforced the existing social and cultural harmony between the religious life, the transitional episodes of adulthood, and the experiences of married woman. Properly submissive wives could easily identify with marriage and humiliation to Christ in regeneration, while, for dominant husbands and fathers, the achievement of true piety demanded an abrupt reversal in roles.

New England ministers also used other types of images that at certain times seemed more applicable. In the 1650s, 1660s, and 1670s, when first-generation patriarchs controlled New England, the image of the angry and wrathful God the Father demanding obedience and submission from his children predominated as people sought to understand the apparent impiety and waywardness of the rising generation. Many divines turned to the Old Testament to decry the present backsliding and found in another kind of familial arrangement—the required subordination of son to father—an image to aid in bringing about regeneration and the submission of people to the Lord.[25] Thomas Hooker had used the metaphor with special force:

Thus the Lord deals with us as a wise father doth with his child, he seeth if he had his portion in his hands he would be riotous and carelesse, and therefore it is wisedome not to trust him with his estate, but to keep him low, and to keep him upon dependance, that he may have better subjection from his hands. So it is with the Lord, he seeth that we have unruly hearts, and that if we had that evidence of Gods mercy made knowne to us that we would have, we would be so proud, and so haughty, and so full of contempt, and so censorious, that there were no living with us: and the more dependance the soule hath, the more observance hath the Lord from us.[26]

But to exhort this way meant to risk losing completely the religious support of second-generation sons, who were struggling to come to terms with a patriarchal God in regeneration and to live up to their fathers before admission.[27]

With the 1680s and 1690s and the passing of the fathers, the Old Testament figure of a vengeful God became less pervasive than the New Testament one of a loving, gentle, and protective Christ—the brother, bridegroom, or husband to the saved.[28] Second-generation ministers sought to cure their parishioners of their spiritual inhibitions, comfort them in a time of social and political transition but emerging confidence, and excite them into religious action. Ministers employed the metaphor of regeneration as marriage to Christ to inspire conversions and adopted new methods to encourage church membership. Some supported the Half-Way Covenant, believing that it might stir interest in full membership; others supported a sacramental piety in the hope of assuaging scruples about partaking of the Lord's Supper.[29] During the 1690s, Cotton Mather began promoting a "New Piety" centered upon the experience of the new birth, a piety that retained humiliation as a key spiritual event but discarded the notion of preparation.[30] Moreover, Solomon Stoddard of Northampton, Massachusetts, started using the Lord's Supper as a "converting ordinance" and as a means through which the people of the town could grow in grace.[31]

Such efforts to bring about conversions and broaden church membership perhaps touched off the predominantly female revivals in admission which occurred especially during the 1690s. Congregations were becoming top-heavy with women, and some ministers, including

Cotton Mather, attempted to explain why they were so visible in membership. Maybe, he noted, there was simply a greater abundance of women than men in the population. But a deeper appreciation of their religious fervor demanded an inquiry into their experiences apart from men. He observed that "the *Curse* in the *Difficulties* both of *Subjection* and of *Child bearing* which the *Female Sex* is doom'd unto, has been turn'd into a *Blessing,* by the *Free Grace* of our Most Gracious God. God Sanctifies the *Chains,* the *Pains,* the *Deaths* which they meet withal; and furthermore, makes the *Tenderness* of their Disposition, a further Occasion of Serious Devotion in them." In addition, most women "have more *Time* to Employ in the more Immediate Service of (their) Souls, that the *Other Sex* is owner of." They "are Ordinarily more within the *House,* and so may more mind the Work within the *Heart,* then *We.*"[32]

Benjamin Colman of Boston's Brattle Street Church made similar observations. Women were less a part of the world than men and hence more religious (Puritan divines were always decrying the secular distractions created by man's involvement in the profane), but their zeal was particularly due to their "MULTIPLIED SORROWS." The "*Curse pronounc'd upon our first Mother EVE,*" Colman explained to an assembly of women, has been "*turn'd into the greatest Blessing to Your Souls.*" He continued that "*Your frequent Returns in Your own Apprehension towards the Gates of Death, by which We all receive our LIFE, suitably leads you to a returning serious Tho'tfulness for your Souls and of Your Spiritual State.*" The fears of the mother awaiting childbirth were more apt to "*terrify*" than the anxieties arising out of illness, for the "*Impressions*" of "*Fits of Sickness*" soon disappear, while the experiences of pregnancy are of greater duration and tend not to vanish but linger in the mind.[33]

At the close of the seventeenth century and beyond, ministers who faced congregations filled with regenerate women not only tried to understand the source of their piety but also were increasingly willing to extol their sanctity and virtue. A "typology of the female as a model for the regenerate" emerged in the literature alongside an idealized picture of the virtuous woman. As portrayed especially by the funeral sermons of the period from 1690 to 1730, the ideal woman sought God early, prayed and fasted, attended church frequently, and submitted to the will of God. She also read and wrote and was a teacher to her children. This does not mean that Puritan piety became feminized or that woman's virtues began to be praised at the expense of the man's.

Puritan divines stressed the need for a virtuous mankind and a common Christianity in working for the conversion of all New Englanders and were quick to point out that experience, not nature, accounted for her more fervent piety.[34] Yet, by upholding the equality of men and women before God and by promoting the ideal of virtuous woman-hood, they might have inadvertently created conditions capable of nurturing gendered definitions of piety. The Puritan discovery of virtuous womanhood was thus a transitional episode in the feminization of New England piety.

Although the history of women and the New England church in the eighteenth century is beyond the purview of this chapter, several significant developments are worthy of note. One is the continuation of female preponderance at admission. Even as ministers continued to extoll the piety of Puritan maidens, the conversion of males remained a clerical priority. Virtuous women attracted so much clerical attention in part because of the important role they could play in the conversion of their husbands.[35] Yet males remained generally unresponsive to preachers' initiatives. The percentage of women entering New England churches hovered around sixty throughout the early eighteenth century, even during the Great Awakening, which has been interpreted as a phenomenon appealing particularly to males.[36] Yet, aside from several communities, whose inhabitants were involved in the traditional, male task of planting new churches, the awakening did not stem the tide of feminization.[37] After the 1750s, the feminization of church membership intensified, so much so that, by the eve of the American Revolution, the median percentage of women at admission had reached 65. Of the many sources of this development, one was surely the ministry's preoccupation with the ideology of virtuous womanhood. Another was the increasing autonomy of women in matters of religion. As women became increasingly able to join the church alone, men, who had formerly relied on their wives for support at admission, were reluctant to act alone. Such a conclusion finds confirmation in data on declining rates of same-day admissions among spouses and on rising rates of female conversions experienced before or in the complete absence of husbands.[38]

Another significant development in the area of eighteenth-century religion and gender involved the relationship of feminine piety to the life course. The clergy's increasingly fervid promotion of early piety for women (and for men as well) narrowed the temporal limitations on the proper age for conversion, threatening to upset customary connections between vital events and church membership. Rising expectations regarding the propriety and even necessity of early piety lowered expectations concerning the probability of later piety, inducing in parishioners a heightened sense of personal urgency over the passage of time and thus of opportunities for salvation. In East Windsor, Connecticut, for example, Hannah Bancroft, who was thirty-six years of age at the time of her admission in 1700, had learned from her minister, Timothy Edwards, "that men or persons were usually converted before they were thirty years of age" but, when she "went for counsel in private" with Edwards, was somewhat relieved to discover that, though she "was too old (for my age was ready to discourage me), yet there was hope for me." Even then, she still thought it was "too late for me to seek mercy." Similarly, Daniel Skinner, who was thirty-one years of age when he joined the East Windsor Church in 1700, had heard "that some thought there was but a mercy for [those] that lived to thirty years of age before they was converted that ever was converted," which "afterwards much terrified" him, for he thought he "had out-stayed my time."[39] Other candidates for communion related similar fears of "losing time," of being "left" behind, of passing "my day of grace," and that "the great work of the soul must be done now or never."[40]

Though such anxieties were not confined to either gender, women may have expressed them more in behavior, as the church records of the early eighteenth century suggest. In the face of rising clerical appeals for early piety, women started joining churches at increasingly lower ages until the 1740s, the period of the Great Awakening, when nearly 50 percent of female converts were under the age of twenty (as opposed to 26, 21, 9, and 11 percent, respectively, for the previous decades), but only 27 percent of male converts were under twenty (as opposed to 9, 8, 4, and 2 percent for the previous four decades).[41]

This chapter raises other issues that need to be explored in future studies of women and the New England church. What of the experiences of males apart from females? Were there implicit, gendered distinctions in Puritan piety? What explains the local variations in sex ratios, which were considerable at certain times and places?[42] By shifting focus from broad patterns over time to the parish and by using techniques of comparative history, future studies might produce answers to these and other questions concerned with the possible connections between changes in communities and admission patterns. Additional demographies of gender and church membership can only deepen our understanding of the important historical background to feminine experience and behavior in antebellum America.

Notes

1. See, for example, Barbara Welter, "The Feminization of American Religion, 1800–1860," in her *Dimity Convictions: The American Woman in the Nineteenth Century* (Athens, Ohio, 1976), 83–102; Nancy F. Cott, *The Bonds of Womanhood: "Woman's Sphere" in New England, 1780–1835* (New Haven, Conn., 1977); Mary Maples Dunn, "Saints and Sinners: Congregational and Quaker Women in the Early Colonial Period," in *Women in American Religion,* ed. Janet Wilson James (Philadelphia, 1980), 27–46; Sue Juster, "In a Different Voice: Male and Female Narratives of Religious Conversion in Post-Revolutionary America," *American Quarterly* 41 (1989): 34–62; Carol F. Karlsen, *The Devil in the Shape of a Woman: Witchcraft in Colonial New England* (New York, 1987); Margaret Masson, "The Typology of the Female as a Model for the Regenerate: Puritan Preaching, 1690–1730," *Signs: Journal of Women in Culture in Society* 2 (1976): 304–15; Gerald F. Moran, "'The Hidden Ones': Women and Religion in Puritan New England," in *Triumph over Silence: Women in Protestant History,* ed. Richard L. Greaves (Westport, Conn., 1985), 125–49; Edmund S. Morgan, "New England Puritanism: Another Approach," *William and Mary Quarterly,* 3rd ser., 18 (1961): 238–39; Robert G. Pope, *The Half-Way Covenant: Church Membership in Puritan New England* (Princeton, N.J., 1969); Mary P. Ryan, *The Cradle of the Middle Class: The Family in Oneida County, New York, 1790–1865* (New York, 1981); Richard D. Sheils, "The Feminization of American Congregationalism, 1730–1835," *American Quarterly* 33 (1981): 46–62; and Laurel Thathcher Ulrich, "Vertuous Women Found: New England Ministerial Literature, 1668–1735," in *Women in American Religion,* ed. Janet Wilson James (Philadelphia, 1980), 67– 87.

2. All data on church membership come from the following records: Milford, Connecticut, First Congregational Church Records, Connecticut State Library (CSL), Hartford, 1:1–3, 7–10, 19–22; Henry Stiles, *The History and Genealogies of Ancient Windsor, Connecticut,* 2 vols. (New York, 1859), 2:873–74, 886–88; Franklin Bowditch Dexter, comp., *Historical Catalogue of the Members of the First Church of Christ in New Haven, Connecticut* (New Haven, Conn., 1914), 1–39; "Records of Farmington in Connecticut," *New England Historical and Genealogical*

Register 11 (1857): 323–26, and 12 (1858): 34–37; Stonington, Connecticut, First Congregational Church and Ecclesiastical Society Records, CSL, 3:1–8; Woodbury, Connecticut, First Congregational Church Records, CSL, 1:3–22; Edwin P. Parker, *History of the Second Church of Christ in Hartford* (Hartford, Conn., 1892), 291–94; New London, Connecticut, First Congregational Church Records, CSL, 1:5–10; Middletown, Connecticut, First Congregational Church Records, CSL, 1:1–22; Don Gleason Hill, ed., *The Record of Baptisms, Marriages and Deaths, and Admissions to the Church . . . in the Town of Dedham, Massachusetts: 1638–1845* (Dedham, Mass., 1888), 21–39; Charles Pope, ed., *Records of the First Church at Dorchester in New England, 1636–1734* (Boston, 1891), 2–29; Richard D. Pierce, ed., *Records of the First Church in Boston 1630–1868*, Colonial Society of Massachusetts, *Publications* 39 (1961): 13–98; "Early Records of Rowley, Mass.," *Essex Institute Historical Collections* 34 (1898): 77–86; "Beverly First Church Records," *Essex Institute Historical Collections* 35 (1899): 185–211; "Record Book of the First Church in Charlestown," *New England Historical and Genealogical Register* 23 (1869): 190–91, 279–84, 435–42; *Roxbury Land and Church Records, Reports of the Record Commissioners* 6 (1881): 73–102; *An Historical Catalogue of the Old South Church* (Boston, 1883); Richard D. Pierce, ed., *The Records of the First Church in Salem, Massachusetts, 1629–1736* (Salem, Mass., 1974), 5–183.

3. "Beverly First Church Records," 177; Parker, *History of the Second Church in Hartford*, 290–91.

4. "Records of Farmington," 12, 35–36; New London Congregational Church Records, 1:5, 7; Middletown Congregational Church Records, 1:D; Pierce, *Records of the First Church in Boston*, 84–90.

5. Patrick Collinson stresses the importance of the laity to English Puritanism in *The Elizabethan Puritan Movement* (Berkeley, Calif., 1967); and *The Religion of Protestants: The Church in English Society, 1559–1625* (Oxford, 1982).

6. Christopher Hill, *Society and Puritanism in Pre-Revolutionary England* (New York, 1964), chap. 13; Charles H. George and Katherine George, *The Protestant Mind of the English Reformation, 1570–1640* (Princeton, N.J., 1961), 269–70; Lawrence Stone, *The Crisis of the Aristorcracy 1558–1641*, abr. ed. (New York, 1967), 281.

7. In Dedham, for example, 70 percent of the town's taxpayers were church members by 1648. Kenneth Lockridge, "The History of a Puritan Church, 1637–1736," *New England Quarterly* 40 (1967): 409. Also, in Milford 82 percent of the male inhabitants and 77 percent of their wives had joined the church by the end of 1644, and during the 1640s 66

percent of the married men and women who became communicants did so on the same day or within a year of their spouses. See chapter 2.

8. Slightly over 50 percent of Dedham's taxpayers were communicants in 1670, for example, and only 36 percent of Milford's male inhabitants in 1669. Lockridge, "History of a Puritan Church," 411; also see chapter 2.

9. Of the churches experiencing increases in admissions during the 1660s, Boston First added more than the average number of new members in 1661 and 1664–67; Salem did so in 1662–63 and 1666–67; and Milford did so in 1669, when forty-six people became communicants. Boston First, Dorchester, Roxbury, and Charlestown saw membership increase during the 1670s, as table 4.1 indicates.

10. Thomas Shepard, *The Church Membership of Children,* in *The Works of Thomas Shepard,* ed. John A. Albro, 3 vols. (New York, 1967) 3:531; Thomas Hooker, *The Unbelievers Preparing for Christ* (London, 1638), 199–200. John Norton is quoted in Ross W. Beales, Jr., "In Search of the Historical Child: Miniature Adulthood and Youth in Colonial New England," *American Quarterly* 27 (1975): 386–87. On "middle age" in colonial America, see John Demos, *Past, Present, and Personal: The Family and the Life Course in American History* (New York, 1986), chap. 6.

11. In the four Massachusetts churches studied by Pope, for example, women nearly always became communicants at earlier ages than men. See *Half-Way Covenant,* appendix.

12. The numbers of children belonging to new members in Connecticut were distributed thus:

Males

No. of Children	0	1	2	3	4	5	6	Over 6
New Members	28	33	26	28	16	11	11	14

Females

No. of Children	0	1	2	3	4	5	6	Over 6
New Members	46	50	46	30	28	20	16	23

13. David E. Stannard, *The Puritan Way of Death: A Study of Religion, Culture, and Social Change* (New York, 1977), esp. chap. 4. Because of their sensitivity to death, Puritans overestimated the rate of mortality in New England, as indicated in chapter 7.

14. The recent literature on childhood mortality rates in early New England is surveyed in Stannard, *Puritan Way of Death,* 54–56. In Andover,

Massachusetts, one of the healthier communities of New England, some three of nine children born to the average family during the seventeenth century died before attaining their twenty-first birthday. Mortality rates were considerably higher in port areas like Boston and Salem.

For mortality rates among women, see John Demos, *A Little Commonwealth: Family Life in Plymouth Colony* (New York, 1970), 66; Philip J. Greven, Jr., *Four Generations: Population, Land, and Family in Colonial Andover, Massachusetts* (Ithaca, N.Y., 1970), 27–28; Maris A. Vinovskis, "Mortality Rates and Trends in Massachusetts before 1869," *Journal of Economic History* 32 (1972): 201; also see chapter 7.

15. Linda Auwers Bissell examines the mobility rates of women, in "From One Generation to Another: Mobility in Seventeenth-Century Windsor, Connecticut," *William and Mary Quarterly*, 3d ser., 31 (1974): 87–88. In Milford 17 and 9 percent of the new members added by the church in 1660–84 and 1685–99 were female newcomers, most of whom had entered town to marry. See chapter 2.

16. Elizabeth White, *The Experiences of God's Gracious Dealings with Mrs. Elizabeth White. As they were written under her own Hand, and found in her Closet after her Decease, December 5, 1669* (Boston, 1741), 3. Though White lived her entire life in seventeenth-century England, her conversion was considered of sufficient relevance to Americans to be published here for an American audience. On the English provenance of White's *Experiences,* see Patricia Caldwell, *The Puritan Conversion Narrative: The Beginnings of American Expression* (New York, 1983), 8– 25.

17. White, *Experiences,* 4, 6, 9–13.

18. Shepard, *The Sound Believer,* in *Works of Shepard,* 1:179, 186; Hooker, *The Unbelievers,* 94.

19. Peter Bulkeley, *The Gospel-Covenant; or, the Covenant of Grace Opened,* 2d ed. (London, 1651), 50, quoted in Edmund S. Morgan, *The Puritan Family: Religion and Domestic Relations in Seventeenth-Century New England,* rev. ed. (New York, 1966), 161.

20. See, especially, Demos, *Little Commonwealth,* chap. 5; and Roger Thompson, *Women in Stuart England and America: A Comparative Study* (Boston, 1974).

21. Morgan, *Puritan Family,* 44–45.

22. So said Benjamin Wadsworth in *The Well-Ordered Family* (Boston, 1712), 28, as noted by Ulrich, "Vertuous Women Found," 76.

23. Cotton Mather, *A Glorious Espousal: A Brief Essay to Illustrate and Prosecute the Marriage, Wherein Our Great Saviour Offers to Espouse unto Himself the Children of Men* (Boston, 1719), 42, quoted in Masson, "Typology of the Female," 308.

24. Morgan, *The Puritan Family,* 161–65.

25. Emory Elliott, *Power and the Pulpit in Puritan New England* (Princeton, N.J., 1975), 13–15 and passim. Elliott notes that in the sermons "before 1650 passages from the New Testament concerning mercy and grace predominate; between 1650 and 1680 there were fifty-seven published sermons based on Old Testament texts and only fifteen on texts from the New Testament; from 1681 to 1695 verses from the Gospel served as the texts for eighty-nine sermons while there were fifty-six texts from the Old Testament" (14).

26. Thomas Hooker, *The Soules Implantation* (London, 1637), 133.

27. John Murrin, in "Review Essay," *History and Theory* 11 (1972), suggests that "most second-generation men (women had less difficulty) could not experience a psychologically convincing conversion so long as their fathers were still alive to provide thunderous comparisons from the 1630s. Viewed from this perspective, scrupulosity blends indistinguishably into awe of the patriarch" (236).

28. Elliott, *Power and the Pulpit,* 14, 129, 176–77.

29. E. Brooks Holifield, *The Covenant Sealed: The Development of Puritan Sacramental Theology in Old and New England 1570–1720* (New Haven, Conn., 1974), chap. 7.

30. Robert Middlekauff, *The Mathers: Three Generations of Puritan Intellectuals, 1596–1728* (New York, 1971), chaps. 13, 17.

31. Paul R. Lucas, *Valley of Discord: Church and Society in the Connecticut Valley, 1636–1720* (Hanover, N.H., 1976), chaps. 7–9.

32. Cotton Mather, *Ornaments for the Daughters of Zion; or, the Character and Happiness of a Vertuous Woman* (Cambridge, Mass., 1692), 44–45.

33. Benjamin Colman, *The Duty and Honour of Aged Women, Deliver'd after the Funeral of the Excellent Mrs. Abigail Foster* (Boston, 1711), ii–iii.

34. Masson, "Typology of the Female," 304–15; Ulrich, "Vertuous Women Found," 67–87.

35. As Cotton Mather once told his parishioners, the wife's "fidelity is no where more signalized, than in her solicitude for the eternal salvation of her husband. . . . Thus every Paul may have Women that labour with him in the Gospel. Vast opportunities are those that a Woman has to bring over Her Husband unto real and serious Godliness." *Ornaments for the Daughters of Zion; or, the Character and Happiness of a Vertuous Woman* (Cambridge, Mass., 1692), 96.

36. See, for example, Cedric Cowing, "Sex and Preaching in the Great Awakening," *American Quarterly* 20 (1968): 624–44.

37. Gerald F. Moran, "'Sinners Are Turned into Saints in Numbers': Puritanism and Revivalism in Colonial Connecticut," in *Belief and Behavior: Essays in The New Religious History,* eds. Phil R. VanderMeer and Robert P. Swierenga (New Brunswick, N.J., 1991), 38–62; and "Christian

Revivalism and Culture in Early America," in *Modern Christian Revivals,* ed. Randall Balmer (Urbana, Ill., forthcoming); Shiels, "Feminization of American Congregationalism," 47–49.

38. Stephen R. Grossbart, "Seeking the Divine Favor: Conversion and Church Admissions in Eastern Connecticut, 1711–1832," *William and Mary Quarterly,* 3rd ser., 46 (1989): 733–35.

39. Kenneth P. Minkema, ed., "The East Windsor Conversion Relations, 1700–1724," Connecticut Historical Society *Bulletin* 51 (1986): 27, 45.

40. Minkema, "East Windsor Conversion Relations," 25, 30, 43, 50.

41. These calculations are based upon the church, town, and vital records of the Connecticut towns of Canterbury, Milford, New London, North Stonington, Preston, Stonington, Stonington East, Suffield, and Woodbury, all of which are to be found in the Connecticut State Library.

42. Such variations or sexual imbalances in church membership, however, were not the result of skewed sex ratios within the population. The Connecticut census of 1774 allows an examination of sex ratios by town and over time, and it reveals that women made up only 49.4 percent of the colony's population. More than two-thirds of the towns listed on the census contained more men than women, while the percentages of women per town ranged from 46.2 to 55.7. Older communities tended to contain higher percentages of women than more recently settled towns, although the association proved insignificant ($r = +.26$). The mean percentages of women residing in towns settled at twenty-five-year intervals from 1635 to 1774 were as follows: 49.7, 49.6, 49.9, 49.7, 48.5, and 48.3. Even if seventeenth-century communities differed from their eighteenth-century counterparts and often contained more women than men, we would be forced to look elsewhere to explain sex ratios in membership which frequently exceed 65 percent women, and at times 70 percent. The 1774 census can be found in the *Public Records of the Colony of Connecticut,* vols. 1–3, ed. J. H. Trumbull; vols. 4–15, ed. C. J. Hoadly (Hartford, Conn., 1850–90) 14: 485–91.

The Great Care of Godly Parents: Early Childhood in Puritan New England

The study of the child in the past is important because it suggests that we have not always perceived or treated children the same way through-out history. Our approaches to children are very much influenced by changes in our general attitudes as well as alterations in the socioeco-nomic contexts in which children are reared. By studying the different views of the child over time as well as the factors that precipitated any changes, we may be more capable of anticipating, understanding, and coping with any shifts in our views and treatment of young children in our society today.

Yet the history of early childhood in premodern America remains to be written. While interest in early American childhood has been high since the 1960s and the advent of the new social history, most studies have focused on older children—particularly adolescents. Sur-prisingly little effort has been made to analyze the images and care of young children. This neglect is unfortunate, since the interaction of efforts on behalf of young children by their families, churches, and schools can provide us with useful insights not only about the child but also about the dynamics of these institutions in the socialization of the young.

Although the Puritans conceived of "young children" in vague chronological terms, we will use it to refer to children below the ages of seven. In addition, while we will try, whenever possible, to consider the behavior or view of young children themselves, we will be con-cerned primarily with adult perceptions and treatment of young chil-dren. Puritanism, as we will see, was a powerful force in the develop-ment of Puritan attitudes toward children. But we will not attempt to distinguish it from New England or Protestant culture in general, which overlapped in many areas of child rearing.

This chapter will focus on three aspects of the young Puritan child in the seventeenth and eighteenth centuries. First, we will examine Puritan ideology and how it may have influenced attitudes toward children—especially how views of infant damnation and of the child's will may have affected the responses of adults. Second, we will investigate whether Puritans really saw young children as distinct and different from others or whether they regarded them merely as miniature adults. Finally, we will analyze early childhood education in New England, considering the roles of the family, the church, and the schools in the socialization of young children and speculating on the relative importance of the mother and the father in this process. While this chapter should be regarded only as a tentative foray into the analysis of the care of young children in the past, it will offer a synthesis of previous investigations and will serve as a guide for further research.

Puritan Ideology and the Child

No aspect of New England theology has been more damaging to the historical reputation of Puritan treatment of childhood than the doctrine of infant damnation. Historians have asked, how could the Puritans have loved their children and at the same time have consigned deceased infants to eternal damnation? In theory, all infants and children who died unconverted suffered the eternal torments of hell. Since few infants were thought to experience conversion, this meant that the great majority of deceased infants were considered damned. As Stannard notes, "If there was any chance of an individual child's salvation, it was not a very good chance—and in any case, ultimate knowledge of who was chosen for salvation and who was not was not a matter for earthly minds." [1] The awful fate awaiting children at their demise was magnified in the minds of Puritans by their depiction of hell as a place of unremitting and unmitigated torment and horror, a picture presented most vividly in Michael Wigglesworth's *Day of Doom*. The Puritans, as some historians argue, were terrified of death, a feeling that was not lost on their children. David Stannard, for example, observes that

Puritan diaries and sermons were filled with references to . . . childhood responses to the terrors of separation, mortality, and damnation. . . . these fears followed the Puritan child into adulthood and combined there with the disquieting complexities of Puritan theology and Christian tradition to produce a culture permeated by fear and confusion in the face of death. To the adult Puritan the contemplation of death frequently "would make the flesh tremble." To the Puritan child it could do no less.[2]

The theory of infant damnation remained generally unchallenged among orthodox New Englanders well into the eighteenth century. But in actual practice, the Puritans avoided the implications of the doctrine. New England ministers were reluctant to dwell on the subject and avoided discussing it in detail, while Puritan parents often refused to apply the doctrine to their own deceased children. "Instead of directly affirming the presence of infants in hell," says Peter Slater, "ministers denied that all of them went to heaven. It was infant damnation by default, often by implication."[3]

Puritan parents could not escape dwelling on the afterlife of children because of the high infant morbidity and mortality rates in early New England. But much as adults made personal exceptions for themselves while contemplating the fate of their souls after death, so did Puritan parents for their children.[4] It was a great temptation to consider a dead infant among the few God had selected for salvation and had thus exempted from the fires of eternal perdition. In such cases, the character of the deceased child was idealized and the meaning of his or her death rationalized. Their demise was considered a welcome departure from the cares and sorrows of the world, while he or she was invested "with superior characteristics, often in invidious contrast to still living siblings."[5] Some parents also sought to sustain relationships with dead children, as the gravestone iconography of the period suggests.

In time, Puritans also began to accept the possibility of infant regeneration. Such was the increasing emphasis placed on the proneness of elect babies to achieve salvation at death that, by the time of the Great Awakening in the early 1740s, the New Lights, who subscribed in theory to the doctrine of original sin and infant damnation, had difficulty in practice consigning unregenerate infants to hell. Even Jonathan Edwards, one of the most ardent defenders of infant damnation, concluded that "'tis generally supposed to be a common thing that the infants of the godly die in infancy are saved."[6] As Norman Fiering has recently noted, it was the doctrine of infant damnation that "was most unassimilable in the eighteenth century and after and was probably responsible for more covert disaffection with orthodox church teaching than any other article of faith."[7] As a result, the concept of infant damnation was jettisoned by the religious liberals of the eighteenth century and increasingly ignored by Old Light Calvinists.

Another aspect of New England theology which has damaged the historical reputation of Puritan treatment of children is original sin. According to most historians, the doctrine of original sin and human depravity was responsible for Puritan repression of children. As Lawrence Stone argues, "The doctrine of Original Sin strongly encouraged the stress on repression (of Puritan children) rather than encouragement as the core of educational theory."[8] "The New English child on the eve of the revolution," James Axtell claims, "was still largely shaped after the religious model of his Tudor ancestors. . . . Until John Locke's rejection of original sin was heard, the children of New England were condemned to replay painfully adult roles in the drama of salvation."[9] According to John Demos, "In all likelihood, the first raw strivings of the infant self seemed to sincere Puritans a clear manifestation of original sin. . . . Such being the case, the only appropriate response from parents was a repressive one." The child's "earliest efforts at self-assertion," he continues, "were met with a crushing counterforce." Puritan parents sought to counteract original sin in children by breaking and beating down their wills. Once established, this mode "of parental discipline was probably maintained for quite a number of years."[10]

Central to the argument of Demos and others is the child-rearing theory of John Robinson, an early seventeenth-century English minister and the Pilgrim's first pastor. In a treatise published in 1625, "Of Children and Their Education," Robinson writes:

And surely there is in all children, though not alike, a stubborness, and stoutness of mind arising from natural pride, which must, in the first place, be broken and beaten down; that so the foundation of their education being laid in humility and tractableness, other virtues may, in their time, be built thereon. . . . For the beating, and keeping down of this stubborness parents must provide carefully . . . that the children's wills and wilfulness be restrained and repressed, and that, in time; lest sooner than they imagine, the tender sprigs grow to that stiffness, that they will rather break than bow. Children should not know, if it could be kept from them, that they have a will in their own, but in their parents' keeping; neither should these words be heard from them, save by way of consent, "I will" or "I will not".[11]

Robinson's is perhaps the most frequently cited passage in the secondary literature on Puritan childhood. But how representative of English and American Puritans were Robinson's attitudes toward children? Some historians argue that they were typical of the seventeenth century,[12] while a few others contend that they were not.[13]

Despite the popularity of Robinson's views among historians of the child, we suspect that he was not as representative of seventeenth-century Puritans as has been suggested. Robinson was a radical separatist—a sect with only a very small following in England, very few of whom migrated to New England. In addition, a recent study by Philip Greven suggests that the repressive mode of child rearing was not typical of all Puritans but was common only among those of an evangelical temperament.[14] But how prevalent was evangelicalism in the seventeenth century?

Greven emphasizes continuity over change, arguing that evangelicals and their authoritarian mode of child rearing persisted over the course of three centuries—from the seventeenth through most of the nineteenth. While he is reluctant to indicate the extent of repressive child-rearing methods in early New England, he does suggest a crucial connection between evangelicalism and religious revivalism, one that allows us to add a temporal dimension to his analysis.[15] Revivals were not common to all periods of New England history but ebbed and flowed across the eighteenth and nineteenth centuries. If one can establish a connection between the periodic eruption of religious revivals and the popularity of authoritarian child-rearing practices among the participants, then the static picture of child care suggested by Greven should be modified.

A recent history of the English family suggests such a link between religious revivals and authoritarian modes of child rearing. Lawrence Stone argues that

in England an era of reinforced patriarchy and discipline lasted from about 1530 to about 1670, with the high point in the 1650s. This in turn gave way to an era of growing individualism and permissiveness which was dominant in the upper middle and upper classes from about 1670 to 1790. The next stage in the evolution of the family was marked by a strong revival of moral reform, paternal authority and sexual repression, which was gathering strength among the middle classes from about 1770.

"The driving force behind this movement," he goes on to say, "was the spread of Evangelical piety. God was again seen as directly controlling day-to-day events within the household, in which capacity he was a severe and pitiless masculine figure." "With this reassertion of patriarchal authority in the early nineteenth century, the status of women inevitably declined." Moreover, there was a

renewed stress on the preeminence of the father, and the subordination of the children. The family became increasingly "a stifling fortress of emotional bonding," while relations between parents and children grew more intrusive. Supervision was more intense and oppressive since it was now motivated by an intense religious zeal. The seventeenth-century Puritan theory of the innate sinfulness of the child was revived.[16]

Stone's analysis parallels that of other historians. In a recent work, C. John Sommerville observes that "the phrase 'breaking the will,' which was not very current in the seventeenth century, seems to have increased in popularity" in eighteenth-century England and America.[17] The classic statement of this view comes from the pen of John Wesley, the noted English evangelist, whose preaching helped to bring about the revivals in mid eighteenth-century England. He writes:

If you are not willing to lose all the labour you have been at to break the will of your child, to bring his will into subjection to yours that it may be afterward subject to the will of God, there is one advice which, though little known, should be particularly attended. . . . It is this; never, on any account, give a child anything that it cries for. . . . If you give a child what he cries for, you pay him for crying: and then he will certainly cry again.[18]

Wesley's counterpart in America, Jonathan Edwards, the premier theologian of the Great Awakening, used similar language in his discussions of children and favored the same repressive mode of child rearing. In fact, the Wesley and Edwards families papers have given historians the richest store of evidence on that method of child rearing.

As for the attitudes of the many other families who participated in the same revivals and shared the same temperament, much less is known. But the language of authoritarian parenthood reappeared throughout the remainder of the eighteenth century and into the nineteenth. It surfaced during the early nineteenth century among the descendants of the New England revivalists in Utica, New York,[19] and it persisted among evangelical families in the antebellum South.[20] It also found expression in the writings of a nineteenth-century Baptist minister, Francis Wayland, who wrote in 1835 in his influential college textbook, *The Elements of Moral Science,* that: "The right of the parent is to command; the duty of the child is to obey. Authority belongs to the one, submission to the other." "In infancy the control of the parent over the child is absolute; that is, it is exercised without any due respect to the wishes of the child."[21]

A few individuals, like Robinson, who advocated the breaking of the wills of young children could be found in the seventeenth century, but they were not typical. Moreover, considerable evidence exists to suggest that the early Puritans were not the snake in the child's paradise, as the traditional historiography would have it. As Edmund Morgan argued as early as 1944, Puritan parents loved their children as much or even more than modern parents, sometimes even to the extent of allowing them to usurp a higher place than God in their affections. "Like Adam," Morgan observed, New England parents "had upset the order of creation, had placed love of creature over the demands of the creator."[22] The Reverend Samuel Willard, a typical New England minister, expressed in vivid language the positive assessment of children which was characteristically Puritan: "The Love of Parents of their children is such as admits not of suitable words to express it, it being so intense and influential, so that God himself is pleased to resemble His Love to His Children by this, there being no Comparison that better resembleth it."[23] As William Gouge, an English Puritan, wrote in 1622:

The Fountains of parents duties is Love. . . . Great reason there is why this affection should be fast fixed in the hearts of parents towards their children. For great is that paine, cost, and care, which parents must undergoe for their children. But if love be in them, no paine, paines, cost, or care will seeme too much. Herein appeareth the wise providence of God, who by nature hath so fast fixed love in the hearts of parents, as if there by any in it aboundeth not, he is counted unnaturall.[24]

We could continue indefinitely with such examples, for Puritan literature is suffused with discussions of adult affection for children. But in other ways as well, the Puritans expressed fondness for their offspring. The literature of the Great Migration contains numerous references to parental solicitude for children as a compelling motive for the exodus. In the privacy of their diaries, many parents contemplated how removal to America might protect their progeny from Old World corruption and profanity and might ensure their physical and especially spiritual well-being. In addition, the 1660s in New England offer an unusual spectacle of a whole society caught up in a dramatic dialogue over the religious fate of children. The eventual outcome of this debate was the Half-Way Covenant, which extended baptism to the children of the unregenerate sons and daughters of the elect. Moreover, as one historian has argued, New England parents put their children out to other families lest they spoil them with lavish displays of affection. Simply put, they did not trust themselves with their own children.[25]

This is not to say that seventeenth-century Puritans were always positive in their assessment or treatment of children, nor does it mean to imply that they were child-centered, as were many nineteenth-century Americans.[26] They were far removed from the cult of the child, but they were equally far removed from the indifferent, neglectful attitudes toward children held by many of their contemporaries and forebears. In this respect, they were born "half modern," as Slater has recently noted.[27] Furthermore, they shared with evangelicals an ambivalent attitude toward children, believing that the infant soul was tainted with original sin. In the words of the Reverend Samuel Willard, children were "innocent vipers," prone to commit evil at an early age but not to be held responsible for their acts until they had reached the age of reason. The Puritans held a complex view of human nature, one that is more in accord with modern attitudes than with the romantic version of the nineteenth century.

Whereas evangelicals stressed fear over love in their approach to infants, most early Puritans were more inclined in the opposite direction. They sought a middle way of child rearing, one that balanced discipline with indulgence, severity with permissiveness. They used the rod only as an instrument of last resort. As William Gouge remarked: "Reprehension is a kind of middle thing betwixt admonition and correction. It is rather to be used because it may be a meanes to prevent strokes and blowes, especially in ingenious and good natured children. [Blows are] the last remedy which a parent can use: a remedy which may doe good when nothing else can."[28]

With evangelicals, Puritans shared an intense concern for the spiritual destiny of their children, but they were less anxious about their ability to achieve it. Pride and will posed less of a threat to them. They desired to bend, shape, and mold the will, not to break it. They exercised an authoritative, not an authoritarian, mode of child rearing. Conversion for them was not what it was for evangelicals, a sudden, dramatic event that imposed itself on nature, altering irrevocably the corrupt, polluted character of the converted. Rather, it was processual and gradual in nature, the result of the piecemeal acquisition of grace, reason, and virtue from infancy through childhood and youth to adulthood. Puritan child-rearing efforts were directed less at the will than at the affections and reason. The affections were to be cultivated early in life, so that children would come instinctively to love God and his word. In their attention to affections, the Puritans, especially the women, anticipated the romanticists of the nineteenth century.[29]

Given this stress on the gradual nurture of grace in children, it is not surprising to discover Cotton Mather, whom some historians label an evangelical, sounding much like the nineteenth-century Horace Bushnell, who championed an organic, developmental approach to children:

Would parents thus conscientiously do their Duty to their children. . . . the Children belonging to the Election of Grace, would be so brought home to GOD by the Parental Ministry, and have the Fear of GOD so gradually and effectually insinuated into them, that your Pastors have little to do, but Instruct, and Confirm, and Edify such as have already ben Converted unto serious PIETY, and as it were sucked it with their Mothers Milk, and in a way that would leave them unable to tell the Time of the First Conversion.[30]

Reason was also to be nurtured in children at an early age, so that they could understand the right doctrine and be able to discern the Lord's body at the time of their admission into the church. The child's mind was considered an empty receptacle, one that had to be infused with the knowledge gained from careful instruction and education. While evil had to be restrained in the child, his or her mind had to be enlightened. All good had to come from the outside. In their belief that the infant's mind was a blank receptacle with a great capacity to reason, the Puritans anticipated the child-rearing theories of John Locke and other eighteenth-century Enlightenment thinkers.

Children as Miniature Adults

According to some of the earliest historians of the Puritan child in New England, the notion of a separate and distinct childhood did not exist.[31] Stanford Fleming, for example, argued that colonial children were simply regarded as miniature adults:

Judging from these records it would seem that children had a fairly large place in church life. Literally, such is the case, but in reality the child as a child had no recognition. There was an utter failure to appreciate the distinction between the child and the adult. Children were regarded simply as miniature adults, and the same means and experiences were considered suitable for them as for those older.[32]

The idea that children in the past were regarded and treated as miniature adults received reinforcement from the work of Philippe Ariès, who traced the nature of childhood in Western Europe from the Middle Ages to the seventeenth century. The work of Ariès was particularly significant because American colonial historians in the 1960s and early 1970s relied heavily on his interpretation of the role of the child in the past and assumed that children in early America were also treated as miniature adults.[33] John Demos summarized the nature of childhood as:

Colonial society barely recognized childhood as we know and understand it today. Consider, for example, the matter of dress; in virtually all seventeenth-century portraiture, children appear in the same sort of clothing that was normal for adults. In fact, this accords nicely with what we know of other aspects of the child's life. His work, much of his recreation, and his closest personal contacts were encompassed within the world of adults. From the age of six or seven he was set to a regular round of tasks about the house or farm (or, in the case of a craftsman's family, the shop or store). When the family went to church, or when they went visiting, he went along. In short, from his earliest years he was expected to be—or try to be—a miniature adult.[34]

Yet Puritans did see children as different and separate from adults. Children below age six or seven were treated very differently than were older ones, and even older children were distinguished from adults.[35]

Indeed, it is important to note that, much like contemporary parents, Puritans believed that different children possessed different abilities and temperaments and that child rearing had to be molded to fit the particular "temper" of each child. Every infant was considered an individual, an attitude reflected in the personalized naming patterns of the Puritans.[36] As Anne Bradstreet observed, "Diverse children have their different natures; some are flesh which nothing but salt will keep from putrefaction; some again like tender fruits are best preserved with sugar: those parents are wise that can fit their nurture according to their nature."[37] Perhaps particular deference was accorded the eldest son, whose responsibility it would be to carry on the traditions of the family after the death of the parents. In any case, Puritan parents had to know their children well and had to raise them accordingly. As one historian observed, "Here is no disposition to allow the unimpeded development of personality, but at least children were not subjected to a preconceived discipline without reference to their individual needs and capacities."[38]

Similar distinctions were made with respect to the capacities of consecutive age groups of children, as indicated by Puritan catechisms, which offer a rich but unexamined source of information on New England views of the intellectual and moral development of children. Of the many catechisms that were published during the seventeenth century, a good number were written especially for children of different ages. Some were written so that even the youngest children could begin learning the rudiments of Christian doctrine. In some instances, ministers assembled graduated catechisms in one volume, as was the case with the Westminster Assembly. Special catechisms were also developed for mothers for the "catechising of children in the Knowledge of God, Themselves, and the Holy Scriptures."[39] It was also the parents' responsibility to know the individual abilities of their children and to adjust their instruction of them accordingly.

While Puritans did distinguish between adults and children and even among children, their conception of the intellectual capabilities of young children was quite different from contemporary views of young children today. Puritans believed that children developed intellectually more rapidly than we usually expect young children to develop today. To observe these differences, it is useful to consider the ages at which Puritans expected children to learn to read as an index of their view of the intellectual capabilities of the child.

Since most early Americans simply assumed that everyone agreed on the proper age for training young children, they did not devote much time or energy to this topic. On the basis of our reading of colonial documents as well as earlier work in this field, it appears that Puritans expected children to learn to read as soon as possible in order to prepare themselves in this world for salvation in the next. As Cotton Mather put it, "The Children should *learn to read* the Holy Scripture; and this, as Early as may be."[40]

There appears to have been considerable variation in the ages at which children learned to read in colonial America, since there was little effort to synchronize reading with a certain chronological age. Yet the thrust of Puritan religious and educational ideas was to encourage reading as soon as possible. In seventeenth-century England, children were expected to learn to read at early ages, entering school at about four or five in urban areas and six or seven in rural ones.[41] English spiritual autobiographies reveal that most of them began their schooling at age six, although some began as early as four.[42] John Locke, one of the most widely read educators in England and New England, assumed that children should be taught to read as soon as possible but cautioned parents against injuring them or discouraging their natural curiosity:

When he can talk, 'tis time he should begin to learn to read. But as to this, give me leave here to inculcate again what is apt to be forgotten, viz., that great care is to be taken that it be never made as a business to him nor he look on it as a task. . . . I have always had a fancy that learning might be made a play and recreation to children, and that they might be brought to desire to be taught, if it were proposed to them as a thing of honour, credit, delight and recreation or as a reward for doing someting else, and if they were never chid or corrected for the neglect of it.[43]

While both Locke and the New England Puritans agreed on the desirability and possibility of early reading, they differed considerably on the precise age for achieving this objective. Whereas Locke saw early reading as desirable, he was unwilling to coerce the young child into reading. Many New England Puritans, on the other hand, saw the reading of the Bible as indispensable to the child's salvation, especially in a world still characterized by high infant mortality, and therefore encouraged or even forced their offspring into learning to read at very early ages.[44] Thus, the sense of urgency and importance attached to early reading by the Puritans may have been tied to the changes in their own religious beliefs and enthusiasm.

The importance and practice of early reading received a major boost in the early nineteenth century when the infant school movement swept the country.[45] Although initially intended to help poor children ages two to four receive an early education, which would help them to overcome their disadvantaged backgrounds, infant schools were soon opened to the children of middle-class families as well. By the 1830s and 1840s in Massachusetts, for example, as many as 40 percent of three-year-olds may have been enrolled in a public or private school.

Not all infant school instructors were eager to teach such young children the alphabet and the rudiments of reading. But parents, reflecting their view of the intellectual capabilities of the young as well as their desire to have their offspring keep up with the training received by other children, insisted that the infant schools provide their pupils with instruction in the alphabet and reading. Thus, as late as the 1820s and 1830s, almost all parents in America agreed that very young children could be taught to read, although some of them did not believe that early intellectual development was essential—especially since the belief in infant damnation had been abandoned by almost everyone since the seventeenth and eighteenth centuries.[46]

The belief that young children could and should be taught to read at an early age persisted virtually uncontested during the first two centuries of American development. But in the 1830s, partly as a reaction to the growing popularity of the infant school movement, this idea was forcefully and successfully challenged by Amariah Brigham, a physician, who saw early education leading to the insanity of the child:

Many physicians of great experience are of the opinion, that efforts to develop the minds of young children are frequently injurious; and from instances of disease in children which I have witnessed, I am forced to believe that the danger is indeed great, and that very often in attempting to call forth and cultivate the intellectual faculties of children before they are six or seven years of age, serious and lasting injury has been done both to the body and the mind. . . .

I beseech parents, therefore, to pause before they attempt to make prodigies of their own children. Though they may not destroy them by the measures they adopt to effect this purpose, yet they will surely enfeeble their bodies, and greatly dispose them to nervous affections. Early mental excitement will serve only to bring forth beautiful, but premature flowers which are destined soon to wither away, without producing fruit.[47]

The warnings of Brigham were soon picked up and echoed by educators and popularized through the mass media.[48] From about 1830 to 1920, the term *precocity* was applied not to extraordinarily gifted children but to normal ones experiencing pressures for accelerated intellectual or social development, which was increasingly seen as being harmful to their health and development.[49] Advocates of early childhood education now reversed themselves and discouraged intellectual precocity among young children.[50] Furthermore, writers of popular advice books admitted their previous mistake in advocating early intellectual activity.[51]

The effort to convince parents that they should not attempt to teach their young children reading at an early age was not immediately successful, as many of them continued to send their children to infant schools. But most of the infant schools, which had been heavily dependent on the financial contributions from middle-class female reformers, were soon forced to close as this better-educated and more widely read group abandoned the idea of early childhood education.[52] By 1860, the transition was complete; almost no three- or four-year-olds attended school in Massachusetts. Indeed, the start of the kindergarten movement at this time revealed the changes; it was directed at children older than those who had gone to the infant schools, and it did not try to teach them how to read.[53]

This reexamination of the societal views of the young child in the past suggests that, while early Americans did not view their children as miniature adults, they did see them as capable of intellectual development at a very young age. This idea persisted unchallenged for two hundred years and was reinforced in the early nineteenth century by the infant school movement. But starting in the 1830s, the belief that early intellectual activity among children ages three and four was possible and desirable underwent a major change that resulted in an entirely different view of young children by the eve of the Civil War.

Early Childhood Education in New England

The centerpiece of Puritan efforts to educate children was the family. Though household religion was part of the general Protestant tradition in England, the Puritans emphasized it more than other groups. They assumed that the family would play a key role in educating its own children and servants and that the state would intervene only when the family failed in its educational mission. As Gouge, a prominent English Puritan minister, put it in 1622:

For the family is a seminary of the Church and Common-wealth. It is a Bee-hive in which the Stocke, and out of which are sent many swarms of Bees: for in families are all sorts of people bred and brought up and out of families are they sent into the Church and Common-wealth. . . . Whence it followeth, that a conscionable performance of domesticall and household duties, tend to the good ordering of Church and Commonwealth.[54]

The family was expected to instruct its members not only in the art of reading and writing but also in religion. Children were expected to be catechized by their parents at home as a normal part of their initial religious training. In fact, the stress on reading rather than writing was to ensure the ability of everyone to comprehend the Bible. When, for example, Watertown officials admonished parents for not educating their children, they focused only on the ability to read the English language: "William Priest, John Fisk, and George Lawrence, being warned to a meeting of the Selectmen at John Bigulah's house, they making their appearance and being found defective, were admonished for not learning their children to read the English tongue: were convinced, did acknowledge their neglects, and did promise amendment."[55] Similarly, in 1650, the Connecticut court ordered the selectmen in every town to keep "a vigilant eye over their brethren and neighbors so that none of them shall suffer so much barbarism in any of their families as not to endeavor to teach themselves or others their children and apprentices so much learning as may enable them perfectly to read the English tongue."[56]

Though the Puritans relied on the family for the early education of their children, they also developed a comprehensive system of schooling. Most of their initial efforts in formal education were directed toward the creation of grammar schools to prepare those children going on to a university. A few towns such as Salem did maintain petty or dame schools, but most towns simply assumed that the parents would teach their children enough reading and writing for their religious needs or their entrance into grammar school.

The failure of some families to properly educate their children and the unwillingness of many communities to establish either petty or grammar schools led the Massachusetts General Court in 1647 to enact a law requiring the establishment of different types of schools on the basis of the number of households in those communities:

It is therefore ordered, that every township in this jurisdiction, after the Lord hath increased them to the number of fifty householders, shall then forthwith appoint one within their town to teach all such children as shall resort to him to write and read, whose wages shall be paid either by the parents or masters of such children, or by the inhabitants in general, by way of supply, as the major part of those that order the prudentials of the town shall appoint; provided, those that send their children be not oppressed by paying much more than they can have them taught for in other towns; and it is further ordered, that where any town shall increase to the number of one hundred families or householders, they shall set up a grammar school, the master thereof being able to instruct youth so far as they may be fitted for the university.[57]

The passage of the 1647 law gives us a good indication of the attitude of Puritans toward schools. While they expected families to educate their own children in the rudiments of literacy, they called for a comprehensive system of formal schools at the town level for both elementary and advanced education. These schools were usually seen as supplementary to the efforts of the parents and were only intended to replace the role of the parents when they were unable or unwilling to educate their children themselves. Nevertheless, despite the clearly articulated desire for formal schools in the seventeenth century, the 1647 law was never vigorously enforced. As Geraldine J. Murphy has pointed out, although all eight towns required to maintain a grammar school did so, only a third of the towns required to establish reading and writing schools obeyed the law.[58] As a result, although parents in some Massachusetts communities had the option of sending their children to one of the petty schools for reading and writing, in most towns they were forced either to teach their children themselves or to send them to some small private dame school.

While it is difficult to assess the success rate of Puritans in educating their children, an estimate of the literacy of Puritans will at least provide some idea of their achievements in this area. Information on the literacy levels of Puritan parents will also give us some sense of the potential for educating their children at home if they had wanted to do so.

Most analysts assume that New England Puritans were better educated than their counterparts in England or in the other colonies since they stressed the importance of education in their religion more than most other groups. Yet there is a growing debate about the actual extent of literacy in New England as well as about the role of Puritan religion in fostering it.

The most comprehensive study of literacy in colonial New England is Kenneth Lockridge's analysis of signatures on wills, which he uses as a crude index of literacy. After considering a variety of offsetting biases in the use of mark signatures to estimate the literacy of the population, Lockridge concludes that "the biases affecting signatures on wills were of moderate force and appear to cancel" each other. Lockridge found that there were significant differences between the literacy of men and women in colonial New England. Among the early settlers, about 60 percent of the men and only 30 percent of the women could sign their own wills. By the end of the colonial period the literacy of both men and women increased, so that 90 percent of males could sign their names and 50 percent of females signed their wills. In rural New England, however, female literacy continued to be below that of urban women and even declined slightly in the first half of the eighteenth century.[59]

To explain the relatively high rate of literacy among New England males, Lockridge rejects the argument that it was the fear of the wilderness that motivated Puritans to invest so heavily in the education of their children.

Something was lacking in these and other colonies which was present in New England. Neither social mobility nor social concentration is the missing crucial force since insofar as either existed it was present in all colonies and neither in New England nor quite evidently elsewhere did either of these forces alone raise literacy toward universality. Widespread fear of the wilderness was not present in New England, so it is not the vital element, and if such a fear had existed it would have occurred in other colonies where there is no evidence it had any impact. In simplest terms male literacy in these other areas of eighteenth-century America failed to rise toward universality because these areas lacked intense Protestanticism and consequent school laws.[60]

The mechanism for this increase was not the transmission of literacy by the families but the growing availability and efficacy of schools. Whereas in the second half of the seventeenth century the Puritan school laws were ignored by many towns because their population was so widely dispersed throughout the settlement, in the eighteenth century most towns complied with these laws, since the greater concentration of population now made the establishment of public schools feasible.[61]

Lockridge's analysis of the relationship between literacy and Puritanism is both provocative and stimulating. Though one must be extremely cautious in accepting his use of mark signatures as an estimate of the literacy level of the population, since many of the biases in this index may not be as offsetting as he hopes, his work is a model of careful specification of his assumptions and informing the reader of the strengths and weaknesses of his procedures. Rather than simply assuming the importance of Puritanism in raising literacy levels, he tests this proposition by comparing levels and trends in literacy in New England with those of other colonies and of England itself.

Though we agree with may of Lockridge's overall conclusions, we do have some reservations about others—especially those that relate to the differences between male and female literacy. Lockridge argues that:

Scholars agree that the levels of signatures runs below but closely parallels reading skills. While the absolute level of either literacy skill must remain uncertain, comparisons of the signature levels of various groups yield fairly reliable comparisons of their overall literacy. Under this interpretation the most precise absolute definition which could be placed on signatures is that they correspond to the actual level of fluent reading.[62]

Lockridge therefore compares the literacy levels of men and women by simply contrasting their mark signature levels. He does acknowledge, however, the possibility that women who could not sign their names might be able to read fluently since they were often educated only in reading skills. But he rejects this possibility by observing that women also had more delicate motor skills due to their household work and therefore could "fake" a smooth signature when totally illiterate—something which men rarely could do.[63]

Since the Puritans placed such a great emphasis on reading rather than writing, as we noted earlier, it is likely that almost everyone in that society would have been under great pressure to learn to read the Bible. In the seventeenth century, the Puritans were often content to teach women only reading, while encouraging men to learn both reading and writing. Therefore, there may be two limitations in using mark signatures: first, by using the differences between men and women in their ability to sign their signatures as an index of the gap in their literacy, one may exaggerate the extent of their differences in being able to read the Bible; second, the stress on reading rather than writing in Puritan culture because of religious needs in the seventeenth century may result in a rather higher proportion of males who could at least read the Bible than indicated by the 60 percent who were able to sign their own names in the mid seventeenth century. In other words, the great shift in male literacy between the mid seventeenth century and the end of the eighteenth century as well as the male-female differences in literacy may be exaggerated by the reliance on mark signatures as a comparable index of literacy over time and among different groups. In his most recent revision of his literacy analysis, Lockridge acknowledges that mark signatures may not be as useful an index of reading ability for women as for men and that the relationship between reading and writing may vary substantially from one culture to another, depending upon the emphasis within those societies on reading and writing as well as how they are taught.[64]

Another important methodological question that needs to be resolved is whether wills are really the most appropriate source for studying the literacy of colonial women. In a study of female literacy in colonial Windsor, Connecticut, Linda Auwers contends that deeds are a better source of literacy information, especially for women, because of the larger number of signatures available, the possibility of tracing them over time, and the fact that women signing deeds are more representative of the female population than those leaving wills. In addition, signatures on wills may exaggerate male-female differences in literacy during adulthood, since females were less likely to retain the ability to sign their names than men who were more apt to have occasion on which to utilize this skill.[65] Similarly, Ross Beales's analysis of Grafton, Massachusetts, in the mid eighteenth century used both deeds and wills, but he did not try to assess the relative usefulness of the two sources.[66]

While the pattern of female literacy as revealed by wills in Windsor appears to be close to that of Lockridge's New England rural sample, the evidence from the deeds suggests a different picture. Based upon the deeds, female literacy in Windsor dropped during the first decades of settlement in the seventeenth through the first half of the eighteenth centuries, when it became almost universal.[67] Beales also found a higher rate of female literacy in Grafton than suggested by Lockridge's rural sample but considerably lower than the comparable figures for Windsor.[68] William J. Gilmore's study of signatures on deeds in late eighteenth-century rural Vermont found a higher rate of female literacy than suggested by Lockridge's figures.[69] Gloria L. Main also found that colonial women in rural and urban Suffolk County, Massachusetts, were more literate than in Lockridge's sample.[70] Finally, Joel Perlmann and Dennis Shirley, using information from wills, deeds, and later manuscript censuses, conclude that New England's young women were achieving near universal literacy by 1790.[71] Thus, the choice of sources to study colonial literacy becomes particularly important for assessing male-female differences, since the use of wills seems to suggest a much larger differential than does the reliance upon deeds.

Lockridge, Auwers, Bruce C. Daniels, and Lee Soltow and Edward Stevens stress the increasing density of settlement and the resultant growth of primary schools in New England as the major factor in the rise of male and female literacy.[72] Lockridge, at the same time, explicitly dismisses home education as a possible source of increased literacy:

As for home education, a model in which females alone educated the children cannot account for a rise in male literacy on the order of 60% to 80% within a generation and a half in farm areas where female literacy remained below one-third. Very substantial male participation as home educators would be required. Whether male or female, the home educators would have to refuse to educate a large majority of their daughters to the point of signature while educating the overwhelming proportion of their sons to this extent. These are stringent conditions. In view of the previous evidence that a rise in male literacy alone can be accounted for by the public schools and that broad public action was found, it seems better to assume that the rise in male literacy was a product of the public schools.[73]

While we agree with these scholars about the importance of schools in fostering literacy in colonial New England, we also suspect that some of the rudiments of that literacy may have been acquired in the home. That females continued to use mark signatures more than males does not exclude the home or neighborhood as a possible source of literacy. If women were much less likely to be taught to write than their brothers were, then it is not at all surprising that they were less able to sign their names, even though both males and females were taught the alphabet and reading, if not writing, within their own homes or those of neighbors. Furthermore, although Auwers correctly points to the higher rates of female literacy in those areas of Windsor that were closest to the schools, her data on the three settlements furthest removed from the center of the town (Pine Meadow, Poquonnoc, and Wintonbury) suggest a sharp increase in female literacy well before they acquired easy access to local schools. East Windsor was another neighborhood that held a disadvantageous position with respect to school, but the settlement showed a precocious history of rising female literacy rates. In East Windsor, children had to cross the Connecticut River to attend school until 1696, when the town hired a teacher to serve the community three months out of the year. Fifty-eight percent of the women born in 1670–89, however, were able to sign their names on deeds and wills. This percentage increased to 62 women born in 1690–1709, 82 among those born in 1710–29, and 84 for the birth cohort 1730–49.[74] In 1700, East Windsor was established as a separate parish, or school district, but, unlike the town, where the civil authorities managed the school, East Windsor turned the responsibility over to the ecclesiastical authorities, namely the church and its minister, Timothy Edwards, who adopted an aggressive posture toward the education of the community's daughters. It seems that at least in this one village of East Windsor, the family and the church were responsible for much of the changes in female literacy.[75]

Another issue in the socialization of the young in colonial America is the relative role of the mother and the father in teaching children. Many scholars assume that it was unlikely that fathers played a major role in teaching their children.[76] Yet very little effort has been made to ascertain the role of the father in early childhood education. In addition, although much has been written about the mother's role in childhood education in the nineteenth century, relatively little has been said about the maternal care and education of young children in early America.[77]

It appears that fathers played a much larger role in the education of their children in colonial New England than in the nineteenth century. Fathers were expected to play the leading role in the catechizing of their children and servants. According to a 1648 law, for example, the masters of the household (usually the fathers) were expected to catechize the children and servants:

Also that all masters of families do once a week (at the least) catechize their children and servants in the grounds and principles of religion. . . . If any be unable to do so much, that then at least, they procure such children or apprentices to learn some short orthodox catechism without book, that they may be able to answer unto the questions that shall be propounded to them out of such catechism by their parents or masters or any of the selectmen when they shall call them to a trial of what they have learned in this kind.[78]

Whether the father was also expected to teach the children the rudiments of reading and writing is not clear. But since males were usually better educated than females in colonial America, perhaps there was little choice in many households as to which parent would instruct the child. Indeed, Auwers found that female literacy in seventeenth-century Windsor was associated with the literacy of the father but not of the mother.[79] As literacy was often considered a prerequisite for spiritual preparedness, the teaching of reading and the catechizing of children probably occurred simultaneously under the direction of the father and often with the assistance of the mother.[80] Perhaps, in some households, there was even a differentiation of instructional tasks, as some Puritan diaries suggest. In his autobiography, for example, Increase Mather tells how he "learned to read of my mother. I learned to write of my father who also instructed me in grammar learning, both in Latin and Greeke tongues."[81]

In the first generation, most fathers were probably able to carry out their household religious and educational duties, since at least 60 percent of them could sign their names (and many others could probably at least read the Bible) and most belonged to the church. The problems came in the mid seventeenth century, when males increasingly stopped joining the church and the church's membership became feminized.[82] Church records show that, from the 1660s onward, church membership in many New England villages became feminized. By the end of the seventeenth century in some New England communities, as many as three out of four people joining the church were women. Of the seventeen churches for which records are available, 70 percent admitted 61 percent women or better during the 1690s. In Boston, where literacy rates among women increased markedly during the eighteenth century, the two churches with extant records, Boston First and Boston Third, admitted 75 percent and 64 percent women, respectively, during the same decades. In fact, Boston Third contained the highest ratio of women to men of any other New England church.[83]

Did the Puritans entrust the catechizing of households to masters who did not belong to the church—especially since church membership was considered the most important sign of religious orthodoxy? And were the unregenerate masters of households willing to continue the tradition of catechizing and educating their children and servants? Surely some of the anxieties over educational decline in mid seventeenth-century New England stemmed from the fact that many fathers were either no longer thought fit to prepare their children spiritually or unwilling to shoulder the responsibility. By the 1660s, for example, some English preachers even perceived the patriarch as a formidable barrier to the religious education of the family. In 1666, John Bunyan denounced "madbrained blasphemous husbands that are against the godly and chaste conversation of their wives; also you that hold your servants so hard to it that you will not spare them to hear the Word."[84] He felt compelled to denounce patriarchs and to call for a relaxation of parental control in order to expose women, children, and servants to his preaching.

The solution to this dilemma was to reassign the responsibility for catechizing and educating young children to the wives, since they continued to join the church even as their spouses declined to do so. Yet these women were handicapped in carrying out this assignment because they were less literate than their husbands. Furthermore, though Puritans were willing to teach women to read and to allow them to help in the education of their children, they may have been reluctant in the 1640s and 1650s to entrust them entirely with the responsibility of directing and catechizing the children and servants in the wake of the radical religious activities of Anne Hutchinson and her followers during the antinomian crisis of the late 1630s.[85]

Perhaps the dilemma posed by the inability or the unwillingness of many males to catechize their households and the reluctance of the Puritan leadership to entrust women to replace them in this function helps to explain the growing willingness of the churches to catechize the children themselves. At first, the churches merely reminded their brethren of the importance of catechizing their children and servants at home, but gradually they began to offer public catechizing themselves.[86] Whereas in 1650 the Connecticut General Court had given "Masters of families" responsibility to "once a week at least catechize their children and servants in the grounds and principles of religion," in 1680 it ordered "that it be recommended to the ministry of this Colony to catechize the youth in their respective places that are under twenty years of age, in the Assembly of Divines Catechism, or some other orthodox catechism, on the Sabbath days," a practice that observers say was regularly followed. In another revision of past practice, the Connecticut General Court in 1700 stipulated that parents, masters, and ministers be responsible for propounding catechical questions to their children, whereas, formerly, just parents and selectmen put forth the questions.[87]

At the same time, colonial officials sought to establish more local schools. In Connecticut, the general court shifted responsibility for schooling from the town as a whole to the individual parishes, thereby ensuring greater participation in local educational affairs on the part of the church and the ministers. While the effects of this change have not been studied, Auwers's analysis of Windsor suggests that the increased role of the church in local school affairs, at a time when church membership was becoming heavily feminized, led to increasing educational opportunities for women.

Though Puritan ministers appear to have been reluctant at first to place the full responsibility for catechizing and educating children on the women's shoulders, they gradually changed their minds. As women became increasingly literate, at least in regard to reading the Bible, and as they continued to join the church in larger numbers than males, ministers began to emphasize their role in the religious education of their children. From the late seventeenth century on, they showed an increasing willingness to praise women for piety and literacy skills. For the period 1668–1735, Charles Evans's bibliography lists fifty-five eulogies, memorials, and funeral sermons for women in addition to other works of practical piety devoted wholly or in part to females, with the great bulk of these tracts appearing in print during the 1710s,

1720s, and early 1730s. From these treatises, a composite picture of the Puritans' image of the virtuous woman emerges. Not only did the ideal Puritan woman express her inordinate piety through early seeking of God, fasting, and prayer, but she also conversed well, read Bibles and devotional literature, and wrote.[88]

New England ministers were also increasingly inclined to advise women on their educational responsibilities. Thomas Hooker told women to bring children "up hither, traine them up to be Souldiers of Christ, it is admirable being here."[89] John Cotton echoed Hooker when he advised women to "Keep at home, educating of her children, Keeping and improving what is got by the industry of the man."[90] In a sermon published in 1692, Cotton Mather devoted whole passages to the religious responsibilities of mothers. The devoted mother, he said, introduces to her "little Vessels" such works as "Histories and Sentences fetch'd from the Oracles of God, and Instructs how to pray in secret unto their heavenly Father. She then proceeds to make 'em expert in some orthodox catechisms, and will have 'em learn to read and write, as fast as ever they can make it; and so she passes to the other Parts of an ingeneuous Education with them."[91] The same Cotton Mather advised mothers to "continually drop something of the Catechism on their children, as Honey from the Rock."[92] As Benjamin Wadsworth counseled mothers, "While you lay them in your bosomes, and dandle them on your knees, try by little and little to infuse good things, holy truths into them."[93]

Letters, diaries, and other records provide numerous examples of women teaching children, reading to children, and exerting a general influence over their religious development. In his diary, Richard Brown, who was born in 1675, relates how he was "educated under the wing of my parence [*sic*], especially my mother, who was a pious and prudent woman, and endeavored to instill into [me] the principals of Religion and holiness; . . . she was unwearied in her watchings, instructions, admonitions, warnings, reproofs & exhortations, that she might bring [me] up in the nurture and admonition of the Lord, and continued she to train me betimes, and when she had caused me to read well at home, she sent me to school."[94] Similar statements of the mother's role in the religious and educational training of their children are found in many other records.[95]

One dilemma that might be associated with this redefinition of the role of women and men in the household is that it may have appeared to undercut the traditional authority and responsibility of the father as the head of the household. The solution to this problem was to declare women's particular sensibilities in religious activities and their special skills in raising young children. Thus, the shift in the religious socialization of young children from the fathers to the mothers may have contributed to the development of the idea of special spheres of responsibility for women in the household—eventually leading to the "cult of domesticity" in the nineteenth century.

While the family had been assigned the major responsibility for educating and catechizing its children in the early seventeenth century, by the end of the eighteenth century it was clear that public schools and churches in New England had assumed some of those tasks. Yet, even at that late date, the family was entrusted with the task of teaching its children the rudiments of literacy and religion, since many public schools and churches expected to deal only with children who already knew the elements of the alphabet and simple reading. It was not until the late eighteenth and early nineteenth centuries that the responsibility of the family for early childhood education changed, as primary schools throughout New England began to take over the tasks of teaching students how to read and write. Furthermore, this transfer of functions from the family to the public schools was not one that was imposed on reluctant families by an aggressive school system; rather, it was a responsibility hesitatingly accepted by most schools and teachers, who would have preferred to leave the care of very young children to their parents.[96] Indeed, by the twentieth century, the role of the state in the provision of education is virtually unchallenged.

Notes

1. David Stannard, *The Puritan Way of Death: A Study in Religion, Culture, and Social Change* (New Haven, Conn., 1977), 49.
2. Stannard, *Puritan Way of Death,* 69.
3. Peter Slater, *Children in the New England Mind: In Death and Life* (Hamden, Conn., 1977), 26.
4. See chapters 1 and 7.
5. Slater, *Children in the New England Mind,* 39.
6. Norman Fiering, *Jonathan Edwards's Moral Thought and Its British Context* (Chapel Hill, N.C., 1981), 210.

7. Fiering, *Jonathan Edward's Moral Thought*, 209.
8. Lawrence Stone, *The Family, Sex, and Marriage in England, 1500–1800* (New York, 1977), 174–75.
9. James Axtell, *The School upon a Hill: Education and Society in Colonial New England* (New Haven, Conn., 1974), 49.
10. John Demos, *A Little Commonwealth: Family Life in Plymouth Colony* (New York, 1970), 136–37, 139.
11. Quoted in Robert Ashton, ed., *The Works of John Robinson*, 3 vols. (London, 1851), 1:246.
12. Axtell, *School upon a Hill*, 147.
13. C. John Sommerville, *The Rise and Fall of Childhood* (Beverly Hills, Calif., 1982).
14. Philip J. Greven, Jr., *The Protestant Temperament: Patterns of Child-Rearing, Religious Experience, and the Self in Early America* (New York, 1977).
15. Greven, *Protestant Temperament*, 10, 142.
16. Stone, *Family, Sex, and Marriage*, 666–69.
17. Sommerville, *Rise and Fall of Childhood*, 124–25.
18. Quoted in Sommerville, *Rise and Fall of Childhood*, 125.⌐
19. Mary P. Ryan, *Cradle of the Middle Class: The Family in Oneida County, New York, 1790–1865* (New York, 1981), 70–71.
20. Donald G. Mathews, *Religion in the Old South* (Chicago, 1977), 98–101.
21. Quoted in Greven, *Protestant Temperament*, 39.
22. Edmund S. Morgan, *The Puritan Family: Religion and Domestic Relations in Seventeenth-Century New England*, rev. ed. (New York, 1966), 185–86.
23. Samuel Willard, *A Complete Body of Divinity on Two Hundred and Fifty Expository Lectures on the Assembly's Shorter Catechism* (Boston, 1726), 601.
24. William Gouge, *Of Domesticall Duties* (London, 1622).
25. Morgan, *Puritan Family*, 77.
26. P. Hoffer and N. E. H. Hull, *Murdering Mothers: Infanticide in England and New England, 1558–1803* (New York, 1981).
27. Slater, *Children in the New England Mind*, 19.
28. Gouge, *Of Domesticall Duties*. Although Greven emphasizes the widespread use of corporal punishment throughout our past, in fact his own evidence suggests that Puritans such as Cotton Mather were reluctant to use physical punishment except when other methods of disciplining children had failed. Philip J. Greven, Jr., *Spare the Child: The Religious Roots of Punishment and the Psychological Impact of Physical Abuse* (New York, 1991), 84.
29. Laurel T. Ulrich, *Good Wives: Image and Reality in the Lives of Women in Northern New England, 1650–1750* (New York, 1982).
30. Quoted in Richard F. Lovelace, *The American Pietism of Cotton Mather: Origins of American Evangelicalism* (Grand Rapids, Mich., 1979), 93–94.

31. Alice Morse Earle, *Child Life in Colonial Days* (New York, 1899); Sanford Fleming, *Children and Puritanism: The Place of Children in the Life and Thought of the New England Churches, 1620–1847* (New Haven, Conn., 1933).

32. Fleming, *Children and Puritanism*, 59–60.

33. Phillipe Ariès, *Centuries of Childhood: A Social History of Family Life*, trans. Robert Baldick (New York, 1962); Michael Zuckerman, *Peaceable Kingdoms: New England Towns in the Eighteenth Century* (New York, 1970); Demos, *Little Commonwealth;* and "The American Family in Past Time," *American Scholar* 43 (1974): 422–46. Many scholars today continue to accept the idea of children as miniature adults in early America. See, for example, John Modell and Madeline Goodman, "Historical Perspectives," in *At the Threshold: The Developing Adolescent*, ed. S. Shirley Feldman and Glen R. Elliott (Cambridge, Mass., 1990), 93–122; and Walter I. Trattner, *From Poor Law to Welfare State: A History of Social Welfare in America*, 4th ed. (New York, 1989).

34. Demos, "American Family," 428.

35. Axtell, *School upon a Hill;* Carl F. Kaestle and Maris A. Vinovskis, "From Apron Strings to ABCs: Parents, Children, and Schooling in Nineteenth-Century Massachusetts," in *Turning Points: Historical and Sociological Essays on the Family*, ed. John Demos and S. S. Boocock (Chicago, 1978), S539–S580; *Education and Social Change in Nineteenth-Century Massachusetts* (New York, 1980); Stannard, *Puritan Way of Death;* "Death and the Puritan Child," in *Death in America*, ed. David Stannard (Philadelphia, 1975), 9–29.

36. Sommerville, *Rise and Fall of Childhood*, 109.

37. John H. Ellis, ed. *Works of Anne Bradstreet* (Charlestown, Mass., 1867), 50.

38. Morgan, *Puritan Family*, 108.

39. Leonard T. Grant, "Puritan Catechizing," *Journal of Presbyterian History* 46 (1968): 107–27.

40. Quoted in Wilson Smith, ed., *Theories of Education in Early America, 1655–1819* (Indianapolis, 1973), 27.

41. David Cressy, *Literacy and the Social Order: Reading and Writing in Tudor and Stuart England* (New York, 1980).

42. Margaret Spufford, "First Steps in Literacy: The Reading and Writing Experiences of the Humblest Seventeenth-Century Spiritual Autobiographers," *Social History* 4 (1979): 407–35.

43. John Locke, *Some Thoughts concerning Education*, ed. F. W. Garforth (Woodbury, N.Y., 1964), 186–7.

44. On early education among the Puritans, see David D. Hall, *Worlds of*

Wonder, Days of Judgment: Popular Religious Belief in Early New England (New York, 1989), 36.

45. Kaestle and Vinovskis, "From Apron Strings to ABCs"; Kaestle and Vinovskis, *Education and Social Change;* Dean May and Maris A. Vinovskis, "A Ray of Millennial Light: Early Education and Social Reform in the Infant School Movement in Massachusetts, 1826–1840," in *Family and Kin in American Urban Communities, 1800–1940,* ed. Tamara K. Hareven (New York, 1977), 62–99.

46. Slater, *Children in the New England Mind.*

47. Amariah Brigham, *Remarks on the Influence of Mental Cultivation and Mental Excitement upon Health,* 2d ed. (Boston, 1833), 15, 55.

48. Kaestle and Vinovskis, "From Apron Strings to ABCs."

49. John F. Kett, "Curing the Disease of Precocity," in Demos and Boocock, *Turning Points,* S183–S211.

50. Lydia Sigourney, *Letters to Mothers* (Hartford, Conn., 1838).

51. H. Humphrey, *Domestic Education* (Amherst, Mass., 1840), 11–12.

52. May and Vinovskis, "Ray of Millennial Light."

53. Kaestle and Vinovskis, "From Apron Strings to ABCs"; *Education and Social Change.*

54. Gouge, *Of Domesticall Duties,* 17–18.

55. Quoted in Robert H. Bremner, John Barnard, Tamara K. Hareven, and Robert M. Mennel, eds., *Children and Youth in America: A Documentary History,* 2 vols. (Cambridge, Mass., 1970), 1:41.

56. Quoted in G. Stewart, *A History of Religious Education to the Middle of the Nineteenth Century* (New Haven, Conn., 1924), 42.

57. Quoted in Lawrence A. Cremin, *American Education: The Colonial Experience, 1607–1783* (New York, 1970), 181.

58. Geraldine J. Murphy, "Massachusetts Bay Colony: The Role of Government in Education" (Ph.D. diss., Radcliffe College, 1960).

59. Kenneth A. Lockridge, *Literacy in Colonial America: An Inquiry into the Social Context of Literacy and Social Development in the Early Modern West* (New York, 1974).

60. Lockridge, *Literacy in Colonial America,* 83.

61. Lockridge, *Literacy in Colonial America,* 65–69.

62. Lockridge, *Literacy in Colonial America,* 7.

63. Lockridge, *Literacy in Colonial America,* 127.

64. Kenneth A. Lockridge, "Literacy in Early America, 1650–1800," in *Literacy and Social Development in the West: A Reader,* ed. Harvey J. Graff (New York, 1981), 183–200.

65. Linda Auwers, "Reading the Marks of the Past: Exploring Female Literacy in Colonial Windsor, Connecticut," *Historical Methods* 4 (1980): 204–14.

66. Ross W. Beales, Jr., "Studying Literacy at the Community Level: A Research Note," *Journal of Interdisciplinary History* 9 (1978): 93–102.

67. Auwers, "Reading the Marks of the Past."

68. Beales, "Studying Literacy."

69. William J. Gilmore, "Elementary Literacy on the Eve of the Industrial Revolution: Trends in Rural New England, 1760–1830," *Proceedings of the American Antiquarian Society*, 92, pt. 1 (1982): 87–177; *Reading Becomes a Necessity of Life* (Knoxville, Tenn., 1989).

70. Gloria L. Main, "An Inquiry into When and Why Women Learned to Write in Colonial New England," *Journal of Social History* 24 (1991): 579–89. Main also found that at least 14 percent of the women born after 1734 in her rural Massachusetts sample learned to write as adults rather than as children. She attributes the willingness of adult women to learn to write as the result of commercial changes in the rural economy which made writing important and useful. For an interesting and useful discussion of the necessity of reading and writing in rural area Vermont, see Gilmore, *Reading Becomes a Necessity*.

71. Joel Perlmann and Dennis Shirley, "When Did New England Women Acquire Literacy?" *William and Mary Quarterly*, 3d. ser., 48 (1991): 50–67. Perlmann and Shirley also expanded Lockridge's sample of late eighteenth-century Suffolk County wills and discovered a higher rate of female literacy than Lockridge did in his smaller sample of wills from that same area.

72. Lockridge, *Literacy in Colonial America*; Auwers, "Reading the Marks of the Past"; Bruce C. Daniels, *The Connecticut Town: Growth and Development, 1635–1790* (Middletown, Conn., 1979); Lee Soltow and Edward Stevens, *The Rise of Literacy and the Common School in the United States: A Socioeconomic Analysis to 1870* (Chicago, 1981).

73. Lockridge, *Literacy in Colonial America*, 58.

74. Auwers, "Reading the Marks of the Past," 211–12.

75. On the relationship between the literacy of the fathers and their sons among German immigrants to Pennsylvania, see Farley Grubb, "Colonial Immigrant Literacy: An Economic Analysis of Pennsylvania-German Evidence," *Explorations in Economic History* 24 (1987): 63–76. For a useful discussion of overall variations and trends in adult male literacy in England and colonial America, see Farley Grubb, "Growth of Literacy in Colonial America: Longitudinal Patterns, Economic Models, and the Direction of Future Research," *Social Science History* 14 (1990): 451–82.

76. Cressy, *Literacy and the Social Order*; Hall, *Worlds of Wonder, Days of Judgment*; Lockridge, *Literacy in Colonial America*.

77. Anne L. Kuhn, *The Mother's Role in Childhood Education* (New Haven, Conn., 1947).

78. Bremner et al., *Children and Youth in America*, 40.

79. Auwers, "Reading the Marks of the Past."

80. Morgan, *Puritan Family;* Margo Todd, "Humanists, Puritans, and the Spiritualized Household," *Church History* 49 (1980): 18–34.

81. Increase Mather, "The Autobiography of Increase Mather," *American Antiquarian Society Proceedings* 71 (1961): 278.

82. See chapters 2 and 3.

83. See chapter 3.

84. Quoted in Stone, *The Family, Sex, and Marriage*, 241.

85. David D. Hall, ed., *The Antinomian Controversy, 1636–1638: A Documentary History* (Middletown, Conn., 1968).

86. Axtell, *School upon a Hill.*

87. Stewart, *History of Religious Education*, 42, 76–77, 50.

88. Linda M. Malmsheimer, "New England Funeral Sermons and Changing Attitudes toward Women, 1672–1792" (Ph.D. diss., University of Minnesota, 1973); Laurel Thatcher Ulrich, "Vertuous Women Found: New England Ministerial Literature," in *Women in American Religion*, ed. Janet Wilson James (Philadelphia, 1980), 67–87.

89. Quoted in F. Shuffelton, *Thomas Hooker*, 1586–1647 (Princeton, N.J., 1977), 219.

90. Quoted in Morgan, *Puritan Family*, 42.

91. Cotton Mather, *Ornaments for the Daughters of Zion*, 3d ed. (Boston, 1741), 107.

92. Quoted in Earle, *Child Life in Colonial Days*, 132.

93. Benjamin Wadsworth, *A Course of Sermons on Early Piety* (Boston, 1721), 60.

94. Quoted in Axtell, *School upon the Hill*, 174–75.

95. Axtell, *School upon the Hill*, 175; David Ferris, *Memoirs of the Life of David Ferris, an Approved Minister of the Society of Friends . . . Written by Himself* (1825; reprint, Philadelphia, 1855), 16–17; Christopher M. Jedrey, *The World of John Cleaveland: Family and Community in Eighteenth-Century New England* (New York, 1979), 15; Morgan, *Puritan Family*, 96; Slater, *Children in the New England Mind*, 100.

96. Kaestle and Vinovskis, *Education and Social Change.*

CHAPTER 5

Troubled Youth: Children at Risk in Early Modern England, Colonial America, and Nineteenth-Century America

The issue of troubled youth has become a preoccupation of contemporary America. There is rising concern about the substantial number of teenagers who are growing up in dangerous environments that expose them to alcohol, drugs, pregnancy, suicide, and other factors that threaten health and life. Poor and disadvantaged adolescents, often minority youths living in the inner cities, are considered particularly vulnerable. There is also widespread fear that American youths today will be ill prepared to meet the technological and social challenges of tomorrow—especially compared to their better-educated Japanese and West European counterparts. While social scientists and policymakers are tackling these problems, there is little confidence that much improvement will actually occur, in part because of the fragmentation and underfunding of services for our troubled youth.

Unfortunately, contemporary perceptions of troubled youths, however sophisticated, lack historical vision. Most recent analyses of the issue portray it as being uniquely contemporary, implying that earlier times lacked comparable problems or handled them more effectively. As a result, there is little present understanding of the problems of youths in past time, of adult responses to them, and of the strategies devised to handle them. This chapter takes a first step toward making up the deficiency. While an understanding of the history of defining and dealing with troubled youths does not necessarily lend itself to any direct or immediate answers for coping with the problems of adolescents today, it does provide us with a broader framework and perspective by which to assess our current efforts. It also alerts us to the constant need to be aware of how much our own youth policies and programs are a reflection of the particular structural and ideological context of life in the United States today.

To appreciate the importance of a history of troubled youths, it is first necessary to overcome prejudice regarding the absence of a concept of youth in past time. Many scholars continue to accept the idea, first proposed and popularized by Philippe Ariès, that Western society in premodern times lacked a notion of youth, treating the age group simply as "miniature adults," rather than as a distinctive and different segment of the population.[1] As historians continue to investigate the history of the life course, however, evidence continues to mount in support of a contrary hypothesis, that Western youth has a long and venerable history, reaching as far back as the medieval period and perhaps beyond.[2] In her recent study of the family in medieval England, for example, Barbara A. Hanawalt argues that court records and other local evidence dispel "Aries's dreary view of children passing directly into adulthood without experiencing adolescence or having their teenage years recognized as a separate phase of the life cycle. The patterns of work and play, the rather late age of majority, and premarital sexual flirtation all point to teenage years not unlike our own."[3]

This is not to say that England or other Western societies possessed a concept of adolescence similar to the modern one; in fact, as we have come to believe, it is anachronistic to use the word *adolescence* when discussing premodern youth. Although *adolescence* entered the English language as early as the fourteenth century, it was rarely used in England and America until the twentieth. Not once, for example, is the word employed in the entire corpus of William Shakespeare, even though that corpus is suffused with the presence of youth. Hence we refrain from using the word in the present chapter except for the late nineteenth century when G. Stanley Hall popularized that term.[4]

Though the word *adolescence* was thus generally missing from premodern life course vocabularies, early modern English and Americans nevertheless had clear and concise ideas about the life stage that they termed *youth,* and they used the term in a way not unlike we use it today. They, like us, believed that the teenage years, along with the early twenties, comprised a discrete, transitional period in the development of an individual, one that involved abrupt alterations in human growth patterns, sexuality, social behavior, and work activity. They believed, as Hanawalt has recently pointed out, that youth was "a time of transition" and was distinguished from other stages by puberty, sexual initiation, leaving home, and entry into work, among other experiences.[5]

Not only did premodern Westerners have a clear conception of youth, but they were also, at times and places, as deeply preoccupied by youth as we are today. Such was the case in early modern England, where policymakers and reformers were deeply concerned about the problems of youth. As Lawrence Stone has argued, "The idea that adolescence only became a social problem in the nineteenth century is sheer historical fantasy," for "the problems of adolescence were a common preoccupation of the early modern period."[6] Such a preoccupation stemmed, in part, from common anxieties over youths' natural propensities for vice and rebellion. Thus, in *A Winter's Tale,* Shakespeare's shepherd remarks, "I would there were no age between sixteen and twenty-three, or that youth would sleep out the rest; for there is nothing in the between but getting wenches with child, wronging the ancientry, stealing, fighting." At the same time, premodern preoccupation with youth flowed from socioeconomic changes that stimulated public awareness and/or concern over troubled youths. Among the most important of the changes were demographic growth and urbanization, which severely disrupted the lives of vulnerable youths wherever they occurred.

This chapter will explore the history of troubled youths in several premodern societies: early modern England, the colonial Chesapeake and New England, and nineteenth-century America. Elizabethan and Carolinian England offers a particularly striking example of how policymakers and reformers in premodern times identified and addressed the problems of troubled youths. In the colonial Chesapeake, the situation was quite different; there, youths suffered severe trauma, but the leaders generally ignored them. In New England, on the other hand, youths had far fewer problems than their southern counterparts but commanded far more interest from adults, a disparity that reveals the power of religious ideology over attitudes toward children. Finally, the nineteenth century in America, a time of rapid socioeconomic change, produced increasing interest in and concern about troubled youths, paving the way for the emergence of modern adolescence.

Youth in Medieval and Early Modern England

Early modern English preoccupation with youth stemmed in large part from profound demographic, economic, and social changes that impinged directly upon the young, altering significantly the contexts of their everyday lives and placing them increasingly at risk. English population grew unusually rapidly in the early modern period, escalating from three to five million people in the 150-year period 1550–1700.[7] At the same time, rapid commercial growth and enclosure had disastrous socioeconomic effects, including the dispossession and dislocation of the peasantry, increasing unemployment, wage deflation, rapidly rising geographical mobility, and urbanization.[8]

The chronic social and economic instability of early modern England left few age groups unscathed, but it affected most dramatically the country's youths, especially the sons and daughters of farming families suffering from overpopulation or dispossession. Thrown off the land at a time of rising competition for agricultural and industrial jobs, youths were forced from parents, family members, and kin. Consequently, geographical mobility became a common characteristic of English youth.[9]

The customary destination for England's mobile youths was London, whose dramatic population growth was made possible by the thousands of youthful immigrants who flooded the capital each year.[10] Rather than finding housing and employment in London, however, the young immigrants instead found unemployment, idleness, poverty, and entrapment in slums that served increasingly as breeding grounds for crimes against property and persons. Rural depopulation and urbanization had thus created new and dangerous conditions for English youths, ripping them from home and hearth and placing them in environments that exposed them to delinquency, crime, incarceration, and death.[11]

As early as the mid sixteenth century, the English state responded to the worsening social conditions by erecting social legislation pertaining to crime which was less rehabilitative than punitive in nature. The state sought to cure vagrancy by criminalizing it, labeling unemployment as a dangerous crime. Though vagrancy legislation dates from the fourteenth century, it achieved its fullest development during the sixteenth and seventeenth centuries, when growing numbers of able-bodied but idle poor compelled government, in defense of orderliness and stability, to expand the law.[12] Thus, the Statute of Artificers of 1563 subjected laborers who refused agricultural work to arrest and incarceration, as did subsequent labor and vagrancy laws. As the state's fear of "masterless men" rose, it prosecuted the law more vigorously, conducting national manhunts for vagrants, which peaked in 1631 to 1639, when 24,867 persons were convicted for vagrancy.[13]

Although vagrancy legislation was directed at a number of groups, "the young were a special worry and were singled out in numerous statutes." The primary purpose of legislation passed in 1576 establishing houses of correction, for example, was that "youth may be accustomed and brought up in Labour and work." Recent demographic analyses of the subject also reveal "that vagrancy was mainly a young person's crime." Youths were picked up and incarcerated on a vagrancy charge far more frequently than other age groups. A list of vagrants imprisoned in Bridewell in 1602 shows that 97 percent were under the age of twenty-one, and 54 percent were under age sixteen; in Norwich in 1595–1609, 72 percent were below age twenty-one, and 52 percent were below age sixteen; and in Crompton in 1597, 75 percent were under age twenty-one, and 50 percent were under age sixteen. Though vagabonds in smaller towns and rural villages were less youthful, still 50 percent were below age twenty-one, and 33 percent below age sixteen.[14]

Statutory and statistical evidence on the youthfulness of vagrants is confirmed in the literary sources, which suggest that vagrancy became associated with youth in the minds of the early modern English. Thus, in 1536, Richard Morison complained about the "young and lusty, [who] neither have, nor yet will learn any honest occupation . . . but continuing in idleness, fall to stealing, robbing, murder, and many other mischiefs." Another social commentator wrote what could be considered one of the first early modern analyses of juvenile delinquency.[15] A primary cause of vagabondage, he argued, was "the bringing up of youths without virtuous exercises." Before age twelve or thirteen, youths were allowed to play in the streets, "which breeds in young age great idleness, a disease hard to be cured." Until their mid-teens, he said, youths were then given odd jobs, gathering firewood and acorns, gleaning wheat, and turning spits at church ales. Finally, by the time they were in their late teens, they were "idle, slothful, and unkempt," and, from age twenty-one on, "fall they to whoredom and set up with a bag and a wallet . . . or else forthwith go to plain thievery."[16]

Aside from punishment and incarceration, the primary cure for youthful vagrancy and delinquency was work;[17] "young people" had to "be found jobs and masters to keep them under control."[18] The authority of masters and local law enforcement officials was strengthened, and the justices of the peace were empowered to draft idle hands for field labor, "on pain, for refusal, of two days and one night in the stocks." In addition, hospitals and houses of correction were charged to care for troubled youths and to put them to work. Thus, as early as 1522, Bridewell of London began to admit not only idle adults but also young people "found unapt for learning" and for whom no service for the moment could be found.[19]

Such measures, initially designed to protect society from troublesome youths, often created new problems for already scarred children. Rural servitude, for example, had a tragic outcome for many of the youths involved. Youths compelled to submit to the authority of a master in a strange and isolated environment were at far greater risk of committing suicide than any other segment and age group of the population, according to a recent study.[20] Similarly, urban apprenticeship promoted the development of a youth subculture, whose members felt more solidarity for each other and less deference toward their masters.[21] The London apprentices developed a particularly notorious reputation for riotous and delinquent behavior, keeping the city's leaders in a constant state of alarm.

As old measures fell short of achieving their intended objective, new and more drastic measures were adopted to discipline seemingly undisciplinable youths, including military service, exportation to America, and indentured servitude. Thus, in some seventeenth-century colonies, as many as three-fourths of the immigrants were indentured servants, and, of these, nearly 70 percent were aged fifteen to twenty-five.[22] The forced exportation of convicts to America after the Transportation Act of 1718 was early modern England's final, drastic cure for troubled youth; some thirty thousand convicts were transported to America in 1718–75, and, of these, nearly 80 percent were aged fifteen to twenty-nine.[23]

In addition to the state, moralists and religious reformers, especially the Puritans, became deeply troubled by youths, though their interests differed from those of Tudor and Stuart policymakers and were focused less on the criminality and dangerousness of delinquent youths than on their sinfulness and religious deviance.[24] Aroused by the torrent of youthful nonconformity unleashed by the Reformation and by local epidemics of immorality (including drunkenness, fornication, and blasphemy) produced by the weakening of family authority, the reformers mounted a moral campaign that had as it primary goals the restoration of the traditional order and also the salvation of youthful souls. The campaign involved, on the one hand, the mobilization of ecclesiastical courts against vice and, on the other, the expansion of education and literacy. In the case of the Puritans, the campaign also involved clerical proselytization of youths, who were viewed as peculiarly prone to immorality and thus especially in need of admonition and religious indoctrination.

As Puritanism rose in the period from 1560 to 1640, so did clerical injunctions against the sins of youth. By the end of the period, Puritan preoccupation with the problem was focused less on the outward social misbehavior of youths than on their inward sinfulness. In other words, youths were perceived as innately sinful, whatever their particular lot. In this sense, Puritan anxiety about youth tended to transcend the imperatives of particular social contexts.

As the Puritans saw it, two types of sins were inherent to youth. One were sins of sensuality, especially sexual lust, which had as its primary concern early sexuality. As Thomas Wythorne said in the late sixteenth century, "After the age of childhood, beginneth the age named adolescency which continueth until twenty and five. . . . In this age Cupid and Venus were and would be very busy to trouble the quiet minds of young folk."[25]

The other major sin was vanity. All age groups were prone to this vice, but the young seemed particularly vulnerable to committing this sin, primarily because of their budding sexuality. Young men, the Puritans charged, often walked and strutted with excessive pride, especially while they were in the company of girls, and often dressed for show, to please the opposite sex. Young men were also inclined to talk without thinking but for effect, in consideration of its impact upon the girls. All such behavior was, according to the Puritans, clearly contrary to God's command to lead life "in holiness and integrity."[26]

While not considered sinful, susceptibility to peer pressure was deemed another dangerous characteristic of youth. Indeed, this was one of the most common injunctions in Puritan sermons and guidebooks.[27]

Since youths were by nature fickle and unstable, it was easy for them to be lured into sin by bad companions, especially considering their innate desire for peer approval. One of the greatest obstacles to religious conversion, young people were told, was bad friends. Apprentices and servants, since they were away from home, were particularly vulnerable to peer pressure. This was especially so in the cities, where youth gangs existed to trap the unsuspecting and unwary.

Thus, organized, troublesome youths were perhaps one of the greatest social concerns of the English Puritans. From statesmen to moralists, early modern English were conscious of the problems posed by the young. Vagabonds, criminals, and the sinful were the deep concern of social policymakers and intellectuals alike.

Youth in Colonial America

In America, transplanted Englishmen hoped to establish stable societies bereft of the social chaos that had plagued youths and distracted the authorities of England. Outside of New England, where immigrant Puritans managed to maintain social harmony for a generation, the social reality in colonial America fell far short of planter expectations. Although colonial communities were less chaotic than some of those the migrants had put behind them, still they were often beset by demographic, social, and economic changes that disrupted the lives of youths, at times severely. While colonial leaders were in general less preoccupied with youths than were their English counterparts, some of them were nevertheless deeply concerned with the problems of youth.

In the seventeenth-century South, indentured servitude dominated the lives of immigrant youths. Though the system, as advertised, held out to English youth the opportunity to acquire land in return for five to seven years of service, it rarely worked that way. Separated from parents, kin, and neighbors and from the protection of English labor laws and customs, immigrant youth were continuously at risk of physical abuse, labor exploitation, disease, and death. More than half of all indentured servants died before their term of service had expired. In addition, terms of service were under constant pressure to expand; youthful servants in their early teens were continuously at risk of laboring for exploitative masters until adulthood. Planter-controlled legislative assemblies passed increasingly harsher labor laws, including some that contained elements of English vagrancy legislation. The rise of such legislation, one historian has recently observed, hints at increasingly conflicted master-servant relationships, which reached the boiling point after the 1650s and climaxed in 1675–76 with Bacon's Rebellion.[28]

Though the rebellion failed, its message was not lost on the authorities. As early as the 1620s, planters had complained about "Vagabonds and bankerupts & other disorderly persons," but not until Bacon's Rebellion did the severity of the vagabond problem hit home.[29] For the next quarter century, the Virginia gentry became preoccupied with control of the group involved in the rebellion. By the early eighteenth century, the "giddy multitude" in colonies such as Virginia had all but disappeared.

With respect to the native-born population, whose size continued to increase relative to that of the immigrant population, high adult mortality rates played havoc with the lives of youth well into the eighteenth century. By the time most native-born children became teenagers, they had either lost a parent or had become orphaned. In one county of seventeenth-century Virginia, 73.2 percent of children had lost at least one parent before they reached age twenty-one or married (whichever came first).[30] While most Creole children were cared for by at least one of their natural parents, most Creole youths were not.

Southern communities were thus forced to assume responsibilities carried on traditionally by the family. Neighborhoods and kin networks were mobilized to provide support, supervision, and education for orphaned youths, while county courts were empowered to appoint guardians to manage properties inherited by youthful minors and to oversee the treatment of orphaned youths bound out to labor until their majority. That such orphan courts often felt compelled to scrutinize the activities of guardians and masters suggests widespread abuse of the system.

The kin network was not entirely successful as a surrogate for the family. In families where youths fell under the care of stepfathers, the potential for abuse was especially high. So was the probability of youthful deviance. "Especially in families where the father had died," one historian holds, "teenaged sons argued with their parents, sought to escape from work and from the authority of others, spent their inheritances imprudently, and got into scrapes with the law." Of the many planter complaints directed at seventeenth-century youths, those from stepfathers were the harshest. One man described his future stepson as "a young Wilde and dissulute person much given to Company Keeping and of such as are debouched and rude fellows, and that hee is uncapable of managing his own estate left by his father being Considerable but living up and downe, or to and fro the County one weeke in one place and a fortnight in another letting his estate fall to Ruine and decay for want of Management." Another man complained that his stepson, seventeen years of age, "takes to idle company, absents himself from the house and endeavors to get his freedom."[31]

Despite the frequency of such complaints, there is no evidence to suggest that adults in the colonial South had anything put a passing, individual interest in the problems and delinquency of youth. While southern courts sought to protect youths, especially those with property, from exploitation or physical abuse, there was no concerted effort on the part of colonial leaders to intervene on their behalf. Rather, age-specific issues, even when recognized as such, took a backseat to problems related to labor, class, and, in time, race. Even though planters could verbalize their concerns with youth, they were far more preoccupied with what they considered to be greater threats to economic development and social stability. Even as eighteenth-century planters intervened increasingly in the lives of their sons and daughters, the colonial authorities remained, as ever, preoccupied with the labor question. By this time, though, the composition of the labor force subject to exploitation had changed from one comprised of English youths to one made up of African and African-American youths.

The history of youth in colonial New England differs dramatically from that of the South, which is due in large part to demographic and religious variables. Low mortality rates combined with the group nature of the Puritan exodus to America to produce stable family life in first-generation New England. Even orphaned youths or unattached servants were raised within patriarchal households, a circumstance dictated by New England legislation. In contrast to the South, strong, viable churches existed to buttress the authority of the family and to help supervise the rearing of children and youths.

In cases of parental neglect or abuse of youths, the state or church was quick to intervene. If there were youths at risk in early New England, they were to be found primarily among Native American societies, whose populations were succumbing rapidly to European disease and war. To the degree that age-related conflict existed in Puritan communities, it was generational in nature, involving disputes between sons desirous of attaining autonomy and fathers desirous of withholding it from them, primarily through the retention of land ownership. Such conflict was only rarely collective in nature; most Puritan youths were content with the delayed achievement of adulthood, marrying late and holding public office and inheriting land even later. In certain respects, early New England was an age relations utopia.[32]

Yet early New England was far more intellectually preoccupied with youth than was the colonial South, a paradox attributable to Puritanism. To the extent that they succeeded in reproducing Old World Puritanism in the New World, New Englanders created Old World anxieties about youth, notwithstanding the stable New World contexts. New England's institutions reflected and, in turn, reinforced traditional Puritan preoccupation with youth. State-supported churches and ministries, which were established primarily to perpetuate the faith, also served as media for the transmission of age-related anxieties about the survival of the faith. Thus, at a very early stage in its development, the Puritan system instituted mechanisms for indoctrinating youths, including youth-specific catechisms, private religious societies, catechetical exercises, lectures, and covenant renewals, in which groups of youths were assembled on the Sabbath to renew their parents' covenants.

When such measures appeared ineffective, Puritan leaders invoked traditional English caveats against the dangers and sins of youth. Starting in the 1660s and 1670s, Puritan presses and pulpits produced a steady stream of jeremiads lamenting the sins of the rising generation.[33] Like their English predecessors, such jeremiads focused on the age-specific, developmental nature of sin. Thus, the Reverend Thomas Foxcroft of Massachusetts observed in 1719 that "the different ages of men have their divers lusts and various corruptions. The impure streams run in distinct channels agreeing to the different complexions of men in several stages of life." Childhood, therefore, was marred by "stubborness" and "falsness," while middle age was stained by "ambition" and old age by "covetousness."[34]

There were two sins that seemed to "hang upon youth and dogg that season of life more than any other," said Foxcroft, and these were "pride" and "sensuality." Both sins, according to Foxcroft and others who expanded upon the theme, were indigenous to youth. Pride was considered the most dangerous sin because it led to many other vices, including disobedience, apostasy, anger, self-conceit, rebellion against family government, blasphemy, Sabbath breaking, and boasting, to cite a few.[35] Pride also made youths unusually resistant to religious conversion and yet uniquely prone to religious deviance. To second-and third-generation ministers, the natural stubborness and rebelliousness of youth helped to explain the pervasive apostasy and immorality of the times.

Sensuality, the second major sin of youth, was also widely condemned by the ministry, for it too was the parent of many other vices, including night revels, fornication, tippling, filthy songs, frolicking, and masturbation, to name a few.[36] Though adult preoccupation with youthful sensuality existed throughout New England's history, it seems to have increased over time.

Rising concern with youthful sensuality found expression in a new genre of sermon devoted entirely to the topic. In 1723, the Reverend Cotton Mather of Boston produced the first American sermon on the subject of youthful masturbation, which condemned the "libidinous practices" of youths "who do evil with both hands" and "have the cursed way of procuring a discharge, which the God of nature had ordered only to be made in a way which lawful marriage leads unto." Mather warned youths of the many serious consequences of the evil act, including impotence, sterility, and "offspring that shall prove a grief of mind." To cure themselves of this dangerous habit, Mather advised youths to think of Christ—"His glorious person," "His Maxims," "His Benefits." "And," he continued, "if these thoughts are in an ejaculatory way darted to the heavens, they may still be more effectual to quench the fiery darts of the wicked one, which are fastening upon you."[37]

Other ministers focused on the collective character of youthful sensuality, and its increased threat to social and familial order. These themes found vivid expression in a treatise written by Reverend Jonathan Edwards of Northampton, Massachusetts, and published in 1737:

Just after my grandfather's death [in 1729], it seemed to be a time of extraordinary dullness in religion: licentiousness for some years greatly prevailed among the youth of the town; they were many of them very much addicted to night walking, and frequenting the tavern, and lewd practices, wherein some by their example exceedingly corrupted others. It was their manner very frequently to get together in conventions of both sexes, for mirth and jollity, which they called frolicks; and they would often spend the greater part of the night in them, without any regard to order in the families they belonged to: and indeed family government did too much fail in the town.[38]

Rising adult preoccupation with youthful sensuality also shows up in the court records of the period. New England courts prosecuted much more vigorously than their southern counterparts crimes against order and morals, and the incidence of such prosecutions, especially against fornication and bastardy, increased dramatically over time. Between 1651 and 1680 in Essex County, Massachusetts, 16.8 percent of all prosecutions for crime were for bastardy and fornication. A century later, the percentage had increased threefold. Between 1760 and 1774 in Middlesex County, Massachusetts, 57.6 percent of all prosecutions were for bastardy and fornication.[39]

The rise of prosecutions for sexual misconduct matched a concurrent rise in premarital pregnancy ratios; by the time the Massachusetts court was vigorously prosecuting sex offenders, nearly half of all Massachusetts brides were pregnant at marriage.[40] Religious declension had combined with rapid population growth, increasing geographical mobility, and the concomitant weakening of patriarchal authority to produce rising numbers of youths at risk of committing sexual and other moral crimes. Some evidence suggests that youths marrying in their teenage years were more frequent sex offenders than other age groups; in one eighteenth-century Massachusetts town, 41 percent of the women marrying at age fifteen through nineteen were pregnant as brides, as contrasted with only 24 percent of those marrying age twenty to twenty-four and 22 percent of those age twenty-five to twenty-nine.[41]

Mobile youths were more prone to sexual deviance than their more stable counterparts, who continued to live under close parental and ecclesiastical supervision.[42] Youths used premarital sex as a weapon against traditional patriarchial authority, forcing parents' hands in decisions regarding marriage. Such deviance posed an increasing challenge to family order, a threat that was not lost on the clergy, as we have seen.[43] The issue of youthful sexuality thus became a point of tension in the generational struggle over youthful autonomy.

Efforts to combat youthful deviance were not confined to clerical jeremiads or court prosecutions. In response to the pressures of social change, eighteenth-century ministers endeavored to protect youths from vice by converting them to faith. Ignoring the traditional Puritan aversion to youthful religious conversion, such ministers promoted a new view of the young in which the capacity for saving grace was stressed over the capacity for committing sin. The clergy, as they emphasized in their sermons and in voluntary societies, sought to mobilize youth around the church in the hope of saving them and, through them, society as a whole.[44]

Clerical evangelicalism touched a responsive chord among many of New England's youths. During the 1740s, the era of the Great Awakening, youths, including many teens, experienced conversion and entered communion in great numbers, dominating, for the first time in the region's history, the admission roles of the established church.[45] Once converted, though, the young did not submit to the authority of that church, as the clergy had hoped they would. Rather, the revival deflected youthful piety into unorthodox channels—including lay exhortation and separatism—and thus rekindled old anxieties about youthful religious deviance. While the opponents of the awakening, the Old Lights, felt most threatened by such deviance, even the New Lights were troubled by the radical turn of events. In the wake of the revival, the old animus against youthful piety returned, and churches closed their doors to the young.[46] For the remainder of the colonial period, religious leaders harped upon the traditional theme of troubled, sinful youth.

Thus, the Great Awakening produced no new commentary on troubled youth, even though its constituency included the poorer youths of inland market towns and coastal seaports, who were particularly vulnerable to the dislocations of war and rapid commercialization. In New London, Connecticut, for example, the separatists "were typically younger and poorer than the Congregationalists," in part because of "the New Light tendency to dissociate the new birth conversion experience from worldly considerations."[47] Despite their radical rhetoric, New Lights were generally oblivious to the plight of indigent, transient youths, whose numbers were growing rapidly in the seaports and market towns of New England.[48] Even in ports outside of New England, such as New York and Philadelphia, where the religious system was weaker, the awakening failed to produce any commentary on the social changes that helped to produce it. Despite their keen interest in early spirituality, revivalists were generally blind to the disruptive effects of commercialization and urbanization upon their youthful constituents. Rather, the poor, young and old alike, "were labelled as deviants and treated as such" and were placed indiscriminately in private homes or workhouses or were warned out of town.[49] Not until the late eighteenth century did Americans begin to distinguish between the "idle" and "industrious poor" and to single out youths for special treatment and care.[50] While an occasional reference was made to the problems of urban youths, little effort was undertaken on their behalf. Like their English and early New England ancestors, late eighteenth-century Americans viewed troubled youths as prisoners of sin and threats to the social order.

Youth and Crime in the Nineteenth Century

The nineteenth century witnessed an increase in general concern about youth and crime. In part, this was a nervous public response to increased urban and industrial development, which weakened the traditional sources of social control by the family and local community. Yet it also reflected a growing recognition of youth as a specific stage of the life course which was especially susceptible to deviance. Particularly in the more economically developed cities of the Northeast, new age-segregated institutions intended to deal with these troubled youths further contributed to the age grouping of youth. By the end of the nineteenth century, contemporary observers such as G. Stanley Hall (1904) described early adolescence as an unsettling and stormy phase of the life course.[51]

Nineteenth-century reformers usually associated youth crime with large cities and the growing urbanization of the country.[52] Only 5.1 percent of the population in 1790 lived in communities with 2,500 or more inhabitants, but, on the eve of the Civil War, nearly one out of five people lived in such towns. By 1900, the proportion living in such communities rose to 39.7 percent. Perhaps even more significant is that, in 1790, there were no cities with fifty thousand inhabitants in the United States; by 1860, nearly one out of ten people lived in these larger cities (and 37.7 percent lived in them in 1900).[53]

There were large regional differences in the degree of urbanization in nineteenth-century America. Whereas more than one-third of people in the Northeast in 1860 and two-thirds of them in 1900 lived in communities of 2,500 or more inhabitants, as late as 1900 less than one out of five southerners lived in a comparable setting.[54] As a result, to the degree that juvenile crime and cities were linked in the minds and experiences of many nineteenth-century Americans, there were considerable regional differences—reminding us to be wary of broad national generalizations based mainly upon the well-publicized accounts from the Northeast.[55]

Another demographic factor was the greater proportion of youths in the past than today. Children ages ten to nineteen were 23.4 percent of the total population in 1850, 20.6 percent in 1900, and 14.2 percent in 1988. An even more dramatic difference is evident if we compute the number of children ages ten to nineteen per 100 adults ages twenty to sixty-four. There were 51.9 children ages ten to nineteen per 100 adults in 1850, 40.0 percent in 1900, and 24.2 percent in 1988.[56] Moreover, cities attracted rural youths seeking employment so that the proportion of young people in urban areas was higher than in the countryside.[57] As a result, the demographic presence of youths in cities was larger in the past than today and reinforced contemporary fears of unrestrained and unruly youths wandering about city streets in nineteenth-century America.

The growth of public schools and the concomitant age grouping that resulted prompted public concern about youth. In colonial America, parents were expected to teach their own children how to read. While some private or public primary schools were established in a few seventeenth-century New England towns, most parents either taught their own children or shared in the paying for a temporary private school teacher.[58] By the early nineteenth century, however, primary schools were established in many Northeast towns and, by the mid nineteenth century, most communities in that region had well-developed public common school systems. In the South, on the other hand, few public schools were created, and, as late as 1900, large numbers of children did not receive much formal education.[59] African-American children were denied equal access to schooling throughout the nineteenth century in most communities.[60]

In rural schools, children of all ages were taught together in a one-room schoolhouse. Rural children from ages three to twenty listened to the same teacher and took turns reciting their lessons based upon their level of achievement rather than their age.[61] As the population of towns grew and schools became more specialized in the mid nineteenth century, there was a rough age grading of pupils in the urban schools. With the growth of northern public high schools in the second half of the nineteenth century, the age segregation of students increased.[62] As a result, many youths in the urban Northeast attended educational institutions that brought them together as teenagers and taught them not only the skills necessary for economic advancement but also the morals deemed necessary to resist the numerous vices and temptations associated with city life.[63]

Nineteenth-century Americans frequently worried about increases in crime and usually associated high crime rates with urban areas. Only a few scholars have attempted to ascertain the actual level of crime in the nineteenth century, and all of them acknowledge the problems of measuring something so elusive.[64] The most detailed and careful comparative study of antebellum crime traces developments in Massachusetts and South Carolina. Using aggregate Massachusetts statistics on total commitments, Michael Hindus found that the rates fluctuated and peaked in the mid-1850s.[65] Surprisingly, South Carolina's crime rates were consistently higher than that in Massachusetts and more focused on personal violence than theft or destruction of property. While assaults continued to dominate South Carolina crimes in both the eighteenth and nineteenth centuries, there was a shift in Massachusetts from crimes against morality in the colonial period to those involving property or liquor-related offenses in the nineteenth century. Urban areas such as Boston, Massachusetts, and Charleston, South Carolina, had higher crime rates than rural areas.[66]

Unfortunately, few of these studies have data on the age of the criminals. The study of Massachusetts and South Carolina, for example, does not provide any information on the age of the criminals.[67] Eric Monkkonen's study of poverty and crime in Franklin County, Ohio, from 1860 to 1885, however, does provide some age-specific information about criminals.[68] He found that about 22 percent of criminals in that county in 1870 were below age twenty-one—considerably fewer than one would find today.[69] Moreover, he found few overall urban-rural differences in crime rates in Ohio during these years and no indication that increasing urbanization led to more crime over time.

Another interesting study of crime and punishment is that of

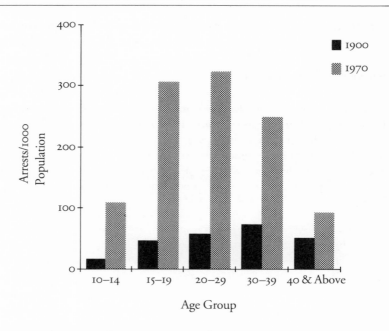

FIG. 5.1. Arrest rates by age group in Oakland, 1900–1970.
(From Lawrence M. Friedman and Robert V. Percival, *The Roots
of Justice: Crime and Punishment in Alameda County, California,
1870–1910* [Chapel Hill, N.C., 1981], 112.)

Alameda County, California, in 1900. Lawrence M. Friedman and
Robert V. Percival discovered that serious crime was declining in
Alameda County in the late nineteenth century so that more police
effort could be directed at enforcing public order by attacking crimes
such as drunkenness and brawling.[70] They also found that arrest rates
were the highest for those ages thirty to thirty-nine, but a substantial
number of older teenagers were arrested as well (fig. 5.1). Youthful
offenders were relatively more likely to be arrested for property crimes
and ordinance violations compared to older adults, who were relatively
more apt to be charged for drunkenness and moral offenses. Perhaps
the most striking finding, however, is that arrest rates at all ages are
much higher today than in the past and that there has been a relative
increase in the proportion of crimes committed by young people.[71]

The growing antebellum attention to youth crime was due, in part,
to the feeling among some commentators that youth was a particularly

important period of change. Authors of advice books for youths did not pay much specific attention to age but believed that this phase of the life course was crucial in the development of proper values and behavior. Austin wrote in 1854:

Early youth is justly considered the most interesting and important, yet dangerous period of human existence. It is *interesting,* because of the innocence, the hilarity, and the zest for enjoyment, which is then evinced. . . . Youth is the most *important* time of life, inasmuch as the habits then begin to lay their foundations—the character commences its formation, and the occupation is to be chosen—upon which depend mainly, the enjoyments and prosperity of after life. And it is the most *dangerous* period, because, ardent, volatile, inexperienced, and thirsting for happiness, the young are exceedingly liable to be seduced into wrong paths—into those fascinating, but fatal ways, which lead to degradation and wretchedness.[72]

Only a few advice books discussed the specific ages of youth. Joel Hawes, a Connecticut Congregational minister and author of a very popular advice book for young men, wrote in 1831 that:

every period of life has its peculiar temptations and dangers. But were I to specify the period which, of all others, is attended with the greatest peril, and most needs to be watched, I would fix upon that which elapses from fourteen to twenty-one years of age. This, pre-eminently, is the forming, fixing period; the spring season of disposition and habit; and it is during this season, more than any other, that the character assumes its permanent shape and colour, and the young man is wont to take his course for life and for eternity. . . . The time we usually denominate one a *young man,* is the most important and perilous period of his whole existence.[73]

Nineteenth-century Americans agreed with Hawes that the period of youth was central in the formation of good character and devoted considerable resources to guide young people through these years. Most children in the North, including many teenagers, were enrolled in public schools.[74] Teachers and school administrators stressed the importance of moral training in the classroom and believed that such education was essential for helping youths avoid the snares and temptations of crime. Indeed, the assumption of most nineteenth-century policymakers was that much, if not all, of youth and adult crime could be prevented with a proper moral education (as opposed to just learning to read and write). As the famous Massachusetts educator, Horace Mann, put it:

Indeed, so decisive is the effect of early training upon adult habits and character, that numbers of the most able and experienced teachers,—those who have had the best opportunities to become acquainted with the errors and the excellence of children, their waywardness and their docility,—have unanimously declared it to be their belief, that, if all the children in the community, from the age of four years to that of sixteen, could be brought within the reformatory and elevating influences of good schools, the dark host of private vices and public crimes, which now embitter domestic peace and stain the civilization of the age, might in ninety-nine cases in every hundred, be banished from the world.[75]

Although some questioned the efficacy of education to prevent crime and pauperism, this continued to be one of the most widely held views throughout the period.[76]

Religious leaders also saw Sunday schools as a valuable tool for combating vice. At first, Sunday schools in the United States in the early nineteenth century were designed for everyone, without any distinction by age, and taught both literacy and morality. While Sunday schools appeared throughout the country, they were often seen as most necessary in cities to prepare their students to combat the urban vices they encountered. As urban public schools were established in the North and taught most children the basics of literacy, Sunday schools concentrated more on teaching religion and morality. In addition, Sunday schools became more age-graded, focusing more on youths than adults.[77]

Sunday schools were only one of many efforts by religious groups to guide youths in the nineteenth century. Bible societies wrote special tracts for youths and distributed thousands of copies to them throughout the nation. Other special institutions such as the Young Men's Christian Association (YMCA) were created in the mid nineteenth century to help young men who were regarded as particularly vulnerable to the temptations of the city. While initially many of these religious efforts and institutions were loosely defined in regard to age, over time they began to target much of their appeals to teenagers and young adults.[78]

Educators and religious leaders tried to provide children with moral training and guidance in an effort to prevent youthful crimes; others sought to work with young offenders to prevent them from becoming hardened criminals. Indeed, much of the nineteenth-century writings and the concerns about youthful deviance comes from Northeast reformers who tried to overcome what they perceived were the dangers and evils of urban life. In their efforts to separate youths from experienced convicts in the newly created penitentiaries, they created special separate institutions for young offenders of both sexes during the antebellum period. While only a minority of youths were ever incarcerated in these reform schools, their construction in Northern cities and the publicity about them helped define the need for special attention for teenage offenders.[79]

Reformers in the early nineteenth century believed that, while all youth were at risk of becoming criminals or getting into trouble, those from certain backgrounds were particularly susceptible to such dangers. They employed an environmental explanation for the causes of crime and poverty—though, at times, it also became racial when African Americans were the subject. Moreover, while reformers often cataloged youthful crimes and misdeeds, they regarded these as particular manifestations of a basically flawed character—frequently the result of parental loss or neglect. Rather than relying only upon specific crimes or misbehaviors to identify troubled youth, they assumed that any children from disadvantaged backgrounds or neglectful parents were at high risk of becoming societal problems. As the New York Society for the Prevention of Pauperism put it in the early 1820s:

Every person that frequents the out-streets of this city, must be forcibly struck with the ragged and uncleanly appearance, the vile language, and the idle and miserable habits of great numbers of children, most of whom are of an age suitable for schools, or for some useful employment. The parents of these children, are, in all probability, too poor, or too degenerate, to provide them with clothing fit for them to be seen in at school; and know not where to place them in order that they may find employment, or be better cared for. Accustomed, in many instances, to witness at home nothing in the way of example, but what is degrading; early taught to observe intemperance, and to hear obscene and profane language without disgust; obliged to beg, and even encouraged to acts of dishonesty, to satisfy the wants induced by the indolence of their parents,—what can be expected, but that such children will in due time, become responsible to the laws for crimes, which have thus, in a manner, been forced upon them?[80]

Most of these ideas about the environmental and familial causes of youthful corruption and criminal behavior continued to be accepted throughout the antebellum period. Yet by the time of the Civil War, some additional nuances had been added as illustrated in the writings of Charles Loring Brace, who worked so closely with the so-called dangerous classes of New York City.[81] Brace divided the causes of crime into "preventible" and "nonpreventible." The list of preventable causes reads much like a catalog of earlier diagnoses: "ignorance, intemperance, over-crowding of population, want of work, idleness, vagrancy, the weakness of the marriage-tie, and bad legislation." The discussion of the nonpreventable (or "those which cannot be entirely removed") causes, however, introduces or emphasizes several elements that reveal a gradual shift in how reformers viewed youths at risk. Among Brace's list of nonpreventable causes of crime are "inheritance, the effects of emigration, orphanage, accident or misfortune, the strength of the sexual and other passions, and a natural weakness of moral and mental powers."[82]

Other reformers in the early nineteenth century had observed that immigrants or their children were more likely to become criminals, but, after the great influx of Irish in the 1840s and 1850s, this theme received even more emphasis. Rather than raising questions about the lower quality of the "stock" of the immigrants, as some late nineteenth-century commentators did, Brace explained the propensity of the children of immigrants to crime in social and environmental terms:

There is no question that the breaking of the ties with one's country has a bad moral effect, especially on a laboring class. The Emigrant is released from the social inspection and judgment to which he has been subjected at home, and the tie of church and priesthood is weakened. . . . Moral ties are loosened with the religious. The intervening process which occurs here, between his abandoning the old state of things and fitting himself to the new, is not favorable to morals or character.

The consequence is, that an immense proportion of our ignorant and criminal class are foreign-born; and of the dangerous classes here, a very large part, though native-born, are of foreign parentage.[83]

Another interesting and significant shift in the thinking of many reformers after the Civil War is seeing some of the sources of youthful crime as the result of inherited characteristics from several generations of degenerate ancestors:

It is well-known to those familiar with the criminal classes, that certain appetites or habits, if indulged abnormally and excessively through two or more generations, come to have an almost irresistible force, and no doubt, modify the brain so as to constitute almost an insane condition. This is especially true of the appetite for liquor and of the sexual passion, and sometimes of the peculiar weakness, dependence, and laziness which make confirmed paupers.[84]

Although Brace's discussion of the inheritability of criminal traits prefigures the more negative and deterministic views of other late nineteenth- and early twentieth-century analysts, it is more optimistic and less rigid than might appear at first glance. Brace saw vice and indulgence as weakening the physical powers of individuals and therefore making them less likely to reproduce themselves than the more virtuous poor. Moreover, these inherited negative characteristics could be overcome by an improvement in a youth's home and neighborhood environment, and therefore timely positive intervention could prevent further degeneration. Despite his belief that the traits of paupers, criminals, or vagrants can be transmitted from one generation to the next, Brace remained optimistic that "the natural drift among the poor is towards virtue."[85]

Finally, Brace, like many other nineteenth-century observers, attached considerable importance to sexual passions in leading to immoral behavior. He made a sharp distinction in the likelihood of reforming wayward boys and girls. Indeed, when comparing male and female delinquents, he almost romanticizes the situation of the boys:

A girl street-rover is to my mind the most painful figure in all the unfortunate crowd of a large city. With a boy, "Arab of the streets," one always has the consolation that, despite his ragged clothes and bed in a box or hay-barge, he often has a rather good time of it, and enjoys many of the delicious pleasures of a child's roving life, and that a fortunate turn of events may at any time make an honest, industrious fellow of him. At heart we cannot say that he is much corrupted; his sins belong to his ignorance and his condition, and are often easily corrected by a radical change of circumstances. . . . It is true that sometimes the habit of vagrancy and idling may be too deeply worked in him for his character to speedily reform; but, if of tender years, a change of circumstances will nearly always bring a change of character.[86]

While Brace was quite optimistic about the chances of reforming boys, he was equally pessimistic about saving delinquent girls:

With a girl-vagrant it is different. She feels homelessness and friendlessness more; she has more of the feminine dependence on affection; the street-trades, too, are harder for her, and the return at night to some lonely cellar or tenement-room, crowded with dirty people of all ages and sexes, is more dreary. She develops body and mind earlier than the boy, and the habits of vagabondism stamped on her in childhood are more difficult to wear off.[87]

Brace viewed boys and girls as fundamentally biologically different in their tendency toward sexual passion and their ability to recover from early sexual activity. He applied a clear double standard to the likelihood of sexually active boys and girls being reformed:

For there is no reality in the sentimental assertion that the sexual sins of the lad are as degrading as those of the girl. The instinct of the female is more toward the preservation of purity, and therefore her fall is deeper—an instinct grounded in the desire of preserving a stock, or even the necessity of perpetuating our race. . . .

This crime, with the girl, seems to sap and rot the whole nature. She loses self-respect, without which every human being soon sinks to the lowest depths; she loses the habit of industry, and cannot be taught to work. . . . If, in a moment of remorse, she flee[s] away and take[s] honest work, her weakness and bad habits follow her . . . and unless she chance to have a higher moral nature or stronger will than most of her class, or unless Religion should touch even her polluted soul, she soon falls back, and gives one more sad illustration of the immense difficulty of a fallen woman rising again.[88]

Thus, while Brace retains some of the optimism and environmental orientation of the early nineteenth-century youth reformers, he also reveals greater attention to the ill effects of immigration, the possibility of transmission of defective traits across generations, and gender differences in the likelihood of being reformed. As with many other American thinkers after the Civil War, the early nineteenth-century native belief that early reform efforts could prevent almost all youthful crimes and indiscretions continued alongside a growing pessimism that there may be limits to what existing large-scale youth institutions could accomplish in practice.[89]

"Scientific" studies of juvenile delinquency appeared in greater numbers in the late nineteenth century.[90] One school of thought, led by the Italian criminologist Cesare Lombrosco, argued that habitual criminals were a distinct and inferior anthropological type distinguished by highly visible physical traits. American scholars such as George E. Dawson and Arthur MacDonald tried to explain juvenile delinquency on the basis of the physical characteristics of children, which they claimed exhibited clear signs of degeneracy.[91] The use of Lombroscian criminology to deal with juvenile delinquency was carried to its logical and absurd extreme by an American physician, Thomas Travis, who wanted to operate upon children to alter the shape of their crania, jaws, and palates in order to alter their appearance and thereby, presumably, their behavior.[92]

Other American analysts emphasized the hereditary aspects of criminal behavior, even though they still thought that much of this deviant behavior could be avoided by altering the environments of potentially troublesome youths. Richard L. Dugdale's famous work, *"The Jukes": A Study in Crime, Pauperism, Disease and Heredity,* seemingly established the familial basis of criminal behavior.[93] And William Douglas Morrison, among others, identified juvenile delinquency with immigrants but, unlike Brace, doubted if a better environment in the New World could entirely overcome the deficient backgrounds and experiences of immigrants:

It is notorious that peoples of the type of the Italians and Hungarians exhibit much less respect for human life than is to be found among the northern races. Contact with the humanizing influences of American civilization no doubt has a wholesome effect in modifying the character and temperament of the children of the emigrants from the south. But family and racial characteristics cannot be altogether obliterated by social surroundings, and it is not at all unlikely that juvenile delinquency of the most serious kind in the United States is in some measure to be set down to the boundless hospitality of her shores.[94]

Nevertheless, despite a new emphasis on the physical and hereditary nature of crime in the late nineteenth century and the questioning of the unbridled optimism of reformers fifty years earlier, most Americans concerned about troublesome youths continued to stress an environmental explanation for delinquency. They continued to believe that early and timely intervention with high-risk youths could prevent or alleviate much, if not all, of juvenile delinquency.[95]

Perhaps the most important scholar of adolescents was G. Stanley Hall. Hall pioneered and then popularized the idea of adolescence as a distinct and tumultuous stage of the life course. While his two-volume study of adolescence dealt only briefly with juvenile delinquency, his views were frequently cited by other scholars and widely publicized through the popular media.

Hall created an evolutionary theory in which the stages of human development recapitulated his notion of the historical changes in Western civilization. He saw adolescence, beginning in ages twelve to fourteen, as particularly prone to rapid and tumultuous change:

Adolescence is a new birth, for the higher and more completely human traits are now born. The qualities of body and soul that now emerge are far newer. The child comes from and harks back to a remoter past; the adolescent is neo-atavistic, and in him the later acquisitions of the race slowly become prepotent. Development is less gradual and more saltatory, suggestive of some ancient period of storm and stress when old moorings were broken and a higher level attained.[96]

Adolescence is also a period of great danger for the growing child. Uneven individual physical and mental development and the particular and unusual strains of modern life make it a perilous period for all youths:

The momentum of heredity often seems insufficient to enable the child to achieve this great revolution and to come to complete maturity, so that every step of the upward way is strewn with wreckage of body, mind and morals. . . . Modern life is hard, and in many respects increasingly so, on youth. Home, school, church, fail to recognize its nature and needs, and perhaps most of all, its perils.[97]

Not surprisingly, Hall found that juvenile delinquency was on the rise and that crimes were now committed at an earlier age:

In all civilized lands, criminal statistics show two sad and significant facts: First, that there is a marked increase of crime of all kinds, and that this increase continues for a number of years. While the percentages of certain grave crimes increase to mature manhood, adolescence is preeminently the criminal age when most first commitments occur and most vicious careers are begun. The second fact is that the proportion of juvenile delinquents seems to be everywhere increasing and crime is more precocious.[98]

Hall was rather eclectic in assembling and accepting a series of explanations, often seemingly contradictory to each other, for the likelihood of adolescents to engage in deviant behavior. Though he rejects the extremes of Lombroso's views, he accepts the identification of crime with physical bearing: "degenerate children are neurotic, irritable, vain, lacking in vigor, very fluctuating in mood, prone to show aberrant tendencies under stress, often sexually perverted at puberty, with extreme shyness or bravado, imitative, [and] not well controlled." Hall stresses, on the other hand, the difficulty for alienated youths of adjusting to the demands of modern society:

The young offender soon comes to feel himself an enemy of society; to regard legitimate business as legalized theft and robbery; religion as a cloak for hypocrisy; clergymen as paid to preach or labor with prisoners; doctors kill or cure as is for their interest; lawyers are licensed robbers or cunning knaves; purity is mere pretense; the world is ruled by selfishness; the courts or justice shops are shams; and those who prey upon the weaker sides of human nature know the foibles of even the good only too well. The seasoned young criminal feels himself superior to the plodder who labors legitimately because he lacks the wit or adroitness to do otherwise.[99]

Hall had no easy solutions for the problem of juvenile delinquency as he saw this as a common experience among developing adolescents in a modern, urban society that placed great temptations and stress on all young people. He rejected strict and rigid punishment as an answer and questioned the efficacy of the current educational system to prevent juvenile delinquency. Perhaps more than anything else, he called for the further scientific study of juvenile delinquency—a call that was heeded by many of his own students, such as William Healy, as well as other scholars in the early twentieth century. Yet, by emphasizing the universality of adolescence, its stormy nature, and the particularly important period of early development at ages twelve to fourteen, Hall helped to reshape the ways Americans viewed children at risk from the nineteenth to the twentieth century.[100]

Conclusion

Some scholars, drawing upon the work of Phillipe Ariès and others, continue to believe that troubled youths, as a group, were not a prob-

lem in early modern England or colonial America because children
were regarded as miniature adults. We strongly disagree. While older
children were often seen as intellectually more precocious and emotionally more mature than many adolescents are regarded today, they were
not viewed or treated as simply miniature adults. On the other hand,
young people in the past were neither as rigidly age segregated as they
are today nor as likely to be called adolescents. Instead, contemporaries
in early modern England and early America were more likely to designate them loosely as youths with varying degrees of economic and social
dependency upon their parents or masters. Therefore, the concept of
troubled youth as a subcategory of the population often did have particular, though often differing, meanings for people in the past.

Concern about youth is sometimes triggered by broader demographic and economic changes. We have seen how, in early modern
England, the combination of rapid population growth and declining
economic opportunities led to increased internal migration and fears
of vagrancy and youthful disorders. Similarly, the growing numbers
of youths in nineteenth-century American cities amid a rapidly changing economy contributed to the increasing anxiety about young people.
These fears in America were heightened by the increasing number of
immigrants who came to the cities in the second half of the nineteenth
century and challenged the existing structures of authority and power
in those communities.

If demographic and economic changes sometimes precipitated fears
of youth, at other times they did not. In the colonial South, for
example, despite the periodic difficulties with young men, societal
anxiety about youth was lower than in either early modern England or
in Puritan New England. Similarly, though there were problems with
youths in the rapidly changing rural areas of nineteenth-century America, the rural youths were not perceived as dangerous as those in the
urban communities. Thus, while demographic and economic factors
certainly play a key role in shaping the experiences of youths and
stimulating and conditioning the general concerns of adults, they do
not, by themselves, determine how societies view or react to troubled
youths.

While concerns about youth have varied from one time period to
another during the past five hundred years, factors such as race, ethnicity, class, and gender have also played a role in how particular subsets
of young people were seen and treated. African-American or immigrant

youths, especially males from economically disadvantaged backgrounds, have usually been seen as more dangerous and threatening to the dominant groups in English and American societies than the children of white, native-born, middle-class parents. Moreover, there usually has been a differential treatment of troubled youths, with those from disadvantaged backgrounds receiving less sympathy and less help than those from more privileged homes. Indeed, one is struck by the extent to which children at risk in the past and even today have been categorized and labeled, to a large degree, by their racial, ethnic, class, and gender characteristics—sometimes unwittingly, even by reformers who were genuinely trying to help these children rather than just trying to protect the rest of society from them.

One interesting difference between today and the past is that we are more likely today to address the specific problems of troubled youth through separate, categorical programs rather than trying to deal with them as individuals as a whole. In other words, many, if not most, of our local, state, and federal programs are designed to help adolescents focus in practice on some particular problem or difficulty, such as an unintended adolescent pregnancy, drug use, school truancy, or juvenile crime. As a result, it is difficult, if not impossible, at times to see and help the adolescent as an individual rather than responding mainly to one or two of the particular difficulties he or she is experiencing.

In the past, the emphasis was almost always on dealing with a troubled youth as a person who had to be thoroughly and completely reformed rather than just addressing one of his or her specific problems. Reformers in early modern England and early America usually saw any deficiencies or problems as ultimately the result of overall moral character weaknesses that had to be reformed before any real and lasting progress could be made. Therefore, for example, nineteenth-century reform schools focused on changing the overall character of the delinquent rather than just addressing any single shortcoming. While the benefit of this approach was that it treated troubled youths as individuals, the danger was that children who challenged or violated any particular law or norm were often quickly and unfairly labeled as having a totally deficient or defective character.

Finally, though the word *adolescence* existed in the English language in early modern England, it was not frequently employed. Similarly, though occasionally one finds mention of "adolescence" by the mid nineteenth century in America, it still is not as commonly used as the word *youth*. Yet by the end of the nineteenth century, the word *adolescence* appears with greater frequency. More importantly, the concept of adolescence as a stormy and often troubled transition from childhood to adulthood, thanks in large measure to the efforts of G. Stanley Hall and his colleagues, gained favor among American social scientists and the public in the early twentieth century. As a result, today most Americans accept the idea of adolescence as a "normal" phase of the life course, even though there appears to be growing disagreement and confusion over the exact nature of that transition.

Notes

1. See chapter 2. For scholars outside of the discipline of history who continue to accept the notion of miniature adults, see M. L. Manning, "Three Myths concerning Adolescence," *Adolescence* 18 (1983): 823–29; R. M. Matter, "The Historical Emergence of Adolescence: Perspectives from Developmental Psychology and Adolescent Literature," *Adolescence* 19 (1984): 131–42; D. W. Proefrock, "Adolescence: Social Fact and Psychological Concept," *Adolescence* 16 (1981): 851–58; R. Teeter, "The Travails of Nineteenth-Century Urban Youth as a Precondition to the Invention of Modern Adolescence," *Adolescence* 23 (1988): 15–18.

2. R. T. Vann, "The Youth of Centuries of Childhood," *History and Theory* 21 (1982): 279–97.

3. Barbara A. Hanawalt, *The Ties That Bound: Peasant Families in Medieval England* (New York, 1986), 188.

4. Thus, our position has changed somewhat since the publication of Gerald F. Moran, "Colonial Adolescence"; and Susan M. Juster and Maris A. Vinovskis, "Adolescence in Nineteenth-Century America," in *Encyclopedia of Adolescence*, 2 vols. (New York, 1991), 1:157–71; 2:698–707.

5. Hanawalt, *The Ties That Bound*, 190. Many scholars use the term *adolescent* indiscriminately and thereby perhaps unintentionally give the reader the false idea that this word was widely employed in early modern England. For example, see A. L. Beier, *Masterless Men: The Vagrancy Problem in England, 1560–1640* (London, 1985); Steven R. Smith, "The London Apprentices as Seventeenth-Century Adolescents," *Past and Present* 61 (1973): 149–61.

6. Lawrence Stone, *The Family, Sex, and Marriage in England, 1500–1800* (New York, 1977), 512.

7. E. A. Wrigley and R. S. Schofield, *The Population History of England, 1541–1871: A Reconstruction* (Cambridge, 1981).

8. London's population, for example, grew at a phenomenal pace, rising from about 120,000 to 350,000 in the period from 1550 to 1650 and from about 550,000 to 900,000 in the period from 1700 to 1800, by which time it was far and away Europe's largest urban center (being twice the size of Paris, its nearest rival). E. A. Wrigley, *Population and History* (New York, 1969), 148.

9. S. Brigden, "Youth and the English Reformation," *Past and Present* 95 (1982): 44.

10. E. A. Wrigley has characterized such people as "household servants of both sexes, apprentices and labourers . . . together with girls in trouble, younger sons without local prospects, fugitives from justice, those unable to find work, the restless and those attracted by the scale and consequence of city life." Quoted in Anthony Fletcher and John Stevenson, *Order and Disorder in Early Modern England* (Cambridge, 1985), 38.

11. The stabilization of demographic and economic factors after 1650 also led to a decline in crime rates and criminal prosecutions. J. A. Sharpe, *Crime in Early Modern England, 1550–1750* (London, 1984). As a result, some of the heightened concern about youth and crime during the period 1550–1650 diminished over the next hundred years.

12. For a general discussion and overview of English policy toward the poor, see Paul Slack, *Poverty and Policy in Tudor and Stuart England* (London, 1988).

13. Beier, *Masterless Men*, 15. Sixteenth-century England also passed laws requiring vagabonds to carry passports stating their place of birth and last residence and mandated badges or "tokens" for convicted or authorized beggars.

14. Beier, *Masterless Men*, 10, 54. We must not exaggerate, however, the centrality of age compared to other factors in English concerns about vagrancy. As Beier has put it,

> From these sources it appears that vagrants had five main characteristics. First, they were poor, lacking any regular income apart from wages from casual labour. Secondly, they were able-bodied— "sturdy," "valiant" and fit to work. Thirdly, they were unemployed, or in contemporary terms "masterless" and "idle." Fourthly, they were rootless: wandering, vagrant, "runnagate." Finally they were lawless, dangerous, and suspected of spreading vice and corruption. The legislation covered other groups as well—the young, certain occupations and ethnic groups—but these were subsidiary to the five main ones. (Beier, *Masterless Men*, 4).

Unfortunately, most studies of crime ignore the issue of age altogether. Sharpe's otherwise excellent review of patterns and trends in English crime, for example, does not consider the issue of age in any detail. *Crime in Early Modern England.*

15. The term *juvenile delinquency* did not become widely used until the late eighteenth and early nineteenth centuries.

16. Quoted in Beier, *Masterless Men,* 55.

17. Though, in practice, local areas were often unable or unwilling to provide special work opportunities for their able-bodied indigent populations. Slack, *Poverty and Policy.*

18. J. Youings, *Sixteenth-Century England* (New York, 1984), 293; Edmund S. Morgan, *American Slavery, American Freedom* (New York, 1975), 65.

19. Youings, *Sixteenth-Century England,* 293, 286.

20. T. R. Murphy, " 'Woful Childe of Parents Rage': Suicide of Children and Adolescents in Early Modern England, 1507–1710," *Sixteenth-Century Journal* 17 (1986): 259–70.

21. Brigden, "Youth and the English Reformation"; Anne Yarborough, "Apprentices as Adolescents in Sixteenth Century Bristol," *Journal of Social History* 13 (1979). "The existence of a large and diverse body of literature about and for apprentices," one historian has written recently, "the evidence of their having met together formally as well as informally, and the frequency with which apprentices acted in concert during the Puritan Revolution to petition the government and to demonstrate in the street indicate that apprentices thought of themselves and were thought of as a separate order or subculture." Smith, "London Apprentices," 157.

22. Among some samples of migrants the age distribution of servants was heavily concentrated in the sixteen to twenty age group, reaching as high as 61 percent among men and 78 percent among women. David Galenson, *White Servitude in Colonial America: An Economic Analysis* (Cambridge, 1981), 27.

23. A. Roger Ekrich, *Bound for America: The Transportation of British Convicts to the Colonies, 1718–1775* (Oxford, 1987), 51.

24. Some historians, like Elton, reject the notion that religious definitions of deviance should be treated alongside more secular definitions of crime. G. R. Elton, "Introduction: Crime and the Historian," in *Crime in England, 1550–1800,* ed. J. S. Cockburn (London, 1977), 2–3. Others, however, persuasively argue that in early modern England contemporaries did not make a clear and sharp distinction between sin and crime. Sharpe, *Crime in Early Modern England,* 4–7.

25. Quoted in Stone, *The Family, Sex, and Marriage,* 512.

26. Steven R. Smith, "Religion and the Conception of Youth in Seventeenth-Century England," *History of Childhood Quarterly* 2 (1974): 500.

27. Smith, "Religion and the Conception of Youth."

28. Galenson, *White Servitude,* 8.

29. Timothy H. Breen, *Puritans and Adventurers: Change and Persistence in Early America* (New York, 1980), 114.

30. Darrett B. Rutman and Anita H. Rutman, "'Now-Wives and Sons-in-Law': Parental Death in a Seventeenth-Century Virginia County," in *The Chesapeake in the Seventeenth Century: Essays on Anglo-American Society,* ed. Thad W. Tate and David L. Ammerman (Chapel Hill, N.C., 1979), 158.

31. Lorena S. Walsh, "'Till Death Us Do Part': Marriage and Family in Seventeenth-Century Maryland," in Tate and Ammerman, *Chesapeake in the Seventeenth Century,* 141, 147–48.

32. Ross W. Beales, Jr., "In Search of the Historical Child: Miniature Adulthood and Youth in Colonial New England," *American Quarterly* 27 (1975): 379–98.

33. For examples of such jeremiads for youth, see Benjamin Colman, *The Warnings of God unto Young People* (Boston, 1716); William Cooper, *How and Why Young People Should Cleanse Their Way, in Two Sermons* (Boston, 1716); *Serious Exhortations Addressed to Young Men: A Sermon Preached May 14, 1732* (Boston, 1732); Increase Mather, *A Sermon Occassioned by the Execution of a Man Found Guilty of Muder . . . Especially to Young Men. To Be Aware of Those Sins Which Brought Him to His Miserable End* (Boston, 1686); Samuel Moody, *The Vain Youth Summoned to Appear before Christ's Bar* (Boston, 1707); Samuel Philips, *Advice to a Child; or, Young People Solemnly Warn'd Both against Enticing and Consenting When Enticed to Sin* (Boston, 1729); and John Webb, *The Young Man's Duty Explained and Pressed upon Him* (Boston, 1718).

34. Thomas Foxcroft, *Cleansing Our Way in Youth* (Boston, 1719), 16.

35. Foxcroft, *Cleansing Our Way,* 16.

36. See N. Ray Hiner, "Adolescence in Eighteenth-Century America," *History of Childhood Quarterly* 3 (1975): 260–61.

37. Cotton Mather, *The Pure Nazarite* (Boston, 1723), 2, 8.

38. Quoted in Jack P. Greene, ed., *Settlements to Society, 1607–1763: A Documentary History of Colonial America* (New York, 1975), 321.

39. Michael S. Hindus, *Prison and Plantation: Crime, Justice, and Authority in Massachusetts and South Carolina, 1767–1878* (Chapel Hill, N.C., 1980), 68. See also Roger Thompson, *Sex in Middlesex: Popular Mores in a Massachusetts County, 1649–1699* (Amherst, Mass., 1986), chap. 1–6.

40. Daniel Scott Smith and Michael S. Hindus, "Premarital Pregnancy in America, 1640–1971: An Overview and Interpretation," *Journal of Interdisciplinary History* 5 (1975): 537–39.

41. Smith and Hindus, "Premarital Pregnancy," 344. On the issue of teenage pregnancies in early America, see Maris A. Vinovskis, *An "Epidemic" of Adolescent Pregnancy? Some Historical and Policy Considerations* (New York, 1988), 3–21.

42. Robert V. Wells, "Illegitimacy and Bridal Pregnancy in Colonial America," in *Bastardy and Its Comparative History*, ed. Peter Laslett et al. (Cambridge, Mass., 1980), 355.

43. Smith and Hindus, "Premarital Pregnancy," 344.

44. Among the many second- and third-generation New England sermons on youthful piety, see Joseph Belcher, *Duty of Parents, and Early Seeking of Christ* (Boston, 1710); Charles Chauncy, *Early Piety Recommended and Exemplified* (Boston, 1732); Benjamin Colman, *A Discourse of Seeking God Early* (Boston, 1713); William Cooper, *Serious Exhortations Addressed to Young Men: A Sermon Preached May 14, 1732* (Boston, 1732); *The Service of God Recommended to the Choice of Young People* (Boston, 1726); and Cotton Mather, *Early Piety Urged* (Boston, 1694).

45. Harry S. Stout, *The New England Soul: Preaching and Religious Culture in Colonial New England* (New York, 1986), 197; J. M. Bumsted and John E. Van de Wetering, *What Must I Do To Be Saved? The Great Awakening in Colonial America* (Hinsdale, Ill., 1976), chap. 7.

46. Stephen R. Grossbart, "Seeking the Divine Favor: Conversion and Church Admissions in Eastern Connecticut, 1711–1832," *William and Mary Quarterly*, 3d ser., 46 (1989): 696–740.

47. Peter S. Onuf, "New Lights in New London: A Group Portrait of the Separatists," *William and Mary Quarterly*, 3d ser., 37 (1980): 635. See also Christine L. Heyrman, *Commerce and Culture: The Maritime Communities of Colonial Massachusetts, 1690–1750* (New York, 1984); Gary B. Nash, *The Urban Crucible: Social Change, Political Consciousness, and the Origins of the American Revolution* (Cambridge, Mass., 1979), 204.

48. L. Withey, *Urban Growth in Colonial Rhode Island: Newport and Providence in the Eighteenth Century* (Albany, N.Y., 1984), 51–76.

49. Withey, *Urban Growth*, 63.

50. J. K. Alexander, *Render Them Submissive: Responses to Poverty in Philadelphia, 1760–1800* (Amherst, Mass., 1980), 48–85.

51. G. Stanley Hall, *Adolescence: Its Psychology and Its Relations to Psychology, Anthropology, Sociology, Sex, Crime, Religion, and Education*, 2 vols. (New York, 1904).

52. Joseph M. Hawes, *Children in Urban Society: Juvenile Delinquency in Nineteenth-Century America* (New York, 1971); Robert S. Pickett, *House*

of Refuge: Origins of Juvenile Reform in New York State, 1815–1857 (Syracuse, N.Y., 1969).

53. Calculated from U.S. Bureau of Census, *Historical Statistics of the United States, Colonial Times to 1970, Bicentennial Edition* (Washington, D.C., 1975), vol. 1, ser. 57–69.

54. Calculated from U.S. Bureau of Census, *Historical Statistics,* vol. 1, ser. 178–79, 202–3.

55. Unfortunately, not much research has been done on troublesome youths in rural nineteenth-century America. There are indications, however, that delinquent youths were present in rural areas but that they usually were not perceived as a serious problem, as in the urban areas. The Board of Public Charities of North Carolina, for example, observed in 1871 that

> doubtless it is true that large cities furnish more of such youthful criminals than do the rural portions of our country. Yet the children of vice and crime will be met from every place where there are neglected orphans—homeless children and ungodly homes that train for crime. Every village depot—every cross-road grog shop will pour out to the traveller's view and annoyance that unrestrained and untutored crew of bad children who make night hideous with their yells and wild songs—who are experts in mischief and who are in training for the prison or the gallows. Quoted in W. B. Sanders, ed., *Juvenile Offenders for a Thousand Years: Selected Readings from Anglo-Saxon Times to 1900* (Chapel Hill, N.C., 1970), 411.

56. Calculated from U.S. Bureau of Census, *Historical Statistics,* vol. 1, ser. 119–34; *Statistical Abstract of the United States: 1990* (Washington, D.C., 1990), table 13.

57. Richard B. Stott, *Workers in the Metropolis: Class, Ethnicity, and Youth in Antebellum New York City* (Ithaca, N.Y., 1990).

58. See chapter 2.

59. Carl F. Kaestle, *Pillars of the Republic: Common Schools and American Society, 1780–1860* (New York, 1983).

60. James D. Anderson, *The Education of Blacks in the South, 1860–1935* (Chapel Hill, N.C., 1988); Thomas L. Webber, *Deep Like the Rivers: Education in the Slave Quarter Community, 1831–1865* (New York, 1978).

61. Wayne E. Fuller, *The Old Country School* (Chicago, 1982); William A. Link, *A Hard Country and a Lonely Place: Schooling, Society, and Reform in Rural Virginia, 1870–1920* (Chapel Hill, N.C., 1986).

62. David Angus, Jeffrey Mirel, and Maris Vinovskis, "Historical Development of Age-Stratification in Schooling," *Teacher's College Record* 90 (1988): 211–36.

63. Carl F. Kaestle, *The Evolution of an Urban School System: New York City, 1750–1850* (Cambridge, Mass., 1973); Stanley K. Schultz, *The Culture Factory: Boston Public Schools, 1789–1860* (New York, 1973).

64. Hindus, *Prison and Plantation;* Eric H. Monkkonen, *The Dangerous Class: Crime and Poverty in Columbus, Ohio, 1860–1885* (Cambridge, Mass., 1975)

65. Hindus, *Prison and Plantation.*

66. While contemporary observers often downplayed rural crimes, Hindus shows that they were quite high in both states. Throughout his analysis, Hindus points out the great difficulties of comparing crime rates in such diverse states as Massachusetts and South Carolina because of differences in their socioeconomic and racial systems as well as in their judicial organizations. *Prison and Plantation.*

67. Hindus, *Prison and Plantation.*

68. Monkkonnen, *Dangerous Class.*

69. Since the records of criminals in Franklin County from 1865 to 1875 did not include age, he matched their names to the individual-level information from the federal manuscript census of 1870. About 32 percent of the defendants between 1865 and 1875 were located in the federal census of 1870. Since teenagers and young adults were more likely to move than older people in nineteenth-century America, this may have reduced their likelihood of being matched to the 1870 census. As a result, Monkkonen's matched criminal and census data set may underestimate the extent of young criminals in the population.

70. Lawrence M. Friedman and Robert V. Percival, *The Roots of Justice: Crime and Punishment in Alameda County, California, 1870–1910* (Chapel Hill, N.C., 1981). The decline of serious crimes in urban areas was not unique to Alameda County. Researchers have found similar declines in crime for many other urban areas both in this country and abroad. Roger Lane, *Violent Death in the City: Suicide, Accident and Murder in Nineteenth-Century Philadelphia* (Cambridge, Mass., 1979); Eric H. Monkkonen, *America Becomes Urban: The Development of U.S. Cities and Towns, 1780–1980* (Berkeley, Calif., 1988). Nevertheless, most contemporary observers believed that urban crimes were increasing rather than decreasing in the late nineteenth century.

71. According to Friedman and Percival, rates of serious crime recently have risen dramatically in Oakland and the police have put much more effort into felony arrests and dealing with the drug problem—areas in which youthful offenders are particularity active. Arrests for crimes such as drunkenness and public disorders, which usually involve older adults, have fallen off and thereby contributed to the disproportionate

number of youth crimes today compared to the past. Friedman and Percival, *Roots of Justice.*

72. J. M. Austin, *A Voice to Youth Addressed to Young Men and Young Women* (New York, 1854), 1.

73. Quoted in Howard P. Chudacoff, *How Old Are You? Age Consciousness in American Culture* (Princeton, N.J., 1989), 22. The word *adolescence,* or *adolescent,* is rarely found in the reform writings of antebellum America. For one of the few occurrences of that term, see the reprint in the New England Female Moral Reform Society's journal of an article from the Boston *Daily Herald* which writes of "those passing from the period of adolescence to manhood or womanhood." *Friend of Virtue* 19 (1 March 1856): 69.

74. Carl F. Kaestle and Maris A. Vinovskis, *Education and Social Change in Nineteenth-Century Massachusetts* (Cambridge, 1980).

75. Massachusetts Board of Education, *Twelfth Annual Report of the Board of Education* (Boston, 1849), 95–96.

76. Charles L. Glenn, Jr., *The Myth of the Common School* (Amherst, Mass., 1988); David J. Hogan, *Class and Reform: School and Society in Chicago, 1880–1930* (Philadelphia, 1985).

77. Anne M. Boylan, *Sunday School: The Formation of an American Institution, 1790–1880* (New Haven, Conn., 1988).

78. Paul Boyer, *Urban Masses and Moral Order in America, 1820–1920* (Cambridge, Mass., 1978); Peter C. Holloran, *Boston's Wayward Children: Social Services for Homeless Children, 1830–1930* (Rutherford, N.J., 1989); Carroll Smith-Rosenberg, *Disorderly Conduct: Visions of Gender in Victorian America* (New York, 1985).

79. Barbara M. Brenzel, *Daughters of the State: A Social Portrait of the First Reform School for Girls in North America, 1856–1905* (Cambridge, Mass., 1983); Hawes, *Children in Urban Society;* Robert M. Mennel, *Thorns and Thistles: Juvenile Delinquents in the United States, 1825–1940* Hanover, N.H., 1973); Pickett, *House of Refuge;* Anthony M. Platt, *The Child Savers: The Invention of Delinquency,* 2d ed. (Chicago, 1977); Steven L. Schlossman, *Love and the American Delinquent: The Theory and Practice of "Progressive" Juvenile Justice, 1825–1920* (Chicago, 1977).

80. N. C. Hart, *Documents Relative to the House of Refuge Instituted by the Society for the Reformation of Juvenile Delinquents in the City of New York in 1824* (New York, 1832), 13.

81. Miriam Z. Langsam, *Children West: A History of the Placing-Out System of the New York Children's Aid Society, 1853–1890* (Madison, Wis., 1964); R. Richard Wohl, "The 'Country Boy' Myth and Its Place in American Urban Culture: The Nineteenth-Century Contribution," *Perspectives in American History* 3 (1969): 77–156.

82. Charles Loring Brace, *The Dangerous Classes of New York and Twenty Years' Work among Them* (New York, 1872), 31.

83. Brace, *Dangerous Classes*, 34–35.

84. Brace, *Dangerous Classes*, 43.

85. Brace, *Dangerous Classes*, 45. Some analysts, like Brenzel, seem to be arguing that there was a shift from an antienvironomentalist, hereditarian explanation for juvenile delinquency to an environmentalist explanation in the antebellum period, which contributed to the development of reform institutions for youth. Brenzel, *Daughters of the State*, 22–24. This represents, however, a misunderstanding of the nature of hereditarian thought at the time and an exaggeration of the extent or nature of any shift. In the early nineteenth century, social problems such as criminality and pauperism were not usually seen in hereditarian terms. The idea of the inheritance of social characteristics gained popularity after 1840 but still was not seen as rigidly determinative until the late nineteenth and early twentieth centuries. Rather, inherited social characteristics were usually seen as a constitutional predisposition toward some behavior but one that could be overcome by early moral education or movement to a more favorable environmental setting. Charles E. Rosenberg, *No Other Gods: On Science and American Social Thought* (Baltimore, 1976).

86. Brace, *Dangerous Classes*, 114–15.

87. Brace, *Dangerous Classes*, 115.

88. Brace, *Dangerous Classes*, 115–16. While many analysts believed that it was more difficult to reform female rather than male delinquents, sometimes they emphasized other arguments besides biological differences. William Douglas Morrison, for instance, agreed that female offenders were more likely to become habitual criminals than male offenders but argued that "this condition of things arises largely from the fact that females are, as a rule, later in being subjected to reformative discipline than males, with the ultimate result that this discipline is less effective when at last it has to be resorted to." *Juvenile Offenders* (New York, 1897), 55. For a useful discussion of the changing attitudes toward female delinquents in the nineteenth century, see Brenzel, *Daughters of the State*. On the differences between male and female delinquents and criminals in the nineteenth century, see Estelle B. Freedman, *Their Sisters' Keepers: Women's Prison Reform in America, 1830–1930* (Ann Arbor, Mich., 1981); Barbara M. Hobson, *Uneasy Virtue: The Politics of Prostitution and the American Reform Tradition* (New York, 1987); and Smith-Rosenberg, *Disorderly Conduct*.

89. There was a general movement in the late nineteenth and early twentieth centuries against any institutionalization of children. Instead, re-

formers felt that children should be kept at home as much as possible. LeRoy Ashby, *Saving the Waifs: Reformers and Dependent Children, 1890– 1917* (Philadelphia, 1984); Michael B. Katz, *In The Shadow of the Poorhouse: A Social History of Welfare in America* (New York, 1986). Some reformers, like Brace, had been arguing against the institutionalization of children as early as the middle of the nineteenth century. Langsam, *Children West.*

90. Mennel, *Thorns and Thistles;* Platt, *Child Savers;* Schlossman, *Love and the American Delinquent.*

91. George E. Dawson, "A Study in Youthful Degeneracy," *Pedagogical Seminary* 4 (1896): 224–56; U.S. Congress, Arthur MacDonald, *A Plan for the Study of Man,* 57th Cong., 1st sess., Senate Doc. 400 (Washington, D.C., 1902).

92. Unlike Lombrosco, Travis did not think many juvenile delinquents or criminals were the result of the deformed physical characteristics of the subject. Rather, a "study of the delinquent with respect to his physical, mental, and ethical conditions shows that at least 90% and probably 98% of first court offenders are normal." Thomas Travis, *The Young Malefactor* (New York, 1908), xxvi. For the few abnormal delinquents who exemplified Lombrosco's theories, however, surgical intervention might be appropriate. He cited the successful work of a physician, E. A. Bogue: "Abnormal palates have been righted; deflected noses made straight; jaws prognathous to half an inch have been made normal. Indeed, the whole cranial form has been so changed that strikingly abnormal heads grow not merely regular, but almost beautiful; and there is often a change for the better in the intellectual and moral life of the child thus treated." Travis, *Young Malefactor,* 209–10.

93. Richard L. Dugdale, *"The Jukes": A Study in Crime, Pauperism, Disease and Heredity* (New York, 1877). Dugdale was not a pessimistic eugenicist but, rather, an optimistic postbellum reformer who felt that proper training of youths could overcome the negative aspects of heredity. Indeed, if proper training were extended over two or three generations, he felt that pauperisms and crime could be largely eliminated. Beginning in the late 1870s and 1880s, however, others increasingly and incorrectly cited Dugdale's work to prove that pauperism and crime were hereditary and predetermined. This increasingly biologically reductionist explanation of poverty and crime became fashionable among many, but certainly not most, American intellectuals and policymakers in the late nineteenth and early twentieth centuries. Y. Rennie, *The Search for Criminal Man: A Conceptual History of the Dangerous Offender* (Lexington, Mass.), 1978; Rosenberg, *No Other Gods.*

94. Morrison, *Juvenile Offenders,* 22.

95. When the German embryologist August Weisman demonstrated as early as 1889 that character traits could not be inherited by offspring, it was no longer possible for scientists to accept the Lamarckian principle that acquired traits could be transmitted from one generation to another. This, in conjunction with the rediscovery of Mendelian genetics, led American social scientists in the early twentieth century to become either more pessimistic about the possibilities of social reforms (if they continued to stress the role of inheritance) or more optimistic (if they abandoned biological explanations of change for cultural ones). For a useful discussion of these changes among early twentieth-century American social scientists, see Carl N. Degler, *In Search of Human Nature: The Decline and Revival of Darwinism in American Social Thought* (New York, 1991).

96. Hall, *Adolescence,* 1:xiii.

97. Hall, *Adolescence,* 1:xiv.

98. Hall, *Adolescence,* 1:325.

99. Hall, *Adolescence,* 335–36, 340.

100. Dorothy Ross, *G. Stanley Hall: The Psychologist as Prophet* (Chicago, 1972).

CHAPTER 6

"Aged Servants of the Lord": Changes in the Status and Treatment of Elderly Ministers in Colonial America

Until recently, the analysis of the status and treatment of the elderly in our past was almost totally neglected. Despite the outpouring of studies in social and family history during the 1960s and 1970s, the elderly were mentioned only in passing. But, with the growth of concern about aging today, historians are now beginning to consider how our colonial ancestors dealt with the aged in the seventeenth and eighteenth centuries. Unfortunately, the recent scholarship on the elderly in colonial America has been rather limited to date. Historians are treating the seventeen and eighteenth centuries as one unit, without really considering if there were major changes in societal reactions to aging during that period. David H. Fischer, for example, writes of the continued exaltation of the elderly throughout the colonial period and only sees a significant change in the attitudes and behavior toward the elderly in the last two decades of the eighteenth century.[1] Similarly, John Demos analyzes old age in early New England with "little attention . . . to issues of chronological development and change."[2] This static view of the status and care of the elderly in early America is reinforced by the tendency of scholars from other disciplines to analyze age relations in preindustrial societies as relatively constant and unchanging over time.

In an effort to construct a more detailed picture of the elderly in early America, this chapter will focus on one particular group—the Puritan ministers of New England. They are an appropriate focus of attention not only because they frequently revealed their ideas about the elderly in published sermons, letters, and diaries but also because their own lives exemplified the ambiguous treatment that was accorded to the elderly in colonial America. Though historians have devoted much time and effort to recreate the intellectual and social experiences of Puritan ministers, they have paid almost no attention to the process of aging—especially among the different generations of ministers.[3] Yet their analyses present a more dynamic portrayal of the experiences of Puritan ministers than the one given by the recent historians of aging in colonial America. Therefore, in this chapter we will draw on the recent literature on Puritan ministers as well as on aging in colonial America in order to suggest some of the possible changes in the status and treatment of elderly ministers.

First-Generation Ministers

To understand the status and treatment of elderly Puritan ministers in New England, it is necessary to reconstruct the lives of the first-generation ministers who came to the New World in the initial waves of the Great Migration during the 1630s and early 1640s. These first-generation Puritan ministers and settlers established the New England churches as well as formulated the relationship between the minister and his congregation which provided the basis for religious practices and controversies for future generations. Though many of the experiences of these first-generation New England ministers were atypical of that of their successors, they set the standards by which subsequent ministers judged their own lives and achievements. As a result, the aging experiences of the first-generation of Puritan ministers in America had a particularly important influence on the way colonial society dealt with their elderly ministers in the seventeenth and eighteenth centuries.[4]

The first-generation of Puritan ministers came to New England in their twenties and thirties.[5] While they fled from the increasing persecution of King Charles and Archbishop William Laud in England, they brought with them the social and cultural heritage of that struggle. Yet, in America, these ministers and their congregations were forced to create their own system of churches based not only upon their religious beliefs but also taking into consideration the particular social and economic conditions in early New England.[6] Though the first-generation Puritans were united in their opposition to the existing

Anglican church, they strongly disagreed among themselves about how to create and run their own churches. Given the congregational form of church organization which they adopted, their early efforts led to a variety of different practices.[7] Yet certain basic features of the Puritan church in New England emerged which had an important bearing on the lives of their ministers in their old age.

One of the fundamental factors in shaping the experiences of elderly ministers is the way in which a religion selects and maintains its clergy. Some religions minimize the role of a separate clergy altogether and simply rely upon members of the congregation to conduct services. Others designate a separate clergy but treat them as part-time ministers who are expected to provide for themselves. Support of ministers in their old age is not a particular problem for these groups, since they do not have a separate or full-time ministry that needs to be maintained by the congregation. In situations where a separate clergy exists, the relationship of the ministers to their congregation becomes very important in determining who provides support for the aging ministers and under what conditions.

The relationship between a Puritan minister and his congregation was never resolved in colonial America. On the one hand, the Puritans believed that the minister was set apart from his congregation and derived his sacerdotal authority from above. On the other hand, Puritans allowed congregations to select their own ministers and encouraged them to participate in many of the decisions of the church, such as the admission of new members or the disciplining of sinners. Throughout the seventeenth and eighteenth centuries, the tension between the clergy and their congregations continued over the exact responsibilities and powers of the minister, which sometimes encouraged parishioners to withhold support for their aging minister.[8]

Once a minister was settled in a particular parish, it was assumed that he would remain there for life, unless, in extraordinary circumstances, both the minister and the congregation mutually agreed upon a termination of his tenure. It was not clear, according to Puritan theology, however, who should pay for the maintenance of the clergy. Initially, the Massachusetts Bay Company paid for the ministers out of its "Common Stock," but it soon shifted that responsibility to the local towns, where it remained throughout the colonial period. The decision to have the local areas pay for their own ministers was important because it passed control of the salaries of ministers from the colony as a whole to the individual towns. In the first decades of settlement, ministers preferred to collect their salaries through voluntary weekly contributions, but most communities quickly abandoned this practice, since it became increasingly difficult to raise sufficient funds unless everyone in the town, whether a church member or not, was taxed for the support of the minister. Since the salary of the minister often comprised at least one-half of the town budget, any decisions involving the support of the minister soon became an issue for all of the citizens rather than just members of the congregation.[9]

Despite the hardships of settling in a new land, the first-generation Puritan ministers did exceedingly well in America. Whereas most Puritan ministers in England had not enjoyed high socioeconomic status, those who migrated to New England in the 1630s and 1640s became prominent social as well as religious leaders of their local communities.[10] In the initial and subsequent divisions of land, ministers usually received among the largest allotments. Reverend John Allin of Dedham, for example, received the largest share of land of anyone in every division before 1656. His overall wealth of over one thousand pounds was unequaled in Dedham before 1700.[11] The prominence of the first-generation ministers was the result not only of their spiritual leadership but also of their unusually high socioeconomic standing within the community—an achievement all the more satisfying to them because of their rapid upward social mobility from their low status in England.

The first-generation ministers enjoyed many other advantages besides access to wealth. Many of them, like Thomas Hooker, migrated to the New World with their old congregations, thus benefiting from continued close association with their old friends and parishioners with whom they had endured so many hardships in England.[12] Furthermore, since one of the major motivations for Puritans to migrate to the New World was to be able to practice their religion, the ministers could assume a much larger role than if they had remained in England, where most people were either indifferent or hostile to them. The importance of their spiritual leadership was reinforced by the heightened sense of excitement and anticipation, during the 1630s and early 1640s, among the New England Puritans due to the expected imminent return of Christ and the inauguration of the millennium. Finally, and perhaps most important of all, the first-generation of Puritan ministers as a whole were unusually charismatic and provided the type of personal leadership for their congregations which was rarely matched by their successors. Ministers such as John Cotton, Thomas Hooker, and Thomas Shephard dominated their congregations by the sheer force of their personalities and intellect, while their successors pleaded unsuccessfully with their parishioners to obtain the same authority that the first-generation ministers had commanded. Thus, though the first-generation of Puritan ministers probably experienced just as many religious controversies, such as the antinomian crisis, as other generations, they were in a much stronger religious and socioeconomic position to deal with these problems both individually and collectively.

Since the local towns were responsible for maintaining ministers throughout their entire lives, any illnesses associated with aging presented a major crisis for the community, if the minister could no longer perform his duties. With such a large proportion of the town budget already expended for maintaining the present minister, it was financially difficult, if not impossible, simply to bring in another minister while at the same time continuing to pay the incapacitated one his normal salary. If the illness was of short duration, the town often either invited neighboring clergymen to fill in temporarily for their stricken colleague on a voluntary and nonremunerative basis or survived without a few Sunday services. But if the illness was more permanent, the town faced a very difficult and unpleasant quandary since its inhabitants did not want to (nor legally could) stop supporting their old minister, while, at the same time, they could not afford to bring in a paid assistant—especially since the harmony of the town was often disrupted over the choice of any potential successor to the ailing minister.

The anguish and cost of dealing with incapacitated ministers was to plague future generations, but it does not seem to have been particularly troublesome for the first generation. This can be explained partially by the fact that many New England ministers remigrated back to England with the outbreak of the English Civil War in 1640 and the availability of positions in Cromwellian England.[13] Many New England communities were thus spared the cost of caring for their aging minister. But even those who remained did not seem to create much of a problem, perhaps because they had accumulated sufficient personal wealth so that they could afford to retire gracefully from office if they became incapacitated and because the community was more willing to shoulder the extra financial burden since they were such outstanding social as well as religious leaders. The combination of the closeness of the remaining first-generation ministers to their parishioners as well as their own financial ability to care for themselves in old age appears to have minimized much of the difficulty experienced by subsequent generations of aging ministers.

To fully understand the impact of the first generation of Puritan New England ministers on their successors, we must look beyond their actual experiences to the ways in which they were remembered. What is most striking about the first-generation ministers is that their achievements and spiritual purity were greatly exaggerated not only by their successors but even by themselves. They created a myth about themselves and their accomplishments which minimized any of the conflicts among themselves and overemphasized the religious zeal of the first settlers.[14] This myth was widely accepted and fostered an image of the first-generation ministers that made all subsequent ones pale into insignificance by comparison. As a result, the very real achievements of the first generation of Puritan ministers was even magnified for their successors through the lenses of their own narratives of the past.

Historians are currently debating among themselves whether the elderly were really venerated in colonial America.[15] Perhaps some of the differences of opinion may stem from the highly favorable image of the role of the elderly in colonial America as exemplified and created by the rather unique experiences of the first-generation ministers. Since much of the material on the portrayal of the elderly in early America is based on the writings and experiences of the New England clergy, it is important to note that, for the first generation of Puritan ministers, old age, wealth, and social status were highly correlated in their own lives—certainly much more than they might have expected if they had remained in England. This relatively favorable personal image of aging was reinforced by the exaggerated exaltation of their achievements and importance by their contemporaries and successors. As a result, it is not surprising that this particular generation emphasized the role of the elderly in society by the example of their own lives as well as in their writings. Perhaps subsequent generations of New England ministers accepted their image of the proper role of the elderly in society, even though, as we shall soon see, their own experiences of aging did not live up to the high expectations created by the first generation.

Second-Generation Ministers

If we define the first generation of New England ministers as those who migrated to the New World in the 1630s and 1640s, the second generation can loosely be designated as their successors, who assumed office mainly in the 1660s and 1670s. While the concept of generations quickly loses its analytical rigor as we move much beyond the early years of settlement, it is a useful distinction initially, since the first generation of ministers saw themselves passing on their spiritual leadership to the next generation of clergymen.[16] Yet the socioeconomic and religious conditions under which their successors labored were much more disadvantageous for fulfilling that trust than the situation that had confronted the first-generation ministers in the 1630s and 1640s.

The first generation of Puritan ministers had risen to prominence during a period of high population growth and economic prosperity due to the rapid influx of settlers. But the Great Migration to New England peaked in 1638, and, with the start of the English Civil War, immigration to New England dropped off dramatically.[17] While new towns had multiplied rapidly during the 1630s and early 1640s, by the 1650s and 1660s very few new settlements were established. As a result, the need for new churches and additional ministers to staff them dropped from a high of eighteen new churches founded between 1638 and 1640 to one new church established between 1647 and 1649.[18] Though the economy gradually recovered, as New England merchants developed trade with the West Indies, the overall economic conditions facing the second generation were not as favorable as those encountered by the first generation.[19]

The economic opportunities available to second-generation ministers were likewise disappointing, especially when compared to the economic success of the first-generation ministers. While the first-generation ministers benefited by receiving some of the largest shares of land in the initial divisions, their successors in the more settled areas were fortunate to receive any land at all, since, by the 1660s and 1670s, much of the town lands had already been allocated. Secondly, though the tax base of the older towns was increasing due to population growth and economic development, the amount available for any particular minister in many areas may have actually diminished because towns were subdivided to form new communities or additional parishes were created in the same town to accommodate the increasingly dispersed population. Finally, by the 1660s and 1670s, most of the older communities had developed an established social elite, which had prospered from the early land divisions as well as the economic improvements made on their property during the past twenty or thirty years. Any young ministers who were now hired by the congregation simply could not match the wealth and social status of many of these earlier settlers or descendants—even if the community tried to be as generous as possible in its provisions for the new minister.[20] Thus, the second-generation ministers who settled in the older communities of New England found it more difficult, if not impossible, to achieve the same social and economic status as their predecessors had attained earlier.

If the second-generation ministers assuming office in the settled communities did not fare as well as their first-generation counterparts, perhaps those who went to the frontier communities, where land was still plentiful and there was no entrenched social elite, did much better. Though this may have been true in a few instances, overall, the second-generation ministers settling in the frontier areas faced at least equally formidable problems. While more land was available, it was less valuable because frontier areas were more distant from the markets.[21] Many of the frontier areas were also considered unsafe, as New England tried to cope with the continued threats from the Indians, which culminated in the bloody King Philip's War in 1675. Finally, whereas the new settlements along the eastern shore of New England in the 1630s and 1640s were in the mainstream of colonial development from the very beginning, those established in the interior were more socially as well as physically isolated from the rest of society—not only in terms of distance but also psychologically.[22] Second-generation ministers who were offered positions in frontier communities often preferred to risk unemployment or underemployment in order to wait for a post in one of the older settlements.[23] Thus, whether one looks at the settled or frontier areas, most second-generation ministers did not have as attractive opportunities available to them as their predecessors.

If second-generation ministers did not fare as well economically as their predecessors, they also faced an audience that seemed less enthusiastic spiritually than the first settlers. Most of the excitement and anticipation of the impending return of Christ had dissipated by the 1660s and 1670s. Many of the sons and daughters of the first settlers did not possess the same religious zeal and self-assurance that had characterized their parents. Whereas New England was the center stage of the Puritan world in the 1630s and early 1640s, by the post-Restoration period, it had lost its special glamor and promise. Though part of this seeming lack of religious interest by the second generation can be seen as the result of the exaggeration of the piety and achievements of the first settlers, it does reflect some real changes that were occurring in that society.[24] Furthermore, while the early congregations had been willing to submit to the strong leadership of the first-generation ministers, parishioners as well as nonchurch members later openly and vociferously challenged the second-generation ministers for the leadership of the parish.[25] As a result, the young ministers who climbed into their pulpits in the 1660s and 1670s faced congregations that were less eager and willing to be guided by the new spiritual leaders of their communities.

If the residents of the New World seemed less pious than their forefathers, their new leaders as a whole were also less capable of inspiring them. While the first-generation ministers were dynamic individuals who led their congregations by the force of their personalities and intellect, their successors were less charismatic and less effective as leaders. Whether this was due to the adverse circumstances under which they labored or the type of training they had received at Harvard University is not clear.[26] In any case, contemporaries as well as most historians have accepted the notion that these second-generation ministers were less capable—a failing that was magnified by the exaggerated stature and achievements of their predecessors.[27]

As the second-generation ministers grew older, they did not possess the same socioeconomic or religious status in their community, nor did they inspire the same awe as their first-generation counterparts. The communities they served also were no more capable or willing to assist them in their old age than they had helped their predecessors. Yet the problems associated with the aging of the second-generation ministers may have been generally reduced if most of them died before reaching old age. While most first-generation ministers lived well into their sixties, perhaps their successors, who entered the ministry at a younger age than when their predecessors assumed office in the New World, had much lower life expectancies.[28]

The burden of providing assistance for elderly ministers is greatly reduced in many preindustrial societies that have high adult as well as high infant mortality rates. In fact, some scholars argue that the issue of retirement does not exist in preindustrial societies since very few individuals survive into their sixties or seventies. This was certainly the case in the colonial South. In seventeenth-century Middlesex County, Virginia, for example, twenty-year-old males could only expect to live another twenty-nine years and their female counterparts only twenty years.[29] If northern ministers also experienced such high adult mortality rates, their parishioners would encounter the problems of an aging minister only infrequently.

Though earlier historians accepted the idea of very high mortality rates in colonial New England, recent work by demographic historians emphasizes the high life expectancy of adults, especially in rural areas.[30] Yet these findings are being challenged by some scholars who question the validity of such high life expectancy for adults in colonial America.[31] Therefore, in order to set the proper demographic context for this analysis, it was necessary to establish more precisely the life expectancy of colonial New England ministers.[32]

The life expectancy at age twenty of Harvard graduates who went into the ministry, temporarily or permanently, from the classes of 1642 through 1749 was 41.1 years.[33] Thus, the average Harvard graduate who preached at least during part of his career could expect to live at least to age sixty.[34] While there are variations in the average age of death of Harvard graduates who went into the ministry over time, there are no strong trends (fig. 6.1).

According to these figures, 58.7 percent of these Harvard graduates from the classes of 1642 through 1749 survived to age sixty. Since most Harvard students were ordained only several years after graduation, the percentage of permanently settled ministers who lived to at least age sixty was even higher.[35] In other words, though in many preindustrial societies the problem of caring for the elderly is lessened by high adult mortality rates, the demographic pattern of New England meant that most ordained ministers were likely to serve their congregations in their sixties and many even in their seventies (36.7 percent of those graduates lived to age seventy).

While it is impossible to estimate what proportion of second-generation ministers became incapacitated, temporarily or permanently, in their old age, it is clear from the fragmentary surviving records that this may have been a more common occurrence among ministers in their sixties, seventies, and eighties than we have suspected. It is certainly evident that even among those elderly ministers who contin-

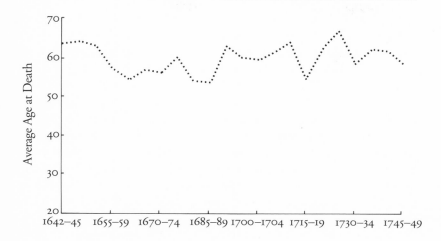

FIG. 6.1. Average age at death of Harvard graduates who preached, by class, 1642–1749. (Calculated from C. K. Shipton and J. L. Silbey, *Silbey's Harvard Graduates,* 16 vols. [Cambridge, Mass., 1873–1972].)

ued to work until they died, old age often brought with it a limitation of their activities.[36] This diminution of the effectiveness of their elderly ministers was generally tolerated by the congregations, both out of respect for their ministers as well as from an unwillingness to pay the extra cost of bringing in an assistant.

There is no evidence that the second-generation elderly ministers were mistreated because of their age. But some of them did suffer in their old age because of the growing contentiousness between the ministers and their congregations over issues of church policy and authority. The newly founded community of Middletown dismissed, with the reluctant acquiescence of the Connecticut General Court, its aged minister, Nathaniel Stow, because he proposed innovations in church discipline. Since Stow was too old to acquire another post and too poor to fend for himself, he appealed to his opponents in the town for a pension; they refused.[37] Though the dismissal of ministers because of disagreements was not commonplace, it was sufficiently frequent to demonstrate how far antagonisms between the ministers and their congregations had developed. In the case of Reverend Stow, it is interesting to observe that neither his age nor his helpless condition elicited any sign of support or compassion from his enemies in the town. While old age was not despised or penalized by these early settlers, neither was it sufficiently venerated or exalted always to help someone who was poor and needed the town's assistance.[38]

Despite the difficulties encountered by second-generation ministers, often in their older years, most of them continued to publicly praise the virtues of aging and the elderly. In fact, they often seemed, if anything, to exaggerate the importance of the elderly in society. In part, this was undoubtedly simply a continuation of the praise of the elderly which had characterized the sermons and writings of the first generation. Perhaps it also reflected the efforts of ministers in the second half of the seventeenth century to bolster order and stability in general as well as to promote their own positions in society as they aged.

Yet underneath this widespread public praise of aging and the elderly there were also indications that the Puritans recognized and abhorred the negative aspects of aging.[39] In fact, some ministers, like Increase Mather, upon his retirement in the early eighteenth century at the age of eighty-two, complained about his loss of identity and uselessness and advised others that "it is a very undesirable thing for a man to outlive his work."[40]

Compared to the experiences of their predecessors, the process of aging for second-generation ministers was often a real disappointment. Their hopes for themselves and their society had been raised to a very high level by the achievements and rhetoric of the first-generation Puritan ministers—so that their failure to live up to those expectations grated all the more. Though most second-generation ministers probably managed to achieve a reasonably comfortable living in their community, very few of them managed to obtain the same social status and admiration that their forefathers seemed to have attained. But, while most second-generation ministers fell short of their own expectations, their local communities were remarkably supportive of them in their old age, unless they became embroiled in a bitter factional fight. Though there were disputes over the payment of the salaries of ministers, especially in the economically backward areas of Plymouth Colony, congregations were usually willing to support their aged minister even when he became partially or totally incapacitated.[41]

Eighteenth-Century Ministers

While the concept of generations had considerable utility in comparing the experiences of first- and second-generation Puritan ministers, it is not of much analytical assistance when we move into the eighteenth century, since the wide range of ages represented by the third and fourth generations make any distinction between them very arbitrary and misleading. Instead, we will focus on the cohorts of ministers in the first half of the eighteenth century, based on their year of graduation from Harvard or Yale universities.[42]

Historians generally are in agreement that the second-generation ministers were disappointed by their religious and socioeconomic achievements compared to those of the first-generation. There is little consensus, however, on the well-being of New England ministers in the first half of the eighteenth century. Some scholars emphasize the stability and prosperity of New England ministers during this period,[43] while others note the disruptions caused by inflation and the Great Awakening.[44] Part of the difference is one of perspective. Those who minimize the difficulties of the ministers in the first half of the eighteenth century write from the vantage point of the nineteenth century, while those who see it more negatively usually do so from the point of view of the seventeenth century. But it also reflects differences in evidence with those who see a more prosperous and less tumultuous early eighteenth century providing much less evidence and analysis than those who differ with them.[45]

In the early eighteenth century, the ministry was becoming a less attractive profession. Whereas most American college graduates in the seventeenth century became clergymen, a much smaller proportion of them did so in the eighteenth century. While 53 percent of Harvard graduates of 1691–1700 became ministers, only 35 percent of Harvard and Yale graduates of 1731–40 climbed into the pulpit.[46] Part of this shift in career choices of college graduates reflects the growing popularity and opportunities in law and medicine rather than in the ministry.[47]

Not only were college graduates less likely to enter the ministry, those that did were no longer the most prominent or promising individuals. Whether measured by the social background of their parents, their birth order, or their class placement, the quality of individuals who went into the ministry declined relative to that of those who entered the other professions.[48] As the eighteenth century progressed, the brightest and most socially advantaged young men no longer pursued a career in the church.[49]

New England ministers in the first half of the eighteenth century did not prosper economically. Though the second-generation ministers did not do as well as those of the first generation, most of them managed to make a reasonable living and accumulate a modest estate. Their successors in the eighteenth century fared even worse economically since, by that time, most towns had already distributed almost all of their land. But even more damaging to the ministers was the effect of inflation and of their fixed salaries.

Most ministers in the eighteenth century, as earlier, served in only one parish once they had been ordained. Among the Congregational minister cohort of 1691–1700, only 8 percent served in more than one charge after ordination, and, among those of the 1731–40 cohort, only 9 percent did.[50] At the time of ordination, the minister usually received some type of settlement, such as land or a house, and was placed on a fixed annual salary, which often included payment in kind as well as cash. By the end of the seventeenth century, most ministers and their congregations relied upon a written contract, which could be renegotiated by mutual agreement of both parties. As a result of these arrangements, the ordained minister was highly dependent upon the stability of the economy or the goodwill of his congregation to agree to any adjustments necessitated by economic fluctuations in the cost of living.

Unfortunately for the well-being of the ministers as well as their parishioners, the New England economy was badly damaged by the cost of King William's War (1689–97) and Queen Anne's War (1702–13). In order to finance these wars, Massachusetts began to issue paper money for the first time in 1690 and continued to do so. Since taxes were not raised sufficiently to retire the money and because of a growing trade deficit, which necessitated additional specie, the value of the Massachusetts paper currency steadily deteriorated (fig. 6.2).

The loss in the purchasing power of Massachusetts paper currency severely affected the clergy, who were on fixed incomes. While many workers were able to negotiate higher wages to offset some of the decline of the Massachusetts paper currency, the ministers were in a particularly weak position because their contracts were not renegotiated

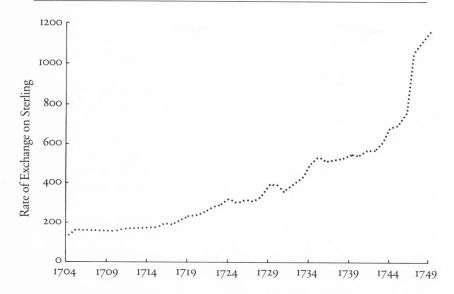

FIG. 6.2. Rate of exchange of Massachusetts paper currency on
sterling, 1704–1749. (From Gary B. Nash, *The Urban Crucible:
Social Change, Political Consciousness, and the Origins of the American
Revolution* [Cambridge, Mass., 1979], 405–6.)

on a regular basis and their bargaining power with their congregations
was limited since they could not leave their parish for another one as
long as the congregation lived up to the terms of the written contract.[51]
Many congregations did try to increase the salaries of their ministers,
but they were limited themselves by the general economic hardships
that affected them individually as well as collectively. The citizens of
many communities could not afford to raise their taxes at a time when
their own wealth had depreciated and their colony taxes had increased
to retire the war debts. Though the economic situation of the colony
varied from year to year in the first half of the eighteenth century, the
position of the ministers, which usually was heavily dependent upon
fixed salaries, continued to suffer disproportionately.[52]

The declining fortunes of ministers in the eighteenth century meant
that many of them were not able to provide adequately for their children as they came of age. Most ministers hoped that at least one of
their sons would follow in their footsteps. Therefore, it was important

for them to be able to send at least one of their sons to either Harvard or Yale. But, as Reverend John Cleaveland of Chebacco Parish in Ipswich, Massachusetts, was to discover, it was often impossible anymore to raise sufficient funds to send even one child to college.[53] In fact, while 63 percent of all Congregational ministers from the classes of 1691–1700 sent at least one son to college, those who graduated from the classes of 1721–30 or 1731–40 were able to send at least one son to college in only 49 percent of the cases.[54] As a result, the percentage of ministers' sons following their fathers' occupation dropped steadily—undoubtedly contributing to the frustration of their parents with their increasingly precarious economic position in society.

In the seventeenth century, there were conflicts between individual ministers and congregations over issues ranging from church policy to payment of salaries. Yet the number of such controversies as well as their severity seems to have increased in the eighteenth century.[55] The number of serious disputes between ministers and their local congregations increased dramatically from twenty-two per one hundred ministers of the cohort of 1691–1700 to fifty per one hundred for the cohort of 1721–30 (fig. 6.3). Throughout the first half of the eighteenth century, the major cause of these disputes was over the salary of the minister, reflecting the tensions created by the runaway inflation.[56]

Another event that was to prove very disruptive to the lives of these eighteenth-century New England ministers was the Great Awakening, which split churches and undermined the authority of many clergymen in the 1740s and 1750s.[57] Ministers who did not agree with the revival risked dismissal or having their congregations split, while those who embraced the New Lights incurred the wrath of their Old Light parishioners. Though, initially, many of the ministers welcomed the revival because it reawakened interest in religion, the bitter controversies generated by the Great Awakening weakened the respect and authority the ministers had hoped would come automatically with their office. Ministers who had been in their pulpits for many years were suddenly called upon by many of their parishioners to defend their own Godliness.[58] Disputes over church doctrine rose steadily among the cohorts of eighteenth-century New England ministers and even exceeded those created by controversies over salaries for the cohort of 1731–40.[59]

The net result of the increases in the number of controversies between ministers and their parishioners in the eighteenth century was the growing number of clergymen who were dismissed—sometimes

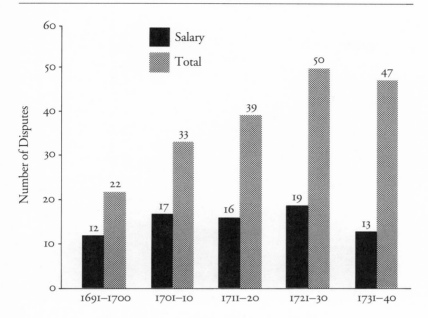

FIG. 6.3. Number of disputes per hundred ministers by decade of college graduation, 1691–1740. (From James W. Schmotter, "Provincial Professionalism: The New England Ministry, 1692–1745." [Ph.D. diss., Northwestern University, 1973], 160.)

by mutual agreement but often unilaterally.[60] The likelihood of dismissal increased over time with over one-fourth of those ministers graduating from the classes of 1721–40 severing their connections with their churches (fig. 6.4). Furthermore, only about a third of those clergymen dismissed continued a career in the ministry by finding another congregation. Thus, while some scholars emphasize the permanence of the eighteenth-century clergy, especially when compared to their nineteenth-century counterparts, there was a trend toward church dismissals which affected a significant proportion of the clergy and alarmed the rest.[61] The eighteenth century was anything but a tranquil and stable period for New England ministers.

The adverse economic and religious conditions of the first half of the eighteenth century undoubtedly hurt many, if not most, of the elderly ministers. Since they had often signed their contracts well before anyone could have anticipated runaway inflation, they were particularly

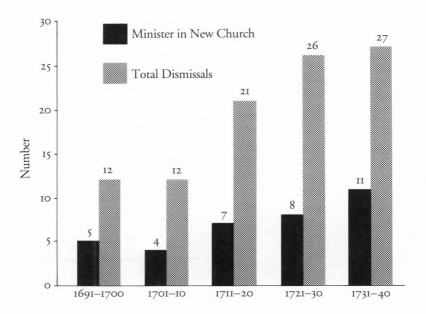

Fig. 6.4. Number of dismissals and subsequent vocation per hundred ministers by decade of college graduation, 1691–1740. (From Schmotter, "Provincial Professionalism," 164.)

hard hit by the depreciation of the paper money. Though many of them did receive some increases in their salaries or special supplements, often they did not keep pace with the depreciation of the currency. While some of the entering ministers managed to include clauses in their contracts to protect them from inflation, most of the new contracts did not have such provisions, and even many of them that did were not sufficient to alleviate entirely the problems caused by the depreciated currency.[62] Furthermore, since fewer and fewer clergy received any land or housing when they were settled, the clergy were less likely to have extensive real estate, which would have acted as a hedge against inflation.[63] Because the salaries of ministers consisted of a combination of payment in kind as well as cash, it is impossible to know exactly how badly the elderly clergy were hurt by the inflation of the first half of the eighteenth century. Yet, if we can believe their own statements as well as those of their contemporaries, most clergymen faced severe cutbacks in their real incomes during these years—a factor that helps to account for the increasing tendency of college graduates to pursue careers in other fields.[64]

The Great Awakening has sometimes been described as a conflict between different age groups, with the young generally favoring it and older individuals opposing it.[65] As a result, one might expect that elderly ministers might have been more willing to oppose the revival and therefore perhaps more likely to suffer from it. This is not the case, however, since the age of the minister, somewhat unexpectedly, does not appear to have any influence on the likelihood of favoring or opposing the Great Awakening.[66] Though the economic disruptions of the first half of the eighteenth century may have hurt the elderly clergy more than their counterparts, the religious turmoil caused by the Great Awakening seems to have affected everyone more equally in terms of age.

Elderly ministers in the first half of the eighteenth century suffered economically and religiously not because of their age but due to the adverse conditions many of them experienced—though, in some areas, such as their economic well-being, elderly ministers may have been particularly vulnerable to these outside forces. Most of them continued, however, to praise the virtues of aging just as their predecessors had done in the seventeenth century and as their successors would continue to do in the early nineteenth century.[67] But the gap between the ideals of aging they espoused and the reality of their own lives probably widened.

Most communities continued to support aging ministers even when they became incapacitated, though some of them tried to reduce the ministers' salaries or even pressured them to retire in order to make way for a successor. One of the major reasons that elderly clergymen refused to retire from office was because few towns were willing to provide adequate pensions for their former ministers, and most of these individuals did not have sufficient wealth to support themselves and their families. Even more distressing and commonplace was the neglect of the widows of elderly ministers. While a very small minority of parishes provided regular pensions for widows, most only granted them an additional six to twelve months of their former husband's salary to help them make that transition. Since many eighteenth-century ministers had been unable to accumulate a very large estate for their surviving spouses, widows were often forced into a rapid remarriage—frequently, if they were relatively young, with the successor to their husband.[68] As a result, in the late eighteenth century, some New England ministers tried to develop an annuity scheme for the support of their widows.[69]

There is one interesting change in the eighteenth century in how towns provided for their ministers. Increasingly in the eighteenth century, as opposed to the seventeenth, the town was expected to show its final respect for its minister by providing him with an elaborate funeral. Whereas the first and even second generation of Puritan ministers opposed the idea of elaborate funerals for anyone, including themselves, their eighteenth-century counterparts expected them.[70] In fact, while public opinion was not outraged by the idea that a widow of an elderly minister did not receive a pension, it was often aroused against any congregation that did not provide for an adequate funeral for its minister. When Reverend John Newmarch of Portsmouth died at age eighty-one in 1749, his children published an accusatory obituary in the Boston newspapers chastising his congregation for failing to provide him with a proper funeral.[71] Though parishioners in eighteenth-century New England may not have accorded their spiritual leaders the same respect and reverence that their forefathers had received, they now remembered them more lavishly at their funerals.[72]

Conclusion

Historians as well as other scholars have tended to see the elderly in colonial America in rather static terms, usually stressing the high status and favorable treatment that the aged received. Our examination of the lives of elderly Puritan ministers, however, casts doubt on this traditional interpretation. The status and care accorded elderly colonial ministers varied over time and cannot be accurately characterized simply by the use of the terms *veneration* and *exaltation.*

The first generation of Puritan ministers come closest to fitting our stereotype of the elderly in preindustrial societies being praised and rewarded for their achievements and leadership. The unique set of circumstances by which the first-generation ministers assumed office as well as their personal characteristics ensured most of them respect, admiration, and power as they aged in the New World. Their substantial accomplishments were quickly glorified into legendary proportions so that the expectations for the role of the elderly ministers in society that they created for the next generations were almost impossible for anyone to attain.

The second generation of Puritan New England ministers experienced a lot of frustration in their lives. Though they achieved relatively comfortable and respectable positions in society, they never were able to attain the religious or socioeconomic position of their immediate predecessors—a failing for which they blamed themselves as well as their parishioners. The increasing conflicts between the ministers and their congregations further eroded the authority of the second-generation clergymen and left some of them vulnerable in old age to bitter attacks from within their churches. Nevertheless, though many of the elderly ministers of the second generation saw their own lives as less than adequate, on the whole they fared well and did not experience any unusual hardships in their old age.

Compared to their seventeenth-century counterparts, New England elderly ministers in the eighteenth century did not do as well. The ministry no longer attracted as talented or socially prominent individuals as before because it could not compete as effectively with the newly emerging professions of law and medicine. Those that did enter the ministry found themselves battling against runaway inflation and the disruptions caused by the Great Awakening. All of these difficulties left the elderly Congregational minister in a weaker religious and socioeconomic position in his community. Though the elderly ministers still did well in eighteenth-century New England compared to many, if not most, of their elderly parishioners, they had suffered a significant loss of status from that of the first-generation ministers—a fact that they frequently and bitterly lamented.

While this chapter, of necessity, has been exploratory rather than definitive in its analysis of the lives of the elderly in colonial America, it does point to the need for further work in this area from a more dynamic perspective. The tendency of scholars to view the status and treatment of the elderly in all preindustrial societies as fixed and given needs to be modified using a life course approach that places the aging process within its proper historical context. Though this will necessitate a much more detailed and laborious effort than simply treating preindustrial societies as static entities, it will yield a richer and a much more accurate picture of the experiences of the elderly.[73]

Notes

1. David H. Fischer, *Growing Old in America,* exp. ed. (New York, 1978).
2. John Demos, "Old Age in Early New England," in *Turning Points: Historical and Sociological Essays on the Family,* ed. John Demos and S. S. Boocock (Chicago, 1978), S248.
3. Emory Elliott, *Power and the Pulpit in Puritan New England* (Princeton, N.J., 1975); David D. Hall, *The Faithful Shepherd: A History of the New England Ministry in the Seventeenth Century* (Chapel Hill, N.C., 1972); Paul R. Lucas, *Valley of Discord: Church and Society along the Connecticut River, 1636–1725* (Hanover, N.H., 1976); James W. Schmotter, "Provincial Professionalism: The New England Ministry" (Ph.D. diss., Northwestern University, 1973), and "Ministerial Careers in Eighteenth-Century New England: The Social Context, 1700–1760," *Journal of Social History* 9 (1975): 249–67; J. William T. Youngs, Jr., *God's Messengers: Religious Leadership in Colonial New England, 1700–1750* (Baltimore, 1976).
4. There is a vast literature of Puritans in early America. See, for example, Michael McGiffert, "American Puritan Studies in the 1960s," *William and Mary Quarterly,* 3d ser., 27 (1970): 36–67. See also chapter 1. While this chapter cannot hope to interact with most of these studies, it will focus on the most recent work specifically dealing with the role of the ministers in New England.

   There is no simple definition of *elderly* in colonial America, but the term was usually first applied to individuals in their sixties. See Demos, "Old Age."
5. Harry S. Stout, "University Men in New England, 1620–1660: A Demographic Analysis," *Journal of Interdisciplinary History* 8 (1974): 21–47.
6. Hall, *Faithful Shepherd.*
7. Lucas, *Valley of Discord.*
8. Hall, *Faithful Shepherd;* Lucas, *Valley of Discord;* Youngs, *God's Messengers.*
9. Lucas, *Valley of Discord.*
10. Hall, *Faithful Shepherd.*
11. Kenneth Lockridge, "The History of a Puritan Church," *New England Quarterly* 40 (1967): 399–424.
12. Frank Shuffleton, *Thomas Hooker, 1586–1647* (Princeton, N.J., 1977).
13. Stout, "University Men."
14. Sacvan Bercovitch, *The Puritan Origins of the American Self* (New Haven, Conn., 1975).
15. W. Andrew Achenbaum, *Old Age in the New Land: The American Experience since 1790* (Baltimore, 1978); Demos, "Old Age"; Fischer, *Growing*

Old; Carole R. Haber, *Beyond Sixty-Five: The Dilemma of Old Age in America's Past* (New York, 1983); Daniel Scott Smith, "Old Age and the 'Great Transformation': A New England Case Study," in *Aging and the Elderly: Humanistic Perspectives in Gerontology,* eds. S. F. Spicker et al. (Atlantic Highlands, N.J., 1978), 285–302.

16. There are many problems as well as advantages in the use of generations as an analytical construct. See David I. Kertzer, "Generation and Age in Cross-Cultural Perspective," in *Aging from Birth to Death: Sociotemporal Perspectives* ed. Matilda W. Riley, Ronald P. Abeles, and Michael S. Teitelbaum (Boulder, Colo., 1982), 27–50; and Maris A. Vinovskis, "From Household Size to the Life Course: Some Observations on Recent Trends in Family History," *American Behavioral Scientist* 21 (1977): 263–87. While some of the second-generation ministers, who were quite old when they assumed office in the New World, experienced old age in the 1660s and 1670s, others, who began their careers in New England at a much younger age, became old only in the late seventeenth or early eighteenth century. In addition, though a minister might be considered second generation in relation to the colony as a whole, he might be of the first generation of settlers in his particular community. Nevertheless, the distinction of generations is worth preserving for the first and second generations of settlers to New England because they viewed themselves in those terms and because the overall age spread within those first two generations was not so broad as to be meaningless.

17. Douglass R. McManis, *Colonial New England: A Historical Geography* (New York, 1975); John E. Pomfret, *Founding the American Colonies, 1583–1660* (New York, 1970); Daniel Scott Smith, "The Demographic History of Colonial New England," *Journal of Economic History* 1 (1972): 165–83.

18. Stout, "University Men."

19. Bernard Bailyn, *The New England Merchants in the Seventeenth Century* (Cambridge, Mass., 1955); Gary M. Walton and James F. Shepherd, *The Economic Rise of Early America* (New York, 1979).

20. One factor that may have helped some of the second-generation ministers was an inheritance of substantial funds from their fathers—especially for those sons whose parents had become prominent and wealthy in the New World. Some historians, like Greven, emphasize the importance of inheritance as a means for the first generation to control the behavior of their children, but others, like Vinovskis, have questioned this interpretation. Philip J. Greven, Jr., *Four Generations: Population, Land, and Family in Colonial Andover, Massachusetts* (Ithaca, N.Y., 1970); Maris A. Vinovskis, "American Historical Demography: A Review Essay," *Historical Methods Newsletter* 4 (1971): 141–48.

21. Walton and Shepherd, *Economic Rise.*
22. Douglas E. Leach, *Flintlock and Tomahawk: New England in King Philip's War* (New York, 1958); Alden T. Vaughan, *New England Frontier: Puritans and Indians 1620–1675* (Boston, 1965); Charles E. Clark, *The Eastern Frontier: The Settlement of Northern New England, 1610–1763* (New York, 1970).
23. Lucas, *Valley of Discord.*
24. While there were real changes occurring in New England society, the effort of earlier historians to portray the experiences of Puritans in terms of declension have not been satisfactory. For a critique of the use of declension, see McGiffert, "American Puritan Studies"; Gerald F. Moran, "Conditions of Religious Conversion in the First Society of Norwich, Connecticut, 1718–1744," *Journal of Social History* 5 (1972): 331–43; and Robert G. Pope, "New England versus the New England Mind: The Myth of Declension," *Journal of Social History* 3 (1969–70): 95–99. See also chapter 1.
25. Lucas, *Valley of Discord.*
26. Hall, *Faithful Shepherd.*
27. Elliott, *Power of the Pulpit;* Hall, *Faithful Shepherd;* Lucas, *Valley of Discord;* Darret B. Rutman, *American Puritanism* (New York, 1970).
28. Stout, "University Men."
29. Darret B. Rutman and Anita H. Rutman, "Of Agues and Fevers: Malaria in the Early Chesapeake," *William and Mary Quarterly,* 3d ser., 33 (1976): 31–60.
30. John Demos, *A Little Commonwealth: Family Life in Plymouth Colony* (New York, 1970); Greven, *Four Generations;* Maris A. Vinovskis, "Mortality Rates and Trends in Massachusetts before 1860," *Journal of Economic History* 32 (1972): 184–213. See also chapter 7.
31. Fischer, *Growing Old.*
32. While some of the early demographic studies of rural New England towns may have exaggerated the expectations of life of adults, Fischer probably had underestimated it. See Demos, *Little Commonwealth;* Fischer, *Growing Old.* For a review of the studies of mortality in early America, see Vinovskis, "Mortality Rates"; and "Recent Trends in American Historical Demography: Some Methodological and Conceptual Considerations," *Annual Reviews in Sociology* 4 (1978): 603–27.
33. To keep the mortality data comparable, it was necessary to calculate the expectation of life at the age of graduation from college. In order to make certain that changes in the mean age of death of ministers were not affected by a rise or fall in the age of college graduation, those data were also gathered and analyzed.

34. Fischer found a mean age of death of 64.9 years for thirty-five New England ministers in the seventeenth century, which is similar to that presented in this analysis. Fischer, *Growing Old*, 45. Yet, in his discussion of the life expectancy of colonial Americans, Fischer repeatedly relies on other data, which gave him a considerably lower estimate.

35. In 1700, the average minister could expect to wait 7.9 years; in 1710, 7.2 years; in 1720, 6.8 years; in 1730, 5.7 years; and in 1740, 5.5 years. Schmotter, "Provincial Professionalism," 185.

36. While Fischer stresses that only three of the thirty-five colonial New England ministers in his sample retired, nearly 14 percent of them who survived to age sixty-five retired. Fischer, *Growing Old*, 44. Furthermore, since many incapacitated ministers continued in their office as long as possible in order to collect their salaries, that 14 percent figure probably is a very low estimate of the likelihood of an elderly minister being incapacitated, partially or totally, in colonial America.

    It would be very difficult to ascertain the nature and extent of physical and mental limitations of aging ministers in colonial America. One might be tempted, for example, to extrapolate from current studies of aging and visual perception of motor performance in order to estimate the disabilities of elderly ministers in the past. But any such simple-minded use of contemporary studies of elderly might be very misleading since the functioning of the elderly is affected by their social environment. In the past, when the elderly were expected to be productive and active members of society, they may not have experienced the same rate of diminution of abilities which is characteristic of societies that encourage or even force their elderly into inactivity and early retirement.

37. Lucas, *Valley of Discord*, 78.

38. Though early Americans may have venerated the elderly, they did so only if they were not dependent upon taxpayers for support or assistance. Demos, "Old Age"; Haber, *Beyond Sixty-Five*. While Fischer acknowledges that the elderly poor did not fare well, the tone of his discussion of the elderly in colonial America tends to exaggerate the positive image and benevolent treatment of elderly in that culture.

39. Demos, "Old Age"; Haber, *Beyond Sixty-Five;* Smith, "Old Age."

40. Quoted in Haber, *Beyond Sixty-Five*, 18.

41. Unfortunately there are no systematic studies of aging of first- and second-generation ministers in regard to their relationship to congregations. There is little indication in the secondary literature of major disputes over matters of continued support simply because a minister had reached age sixty or seventy and was no longer as capable of performing his duties as a younger person.

42. Most of the colonial New England clergy were trained at either Harvard or Yale, and fortunately Schmotter has completed a very useful analysis of their careers.

43. Daniel H. Calhoun, *Professional Lives in America: Structure and Aspiration, 1750–1850* (Cambridge, Mass., 1965); Donald M. Scott, *From Office to Profession: The New England Ministry, 1750–1850* (Philadelphia, 1978).

44. Schmotter, "Ministerial Careers"; Clifford K. Shipton, "The New England Clergy of the 'Glacial Age,'" *Publications of the Colonial Society of Massachusetts* 32 (1933): 24–54; Youngs, *God's Messengers.*

45. Most of the work on the eighteenth-century clergy is highly impressionistic or based only on a few ministers. Only a few studies have tried to reconstruct in detail the careers of eighteenth-century New England ministers. See, for example, P. M. G. Harris, "The Social Origins of American Leaders: The Demographic Foundations," *Perspectives in American History* 3 (1969): 159–344; Schmotter, "Provincial Professionalism"; "Ministerial Careers"; Harry S. Stout, "The Great Awakening in New England Reconsidered: The New England Clergy as a Case Study," *Journal of Social History* 8 (1974): 375–400.

46. Schmotter, "Ministerial Careers."

47. Gerald W. Gawalt, *The Promise of Power: The Emergence of the Legal Profession in Massachusetts 1760–1840* (Westport, Conn., 1979); Joseph F. Kett, *The Formation of the American Medical Profession* (New Haven, Conn., 1968).

48. Schmotter, "Ministerial Careers."

49. Shipton, "New England Clergy."

50. Schmotter, "Provincial Professionalism."

51. Youngs, *God's Messengers.* In some situations, the minister's salary was granted on an annual basis. Jonathan Edwards, for example, was so distressed that the townspeople continued to question his expenditures and style of living that he petitioned them to put him on a fixed annual salary. Patricia Tracy, *Jonathan Edwards, Pastor: Religion and Society in Eighteenth-Century Northampton* (New York, 1979).

52. For a discussion of New England economic conditions in the eighteenth century, see Alice S. Jones, *Wealth of a Nation to Be: The American Colonies on the Eve of the Revolution* (New York, 1980); Gary B. Nash, *The Urban Crucible: Social Change, Political Consciousness, and the Origins of the American Revolution* (Cambridge, Mass., 1979); Walton and Shepherd, *Economic Rise.*

53. Christopher M. Jedrey, *The World of John Cleaveland: Family and Community in Eighteenth-Century New England* (New York, 1979). Even as prominent a minister as Cotton Mather in 1720 admitted to Thomas Hollis, the English philanthropist, that, because of his small ministerial

salary and the rapid increase in inflation, he would have been unable to send his son to college without outside assistance. Youngs, *God's Messengers,* 105. A surprisingly significant proportion of college students, particularly those training for the ministry, received outside support from charitable groups because their own parents could not afford to send them to school. David Allmendinger, *Paupers and Scholars: The Transformation of Student Life in Nineteenth-Century New England* (New York, 1975).

54. Schmotter, "Provincial Professionalism."

55. Schmotter, "Ministerial Careers."

56. While Schmotter acknowledges the negative impact of inflation on the salaries of ministers, he seems to underestimate the seriousness of it. Instead, he tends to explain the increasing concern about the salaries of ministers in the 1720s as a reflection of their growing professional orientation. The stress on the growing professionalism of the clergy in the early eighteenth century is also a theme emphasized by Youngs in *God's Messengers.*

57. C. C. Goen, *Revivalism and Separatism in New England, 1740–1800* (New Haven, Conn., 1962); Stout, "Great Awakening"; Tracy, *Jonathan Edwards.*

58. Youngs, *God's Messengers.*

59. Schmotter, "Ministerial Careers."

60. Schmotter, "Provincial Professionalism."

61. Calhoun, *Professional Lives;* Scott, *From Office to Profession;* Youngs *God's Messengers.*

62. Schmotter, "Ministerial Careers."

63. Schmotter, "Provincial Professionalism."

64. Ola L. Winslow, *Meetinghouse Hill, 1630–1783* (New York, 1952); Youngs, *God's Messengers.*

65. There is an extensive literature on the issue of age and the Great Awakening. For a good introduction to the field, see Philip J. Greven, Jr., "Youth, Maturity, and Religious Conversion: A Note on the Ages of Converts in Andover, Massachusetts, 1711–1749," *Essex Institute Historical Collections* 108 (1972): 119–34; Moran, "Conditions of Religious Conversion."

66. Stout, "Great Awakening."

67. On the images of aging in the nineteenth century, see Achenbaum, *Old Age;* Fischer, *Growing Old;* Jane Range and Maris A. Vinovskis, "Images of the Elderly in Popular Literature: A Content Analysis of Littel's Living Age, 1845–1880," *Social Science History* 5 (1981): 123–70; and Barbara G. Rosenkrantz and Maris A. Vinovskis, "The Invisible Lunatics: Old Age and Insanity in Mid-Nineteenth-Century Massachusetts," in *Aging*

and the Elderly: Humanistic Perspectives in Gerontology, ed. S. F. Spicker et al. (Atlantic Highlands, N.J., 1978), 95–125.

68. Youngs, *God's Messengers.*

69. Maris A. Vinovskis, "The 1789 Life Table of Edward Wigglesworth," *Journal of Economic History* 31 (1971): 570–90.

70. On the ways in which colonial Americans dealt with death and dying, see David E. Stannard, *The Puritan Way of Death: A Study in Religion, Culture, and Social Change* (New York, 1977). See also chapters 1 and 7.

71. The town replied defensively that it had meant to cover the costs of the funeral at the next town meeting but then counterattacked by arguing that the minister had done quite well in his years in office and that his estate was quite capable of bearing the costs of the funeral, if necessary. See C. K. Shipton and J. L. Sibley, *Sibley's Harvard Graduates,* 16 vols. (Cambridge, Mass., 1873–1972), 4:73–75.

72. It is not clear how much of the willingness of the congregation to spend large sums on the funerals of its members in the eighteenth century was in part an effort to soothe the minister while he was alive. It sometimes does appear that in congregations that were badly split, the funeral may have become an important ritual to reintegrate the parish as well as to say good-bye to its minister.

73. For a comparable but more detailed analysis of aging ministers in New Hampshire, see Maris A. Vinovskis, "Aging and the Transition from Permanency to Transiency among New Hampshire Congregational and Presbyterian Ministers, 1633–1849," in *Historical Demography of Aging,* ed. David Kertzer (forthcoming).

CHAPTER 7

Angels' Heads and Weeping Willows:
Death in Early America

Most recent studies of America's past can be placed into one of two distinct and sometimes hostile camps. Traditional historians have continued to rely almost exclusively on literary sources of information. As a result, their work has focused on the ideology and attitudes of early Americans. On the other hand, a small group of historians, borrowing heavily from the other social sciences, have undertaken to recreate the behavioral patterns of American society in the past. Though these two approaches are potentially complementary to each other, there has been very little effort made to integrate them.

This bifurcation of approaches to the study of American history is quite evident in the recent efforts to analyze the role of death in America. Traditional historians have begun to examine the writings of early Americans in order to recreate their attitudes and images of death. Historical demographers have exploited the censuses and vital records to calculate the incidence and timing of death in early America. But no one has attempted to explore systematically the relationship between attitudes toward death and the actual levels and trends in mortality in early America. In part, this is the result of the assumption by most historians that the attitudes toward and the incidence of death in America were identical.

In this chapter, we will demonstrate that many colonists did not accurately perceive the extent of mortality in their society. We will suggest some of the reasons for their misperceptions. It is hoped that this examination will encourage other scholars to integrate attitudinal and behavioral approaches to the study of American history.

Most of us have certain preconceived notions about death in colonial

America. We envision the early settlers of the country facing such a multitude of hazards that death at a fairly early age was practically inevitable. We also imagine that persons surviving to old age were quite rare and extremely fortunate in having escaped the continuous waves of famine and pestilence which swept through the population. The idea that high mortality rates prevailed in colonial America has been reinforced by the numerous instances of entire families or communities perishing in the hostile environment of the New World.

Nearly all of us are familiar with the tragic experiences of the Pilgrims who landed at Plymouth on 11 November 1620. Though only one of the one-hundred-two passengers aboard the *Mayflower* perished at sea, the eleven-week journey had left the rest of them weak, exhausted, and unprepared for the coming winter. William Bradford noted their ordeal in his diary:

But that which was most sadd & lamentable was, that in 2. or 3. moneths time halfe of their company dyed, espetialy in Jan: & February, being the depth of winter, and wanting houses & other comforts; being infected with the scurvie & other diseases, which this long vioage & their inacomodate condition had brought upon them; so as ther dyed some times 2. or 3. of a day, in the foresaid time; that of 100 & odd persons, scarce 50 remained.[1]

Even those settlers who survived the rigors of the first year in the New World faced unforeseen epidemics, which took very heavy tolls on the inhabitants, especially in urban areas such as Boston and Salem. In 1721, there was an outbreak of smallpox in Boston in which over 50 percent of its eleven thousand inhabitants contracted the disease. In that year, the Boston death rate soared to an incredible one-hundred-three deaths per thousand population. Thus, over 10 percent of the city's population died within the space of one year.[2] Only the very small percentage of the people daring enough to try the new technique of inoculation managed to escape the high death rate among those who had smallpox.[3]

Smaller communities were not safe from the terrors of epidemics. In the parish of Hampton Falls in New Hampshire, for example, the "sore-throat distemper" in 1735 nearly decimated the population. This epidemic, later identified as diphtheria, resulted in the deaths of two-hundred-ten persons—or over one-sixth of the entire population of that parish. The outbreak of diphtheria caused fatalities particularly among young people; 95 percent of those who died in Hampton Falls were under the age of twenty. Nearly twenty families buried all of their children that year.[4]

Any person still skeptical of the existence of high mortality in early America would certainly be convinced by one of the few extant life tables for that period—the Wigglesworth Life Table of 1789. Edward Wigglesworth, Hollis Professor of Divinity at Harvard University, became interested in life tables when he was advising the Massachusetts Congregational Charitable Society on how to establish an annuity fund for the widows of ministers. At that time, there were no life tables available for the United States from which to estimate the life expectancies of the ministers and their wives. Therefore, Wigglesworth collected bills of mortality from various New England towns with the active cooperation of the newly established Academy of Arts and Sciences in Boston. From the sixty-two bills of mortality returned, Wigglesworth constructed a life table in 1789. He calculated that the average person in New England could expect to live only 35.5 years—thus reinforcing our grim image of health conditions in early America.[5]

Most writers have argued that death rates in seventeenth-century New England were very high, and there is also a consensus that life expectancy improved significantly in the first half of the nineteenth century. This interpretation is based on a comparison of Wigglesworth's Life Table of 1789 and Elliott's table of 1855 for Massachusetts. On the basis of these two tables, it appears that the average person in the commonwealth could expect to live an additional 4.3 years by 1855.[6]

Thus, the traditional picture of mortality in early America is one of high death rates in the seventeenth and eighteenth centuries followed by a marked improvement in the nineteenth century. A sociologist has summarized the extent of mortality in early America as follows:

Although precise statistical evidence is lacking, the little that scientists have been able to compile from various anthropological and archaeological sources indicates that throughout most of his existence man has had to contend with an extremely high death rate. The brutally harsh conditions of life in the pre-industrial world made human survival very much a touch-and-go affair. A newborn infant had no more than a fifty-fifty chance of surviving to adulthood; the average life expectancy of primitive man was probably not much in excess of twenty-five or thirty years. Even more significant, the survival situation was not a great deal better as recently as the middle of the eighteenth century. Early records for the state of Massachusetts, for example, indicate that average life expectancy in colonial America was still somewhat less than forty years.[7]

Most studies of Puritan attitudes toward death have accepted the notion that death rates in early New England were very high. In fact, the imminence of death in Puritan society is often used by historians to explain the preoccupation of early Americans with the process of dying.

Recent work in historical demography, however, raises serious questions about the validity of the traditional view of death in early America. During the last twenty-five years, historical demographers have used family reconstitution techniques to provide a very different interpretation of mortality levels in New England.[8]

This recent work verifies that death rates were very high in urban areas in colonial New England. Boston deaths averaged thirty to forty per thousand population during the years 1701 to 1774. Furthermore, there were large fluctuations in the death rates in Boston. Most of the sudden rises in the death rate in 1702, 1721, 1730, and 1752 were the result of epidemics, which ravaged that busy seaport.[9]

The newer work also shows that death rates in urban areas such as Boston or Salem were not typical of the rest of the population. In most rural communities, the settlers who managed to survive the hardships of the early years could look forward to many more years of life in the New World. Though data on mortality levels are very scarce for the colonial period, historical demographers have been able to provide some estimates by relying on the reconstitution of families from the vital records of the community. On the basis of detailed investigations of Andover, Dedham, Hingham, Ipswich, and Plymouth, it now appears that life expectancy was much higher in rural New England than was previously believed. These communities experienced death rates of fifteen to twenty-five per thousand, rather than the higher mortality rates in Boston or Salem. Since most people in America in the seventeenth and eighteenth centuries lived in small, rural communities, not unlike these five Massachusetts towns, it is likely that most Americans did not have the same frequent encounter with death that residents of commercial centers did.

Since most seventeenth- and eighteenth-century Americans were English or were at least influenced by an English heritage, it is useful to compare the death rates in New England and the Old World. Generally, death rates in America were lower than in Europe. Death rates for infants in Ipswich and America overall were significantly lower than those in Europe, while infant mortality rates in Salem were comparable to those in Europe. Similarly, death rates after the age of twenty were lower in most Massachusetts communities than in Europe.[10]

These findings appear to be in direct contradiction to the expectations of life according to the Wigglesworth Life Table of 1789. A detailed examination of that life table, however, reveals serious methodological flaws in its construction and coverage. Wigglesworth's table is based only on the ages at death obtained from bills of mortality. Since he did not have data available on the population who were liable to die in that period, he was forced to assume that the age distribution of the deaths in the bills of mortality approximated the actual age distribution of the entire population. Though Wigglesworth realized that this crucial assumption was incorrect, his attempts to adjust his stationary population model must be viewed as intelligent guessing at best. Furthermore, his sample of towns was not representative of the entire region. Most of his data came from towns that were more urban than the area as a whole and consequently probably exaggerated the extent of colonial mortality. As a result, his estimate of life expectancy in colonial New England is probably too low and therefore does not invalidate the results from the family reconstitution studies.[11]

Another problem with many of the interpretations of living conditions in colonial America is that they are based on a faulty understanding of life tables. If the expectation of life at birth is 40.0 years, it means that the average person could expect to live that long. It does not mean, however, that, once this average person had reached age twenty-one, he or she had only nineteen years remaining. When an individual had survived the perils of early childhood and the rigors of early adulthood, his or her chances of continuing to live were actually increased.[12] The average male at age twenty-one in seventeenth-century Plymouth, for example, could expect another 48.2 years of life and the average female at the same age another 41.4 years.[13]

Most of the differences in life expectancy between colonial Americans and Americans of today are due to the much higher rate of infant and child mortality in the past. Adults in colonial New England often could anticipate lives almost as long as each one of us today, especially if they were male. The average male at age twenty-one in seventeenth-century Plymouth had a life expectancy only 4.3 years less than the typical American white male today. The average female at age twenty-one in seventeenth-century Plymouth, however, could expect to live 17.5 years less than her white counterpart today—in large measure because maternal mortality rates in colonial America were very high.[14]

Death rates in early America did not remain constant. In the seventeenth century, there were large rural-urban differences in mortality in Massachusetts, since small agricultural communities such as Dedham, Plymouth, Andover, Hingham, and Ipswich had relatively high life expectancies, whereas Boston and Salem had much lower ones. The eighteenth century witnessed the convergence of these rates, as mortality rose slightly in some of the smaller towns, while death rates fell in Salem. Boston continued to have very high death rates throughout the eighteenth century. In the early nineteenth century, there was a further convergence, as Boston death rates dropped to around twenty per thousand, while mortality in rural areas remained fairly steady.[15]

In order to analyze the level of mortality in nineteenth-century America in more detail and to look especially at the rural-urban differences, life tables for various Massachusetts towns in 1860 have been calculated from the federal census and the state vital records. Since the only previous life table for this period that might be of use to us, Elliott's Life Table of 1855, is inadequate because of several methodological shortcomings, these tables provide an unusual opportunity to assess the presence of death in mid nineteenth-century society.[16]

Life expectancy at birth in Massachusetts in 1860 was relatively high compared to most European countries. The average male at birth had a life expectancy of 46.4 years, while the average female could look forward to 47.3 years of life. Contrary to the assertions of most other scholars, there was very little difference in mortality between rural and urban areas in Massachusetts. The major difference according to town size was between towns with populations under ten thousand and those with populations over ten thousand. Furthermore, socioeconomic differences among these towns could not account for a large proportion of the differences in mortality. In a multiple regression analysis where the age-standardized death rate was the dependent variable and a variety of socioeconomic characteristics of those towns were the independent variables, the resultant equation for the state accounted for less than 15 percent of the variance in the death rates. Put more simply, our detailed statistical analysis of mortality levels among Massachusetts towns in 1860 displayed a remarkable similarity among themselves.[17]

Compared to England and Wales in 1838–54, life expectancy in Massachusetts in 1860 was significantly higher for both males and females. It is interesting to observe the generally similar pattern in life expectancy for both areas. If an American, English, or Welsh child survived the high levels of infant and child mortality, his or her life expectancy increased dramatically.[18]

Though the overall level of mortality in colonial New England was probably much lower than previously estimated, it does not mean that death was not a serious problem—particularly for the young. Adults in rural New England could anticipate reasonably long lives, but their children faced much worse odds. Infant mortality rates in colonial America ranged from 115 per thousand births in seventeenth-century Andover to 313 per thousand births for females and 202 per thousand for males in seventeenth-century Salem. In other words, 10 to 30 percent of the children never survived the first year of life. In the United States in 1986, on the other hand, the infant mortality rate was 10.4 per thousand—or more than ten times less than that of the colonial period.[19]

The higher mortality rate among children in the past can be illustrated by comparing the expectation of life for males in Massachusetts in 1860 with those of males in the United States in 1986. At the later ages, the expectation of life for both groups is very similar, but there is a very substantial difference at birth. The average white male child at birth today can expect to live to age 72.0; if he survives to age ten, he increases his total life expectation by only 0.9 years. On the other hand, the average male child in Massachusetts born in 1860 could anticipate 46.4 years of life; if he survived to age ten, his total life expectancy would increase by 16.6 years.[20]

In addition, since the average family in colonial New England usually had three times as many children as we have today, there was a high probability that most families would experience the loss of a least one child during their lifetimes. The combination of high infant mortality rates and high birth rates increased the likelihood that the typical family in early America would have to deal with the death of a member of their nuclear family.[21]

Our analysis of mortality levels and trends in New England before 1860 suggests that most individuals, especially those who had survived the dangers of early childhood, could look forward to reasonably long lives. Therefore, we might expect that our Puritan ancestors would not have been very concerned or worried about mortality—especially about deaths among adults. Yet New England society seemed obsessed with death, despite the moderate mortality rates for that period. Even more astonishing is the fact that most people in those days greatly overestimated the extent of mortality in their society.

Some colonists, such as Edward Wigglesworth, did realize that death rates in the New World were somewhat lower than in England. But even Wigglesworth, the foremost expert on colonial mortality, seriously underestimated the expectation of life in early New England. The general populace seemed convinced that death rates were very high. Anyone reading through the diaries of these people is immediately struck by the fascination and concern with death. The image of early American society one receives from these writings is that of a very unhealthy environment in which each individual anticipates his or her demise at any moment.[22]

Even as late as the first half of the nineteenth century, many Americans continued to overestimate their likelihood of dying. For example, Samuel Rodman began to keep a diary at age twenty-nine in 1821. He was a very scientifically oriented man, who collected weather data from 1812 to 1876 and was generally calm about discussions of death throughout his diary during the next thirty-eight years. But it is very interesting to observe how he misperceived the dangers to his life well into the nineteenth century.

Rodman often mentions how he should devote more attention to his spiritual needs because he anticipates he may die at any moment. In 1838, he celebrates his birthday by noting in his diary that "this is the 46 anniversary of my birth. I have lived therefore already considerably beyond the average of human life." Three years later, he repeats the general theme: "I should not conclude this note without attesting to the fact that this is my 49 anniversary, and that I have entered on my 50th year. It seems a matter of surprise that I have lived so long, and without yet any material change. I have actually passed beyond the period of youth and middle age and may justly be classed among the old."[23]

If Rodman had had the benefit of our life tables for 1860, he could have taken comfort in the fact that he was likely to survive at least another twenty years at age fifty. The intriguing question is why Rodman, an unusually intelligent and perceptive man, should have underestimated so greatly the extent of longevity in his society. Why did he and so many other diarists of the period feel that death was imminent, when, in fact, the death rates for adults in their communities were not very high?

Perhaps the misperceptions of the extent of mortality in New England society were due to the unusual life experiences of those individuals who kept diaries. Maybe they were less healthy and/or came from families that had experienced higher mortality than the rest of the population. Keeping a diary might be part of an attempt to introduce order and stability into a life that was constantly overshadowed by the presence of death.

In the case of Samuel Rodman, this interpretation does not appear to be valid. Despite his frequent anticipations of dying, he managed to survive to age eighty-four, and his wife lived to be eighty-two. Though two of their eight children did die early, at ages one and three, the remaining six lived to the ages of twenty-three, sixty-one, seventy-seven, eighty-seven, and ninety-one. One might properly object that these figures are misleading because Samuel Rodman had no way of knowing how long he or his offspring would survive. Perhaps he was merely reacting to the much higher mortality of his parents and siblings. Yet his father lived to age eighty-two and his mother to age ninety-five. Furthermore, his sisters survived to the ages of thirty-one, sixty, seventy-eight, and eighty-one.[24] In other words, whatever indications of low life expectancy Rodman had, they probably did not come mainly from the experiences of his immediate family.

Though our analysis of Rodman's longevity suggests that his anticipation of imminent death probably was not based on his own physical frailty, we should be careful not to generalize about the relationship between personal health and preoccupation with death among diarists on the basis of just one individual. Kathryn Kish Sklar has coded data from published diaries of seventy-one American women who lived in the eighteenth and early nineteenth centuries. These data are of particular interest to us because many historians have remarked on the preoccupation of women with items about health and death in their diaries. We already know that women who kept diaries were more educated than the rest of the population and probably came from more affluent backgrounds. Using her data, it is possible to calculate age at death for forty of these women.[25] Therefore, one is now able to estimate the life expectancy of these women who kept diaries.

Of the forty women, the average age at death was 56.4 years. This compares very favorably with the expectation of life at birth for Massachusetts women in 1860 of 47.3 years. This is a very misleading comparison, however, because most women did not begin to keep diaries until they had already survived the perils of early childhood (fig. 7.1).

Instead, we need to take into consideration the ages at which these women began their diaries before calculating their life expectancies. Then we can compare their expectation of life to that of women in the general public (fig. 7.2).

The results indicate that women who kept diaries were in fact less healthy than Massachusetts women in 1860, particularly at ages twenty and thirty. Though this does reinforce the argument that unhealthy people were more likely to keep diaries, it is important to bear in mind that the average woman who kept a diary at age twenty could expect to live another 35.5 years. Thus, most women who kept these diaries were actually quite healthy, and their own prospects of dying in the very near future were not very likely, despite their utterances to the contrary in those diaries.

Since we cannot account for the misperceptions of the level of mortality in early New England in terms of the colonists' personal encounters with death, we need to look at the general context of life in that period to see what factors encouraged people to imagine such high death rates, especially among the adult population. Though death is a biological phenomenon, the reactions of people to it are largely defined by the manner in which society handles its dying. It is our contention that the great emphasis placed on death in early New England led people to overestimate the extent of its occurrence in their communities and lives.

Americans today are remarkably unwilling to discuss death. Our society refuses to face the issue of death openly; thus, death has replaced sex as the major taboo. Geoffrey Gorer, in a very insightful book, has argued that "in the 20th century there seems to have been an unremarked shift in prudery; whereas copulation has become more and more mentionable, particularly in the Anglo-Saxon Societies, death has become more and more unmentionable as a natural process."[26]

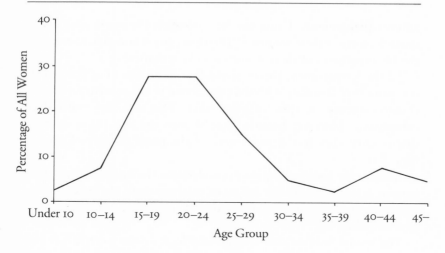

FIG. 7.1. Distribution of ages at which women began to keep their diaries in the eighteenth and nineteenth centuries. (Calculated from data on American diaries collected by Kathryn Kish Sklar of the State University of New York at Binghamton.)

Puritan society had a very different attitude toward death; there was a great fascination and interest in that subject, and people were encouraged to discuss it among themselves. Furthermore, the very process of dying in early New England forced people to come to terms with death rather than pretend that death did not really exist.[27]

The location in which an individual dies is important because it determines the access his or her relatives and friends will have to him during that time. In addition, the place where a person dies also influences the amount of exposure the rest of society will have to the process of dying.

Today there is a debate over whether it is better to die at home or in a hospital. Some elderly actually prefer to die away from home in order to avoid becoming burdens to their families. Yet, when one dies at home, he or she is in familiar surroundings and among friends. A patient who is hospitalized is largely removed from the help and care of his or her family.

Public opinion in America has gradually shifted away from the preference for dying at home. Less than a third of the public now would prefer to have someone die at home. In 1968, a public opinion poll asked: "Do you feel that if an individual is dying and is beyond any

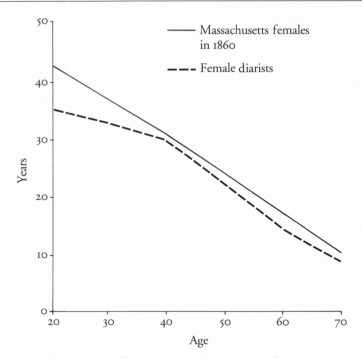

FIG. 7.2. Life expectancy of Massachusetts females in 1860 and eighteenth- and nineteenth-century female diarists. (Calculated from data on American diaries collected by Kathryn Kish Sklar of the State University of New York at Binghamton; Maris A. Vinvoskis, "Mortality Rates and Trends in Massachusetts before 1860," *Journal of Economic History* 32 [1972]: 211.)

available medical aid, that it is more desirable to remove the person to a hospital or other institution, rather than have them remain at home?"[28] The replies are given in table 7.1.

This change in attitude has been accompanied by a shift in the actual location of dying. In 1949, 49.5 percent of all deaths occurred in an institution; by 1982, that figure had risen to 68.1 percent and was even higher in urban areas such as New York City.[29] As a result, most Americans today do not often see the process of dying firsthand. This isolation from death is compounded by the development of "retirement cities" in the United States, where the elderly are, in effect, segregated from the rest of the society. As Robert L. Fulton has so aptly put it,

Here for the first time modern man is able to avoid almost entirely the grief and anguish of death. By encouraging the aged members of the society to congregate in segregated communities, familial and friendship commitments are made fewer by time and distance, and emotional and social bonds are loosened. Physically and emotionally separated from those most likely to die, the modern individual is freed of the shock he would otherwise experience from their death. Herein may lie a form of man's "conquest" of death.[30]

The colonists died mainly in their own homes since there were few hospitals or other institutions in which the aged could be placed. In the absence of a specialized nursing profession, relatives and neighbors attended to the needs of the dying, thus increasing the amount of contact between the living and the dying.

The homes of the early colonists were very small compared to today, especially those built in the early years of settlement. According to the probate inventories, the average number of rooms per house in Suffolk County, Massachusetts, rose from 4.3 in 1675–99 to 5.7 in 1700–1719, and to 6.0 in 1750–75.[31] Thus, there was relatively little privacy available in these homes to shield the dying person from the rest of the family, even if the colonists had desired to isolate him or her.

Finally, since there were no funeral homes in the seventeenth and eighteenth centuries, the dead person remained in his or her own home, where friends and neighbors could view him. As the art of embalming was still in its infancy in colonial America, very little effort was made to preserve or repair the dead body. People were forced to see the dead persons as they were, rather than having them cosmetically preserved or improved to enhance their appearances in death.[32]

The funeral itself encouraged people to come into intimate contact with death. At first, funerals in colonial America were simple affairs,

TABLE 7.1. Should Dying Person Be Removed to a Hospital or Another Institution?

Response	Percentage	N
Yes, this is best for all concerned.	34.1	669
No, death should be at home if at all possible.	28.2	553
Undecided	35.3	692
No answer	2.4	47

Source: Glen M. Vernon, *Sociology of Death; An Analysis of Death-Related Behavior* (New York, 1970), 110.

since there was an effort to avoid the excesses of English funeral practices. One contemporary observer of early colonial funerals described them: "At Burials nothing is read, nor any funeral sermon made, but all the neighborhood or a goodly company of them come together by tolling of the bell, and carry the dead solemnly to his grave, and then stand by him while he is buried. The ministers are most commonly present."[33] Gradually funerals became more elaborate and expensive. The practice of distributing gifts of gloves, rings, or scarves to participants at funerals was a custom brought over from England and which flourished in New England in the late seventeenth and eighteenth centuries. The practice quickly became excessive as the quality of the gifts distributed was supposed to reflect the social status of the deceased. At the funeral of Governor Joseph Belcher's wife in 1736, over one thousand pairs of gloves were distributed. Ministers, who usually received gifts at all the funerals they attended, often accumulated large quantities of such items. Andrew Eliot, for example, minister of the North Church in Boston, received 2,940 pairs of funeral gloves in his thirty-two years in the pulpit. Rather than allow such gifts to overwhelm his household, Reverend Eliot sold them to supplement his modest salary.[34]

As the costs of these funeral items rose, there were numerous attempts by the general court as well as individual citizens to curtail funeral expenses. None of the proposed measures, however, succeeded because our colonial ancestors were just as determined to have extravagant funerals then as we are today.[35]

But these social aspects of funerals provided still greater encouragement for people to attend them. It was expected in the small rural communities of New England that everyone would attend the funerals of any of their townspeople. Given the death rate of that period, it was likely that, in a small village of a thousand inhabitants, there would be at least ten to twenty-five funerals each year. Since most burials were handled by the neighbors and friends rather than by a professional undertaker, the significance of each funeral became even more important to the living. Thus, there was a constant reminder to the entire community of the presence of death, whereas today most of us are not affected by the deaths of anyone except very close friends or relatives.

Finally, the practice of giving funeral sermons became established by the early eighteenth century. Ministers now used the occasion of the gathering at the grave to preach to the living the importance of coming to terms with the inevitability of death. Increasingly these sermons were published and distributed to the congregation as a remembrance of the departed and a reminder of the frailty of life.[36]

The awareness of death by an individual in colonial America did not end with the lowering of the body into the grave. The grave as well as the burial place continued to further the notion of the shortness of life on earth for the survivors. Scholars such as Harriette Forbes, Allan Ludwig, and Dickran and Ann Tashjian have already explored the artistic and symbolic implications of the early gravestones that are dotted throughout the countryside. Rather than simply repeat their interesting analyses of the meaning of these early artifacts, we will try only to reconstruct how these images of death might have influenced the perceptions of our ancestors about the extent of mortality in their communities.[37]

Before 1660, graveyards in New England were quite plain. Often people were buried in convenient locations near their homes rather than being interred in burial grounds near their churches.[38] We can understand this casual attitude toward the burial site if we recall that, in England, the common practice had been to bury many different individuals on the same plot of land. No effort was made to keep a separate spot for each person who died; rather, bodies were buried with the expectation that someone else would share that same area as soon as the previous occupant had decomposed sufficiently. Thus, the Church of St. John the Baptist in Widord, Hertfordshire, buried nearly five thousand people in a plot of less than half an acre in area. Usually these early English burials did not include even placing the deceased in a coffin.[39]

Gradually the burial places became more important to the Puritans as a reminder of the presence of death. As efforts were made to preserve the memory of those who had departed, gravestones were used to identify the bodily remains as well as to provide inspiration for the living. Partly for ornamental reasons but mainly for instructing the living, colonial gravestones began to depict the reality of death.

These symbolic illustrations of death were significant reminders of the frailty of life in a society in which many of its citizens were illiterate and therefore unable to read messages about death from the inscriptions on the gravestones. These grim symbols of death were meant to remind the living that the day of judgment was coming and that all would be called upon to account for their lives.[40]

The symbolic messages of the early New England gravestones were usually simpler and plainer than those on the religious artworks of Europe at that time. The Puritans were very anxious to avoid duplication of symbols that were commonly identified with the Roman Catholic church.[41] The imagery of the early New England gravestones ranged across a wide variety of themes—from emblems of death to symbols of resurrection. Furthermore, there was an evolution in gravestone imagery over time—from the vivid and often harsh depiction of death by the use of death's-heads to the more cheerful and subtle representations of death by winged cherubs and weeping willows in the late eighteenth and early nineteenth centuries.[42]

Probably the single most important factor in reminding early New Englanders of the presence of death was their religion, which placed great emphasis on death and an afterlife for those who had been saved. Ministers frequently preached about death, and the demise of any member of the congregation was seen as an opportunity to remind the living of the proper way of serving God.[43]

Ministers tried to encourage everyone in their congregations to think about the meaning of death. Thus, Cotton Mather, in his work *A Christian Funeral,* advises the survivors that, "when any Person known to me *Dies,* I woud set my self particularly to consider: *What lesson of goodness or Wisdom I may learn from any thing that I may observe in the Life of that Person?*"[44] And, in his *Death Made Easie & Happy,* Mather implores his readers to remind themselves each day that they are to die shortly: "Let us look upon everything as a sort of Death's Head set before us, with a *Memento mortis* written upon it."[45]

Puritan ministers frequently reminded pregnant women of their likelihood of dying during childbirth. This message was often an effective means of getting parishioners to think about their own religious development. Cotton Mather publicized the dangers of childbirth in a broadside elegy on the death of Lydia Minot, who perished trying to deliver her sixth child: "Here lyes the Mother, & the Child, Interr'd in one; Both waiting for the same Bless'd Resurrection. She first to it was Life; Then to't became a Grave, Death in her Womb: To fetch it thence, Death to her gave."[46]

In the early decades of settlement, church leaders were relatively matter-of-fact about the presence and inevitability of death. But, as the children of the original settlers gradually turned away from the church, there was a widespread fear that their "errand in the wilderness" might fail. Ministers now seized upon the terrors of death to persuade their sinful townspeople to return to God's way. Thus, Solomon Stoddard, in his *The Efficacy of the Fear of Hell to Restrain Men from Sin,* wrote, "Many seem to be Incorrigible and Obstinate in their Pride and Luxury and Profaness . . . they are afraid of Poverty, and afraid of Sickness, but not afraid of Hell; that would restrain them from sinful Practices, Destruction from God would be a Terrour to them."[47]

Increasingly these ministers directed their message to young children. From a very early age, Puritan children were admonished to think of their impending doom in hell unless they were saved by God's grace.[48] This message can be seen in an anonymous broadside of that period:

> My Cry's to you, my Children . . .
> Be wise before it be too late.
> Think on your latter end.
> Though you are young and yet you must die,
> and hasten to the Pit.[49]

The idea of an unexpected and sudden death for young children was reinforced through schoolbooks. In the widely used *New England Primer,* children learned their alphabet through rhymed verses such as:

> Xerxes the great did die,
> and so must you & I.[50]

Or they were reminded of the impending doom in longer verses later in their lessons:

> I in the Burying Place may see
>   Graves shorter there than I;
> From Death's Arrest no Age is free,
>   Young Children too may die;
> My God, may such an awful Sight,
>   Awakening be to me!
> Oh! that by early Grace I might
>   For Death prepared be.[51]

People were also encouraged to keep diaries in which they recorded their spiritual progress and failings. New England Puritans were expected to prepare for death throughout their lives. Emphasis was placed on continually thinking about the shortness of one's own life. As Roger Williams put it:

It is further of great and sweet use against the bitterness of Death, and against the bitter-sweet delusions of this world daily to thinke each day our last, the day of our last farewell, the day of the splitting of this vessell, the breaking of this buble, the quenching of this candle, and our passage into the land of Darknesse, never more to behold a sparke of light untill the heavens be no more.[52]

Therefore, it is not surprising that the death of anyone in the community often stimulated these diarists to reflect on their own precarious situation even though the actual conditions of life in that society were much healthier than they imagined.

Perhaps now we are in a better position to account for the misperceptions of early New Englanders of the level of mortality in their society. They came from England, where mortality rates were very high. Their expectations of continued high mortality in the New World were reinforced by the difficulties of the early years of settlement, the uncertainty of life due to the presence of periodic epidemics, and the particularly high mortality of their children. Though their chances of survival in America were actually much better than those of their relatives and friends in the old country, they usually did not realize this fact because of the great emphasis that was placed on death by their religion. The continued reminder of the shortness of their lives whenever anyone died made it difficult for the average person to comprehend the changes in the overall mortality level which had occurred. Furthermore, their incessant preoccupation with death helps to explain why most scholars of colonial history thought that there was such a high death rate in the seventeenth and eighteenth centuries. Since most of these historians relied only on literary evidence, there was no reason for them to suspect that the colonists had incorrectly assessed the living conditions in early New England.

Notes

1. William Bradford, *Of Plymouth Plantation,* ed. Harvey Wish (New York, 1962), 70. For a more detailed discussion of the experiences of the Pilgrims, see George D. Langdon, Jr., *Pilgrim Colony: A History of New Plymouth, 1620–1691* (New Haven, Conn., 1966).

2. On the extent of mortality in Boston, see John B. Blake, *Public Health in the Town of Boston, 1630–1882* (Cambridge, Mass., 1952).

3. Blake, *Public Health,* 74–98; John Duffy, *Epidemics in Colonial America* (Baton Rouge, 1953), 16–112.

4. Duffy, *Epidemics,* 117–18; Ernest Caulfield, "A History of the Terrible Epidemic, Vulgarly Called the Throat Distemper, as It Occurred in His Majesty's New England Colonies between 1735 and 1740," *Yale Journal of Biology and Medicine* 11 (1938–39): 219–72, 277–335.

5. Edward Wigglesworth, "A Table Shewing the Probability of the Duration, the Decrement, and the Expectation of Life, in the States of Massachusetts and New Hampshire, formed from sixty two Bills of Mortality on the files of the American Academy of Arts and Sciences in the Year 1789," *Memoirs of the American Academy of Arts and Sciences,* vol. 2, pt. 1 (1793): 131–35. For an analysis of the gathering of that data as well as its utilization, see Maris A. Vinovskis, "The 1789 Life Table of Edward Wigglesworth," *Journal of Economic History* 31 (1971): 570–90.

6. Warren S. Thompson and P. K. Whelpton, *Population Trends in the United States* (New York, 1933), 228–40. A more recent interpretation of mortality trends by Yasukichi Yasuba argues that death rates probably were increasing just prior to the Civil War because of the increase in urbanization and industrialization. Yasukichi Yasuba, *Birth Rates of the White Population in the United States, 1800–1860: An Economic Study,* Johns Hopkins University Studies in Historical and Political Sciences, vol. 79, no. 2 (Baltimore, 1962), 86–96.

7. Edward G. Stockwell, *Population and People* (Chicago, 1968), 26.

8. Philip Greven, Jr., *Four Generations: Population, Land, and Family in Colonial Andover, Massachusetts* (Ithaca, N.Y., 1970); John Demos, *A Little Commonwealth: Family Life in Plymouth Colony* (New York, 1970); Susan L. Norton, "Population Growth in Colonial America: A Study of Ipswich, Massachusetts," *Population Studies* 25 (1971): 433–52; Kenneth A. Lockridge, "The Population of Dedham, Massachusetts, 1636–1736," *Economic History Review,* 2d ser. 19 (1966): 318–44; Daniel Scott Smith, "The Demographic History of New England," *Journal of Economic History* 32 (1972): 165–83; Maris A. Vinovskis, "American Historical Demography: A Review Essay" *Historical Methods*

Newsletter 4 (1971): 141–48; "Mortality Rates and Trends in Massachusetts before 1860," *Journal of Economic History* 32 (1972): 184–213; "Death and Family Life in the Past," *Human Nature* 1 (1990): 109–22.

These generalizations only apply to the New England area. Mortality rates in the colonial South were considerably higher than in New England, according to some of the recent work in that area. Irene Hecht, "The Virginia Muster of 1624/5 as a Source for Demographic History," *William and Mary Quarterly,* 3d ser., 30 (1973): 65–92; Lorena S. Walsh and Russell R. Menard, "Death in the Chesapeake: Two Life Tables For Men in Early Colonial Maryland," *Maryland Historical Magazine* 69 (1974): 211–27; Darret B. Rutman and Anita H. Rutman, *A Place in Time: Middlesex County, Virginia, 1650–1750* (New York, 1984); Alan Kulikoff, *Tobacco and Slaves: The Development of Southern Cultures in the Chesapeake, 1680–1800* (Chapel Hill, N.C., 1986).

9. Blake, *Public Health,* 247–49.
10. For an analysis of English demographic trends, see E. A. Wrigley and R. S. Schofield, *The Population History of England, 1541–1871: A Reconstruction* (Cambridge, Mass., 1981).
11. Vinovskis, "The 1789 Life Table." Despite the serious problems with the Wigglesworth Life Table, many demographers continue to use it uncritically. See, for example, Richard A. Easterlin, "Population Issues in American Economic History: A Survey and Critique," in *Research in Economic History, Supplement 1 (1977),* ed. Robert E. Gallman (Greenwich, Conn., 1977), 131–58.
12. For an introduction to the use and interpretation of life tables, see Louis I. Dublin, Alfred J. Lotka, and Mortimer Spiegelman, *Length of Life: A Study of the Life Table* (New York, 1949).
13. Demos, *Little Commonwealth,* 192.
14. Demos, *Little Commonwealth,* U.S. Bureau of the Census, *Statistical Abstract of the United States: 1990,* 110 ed. (Washington, D.C., 1990), table 106.
15. Vinovskis, "Mortality Rates."
16. Vinovskis, "Mortality Rates."
17. Vinovskis, "Mortality Rates." The results of this regression analysis have not been published. The use, however, of the 1860 standardized mortality in a regression analysis of fertility differentials in Massachusetts is reported in Maris A. Vinovskis, "A Multivariate Regression Analysis of Fertility Differentials among Massachusetts Towns and Regions in 1860," in *Historical Studies of Changing Fertility,* ed. Charles Tilly (Princeton, N.J., 1978), 225–56.
18. Vinovskis, "Mortality Rates"; Dublin et al., *Length of Life,* 346.
19. U.S. Bureau of the Census, *Statistical Abstract,* table 106.

20. U.S. Bureau of the Census, *Statistical Abstract,* table 106; Vinovskis, "Mortality Rates."

21. Even as late as 1900, most families experienced the death of at least one child or parent during the childbearing years. Peter Uhlenberg, "Changing Configurations of the Life Course," in *Transitions: The Family and the Life Course in Historical Perspective,* ed. Tamara K. Hareven (New York, 1978), 65–97.

22. Various scholars have commented on the preoccupation of early Americans with the issue of death in their writings. See, for example, Lewis O. Saum, "Death in the Popular Mind of Pre-Civil War America," *American Quarterly* 26 (1974): 477–95; and Charles Allen Shively, "A History of the Conception of Death in America, 1650–1860," (Ph.D. diss., Harvard University, 1969).

23. Zepharriah Pease, ed., *The Diary of Samuel Rodman: A New Bedford Chronicle of Thirty-Seven Years: 1821–1859* (New Bedford, Mass., 1927), 180, 218. Puritans often used the occasion of their birthdays or New Year's Day to reflect on their own mortality. Gordon E. Geddes, *Welcome Joy: Death in Puritan New England* (Ann Arbor, Mich., 1981). For examples of concerns about dying early in colonial conversion narratives, see *Connecticut Historical Society Bulletin* 51 (1986): 1–62.

24. Pease, *Diary of Samuel Rodman,* 218.

25. We are deeply indebted to Kathryn Kish Sklar of the State University of New York at Binghamton for allowing us to use her data for these calculations.

26. Geoffrey Gorer, *Death, Grief, and Mourning* (Garden City, N.Y., 1965), 192–99.

27. For analyses of the reactions of Puritans to death, see David E. Stannard, "Death and Dying in Puritan New England," *American Historical Review* 78 (1973): 1305–30; Shively, "History of the Conception of Death."

28. Glen M. Vernon, *Sociology of Death: An Analysis of Death-Related Behavior* (New York, 1970), 110. For a more general discussion of American attitudes toward death, see Richard G. Dumont and Dennis C. Foss, *The American View of Death: Acceptance or Denial?* (Cambridge, Mass., 1972).

29. Jack B. Kamerman, *Death in the Midst of Life: Social and Cultural Influences on Death, Grief, and Mourning* (Englewood Cliffs, N.J., 1988), 40.

30. Robert L. Fulton, "Death and the Self," *Journal of Religion and Health* 3 (1964): 367.

31. David H. Flaherty, *Privacy in Colonial New England* (Charlottesville, Va., 1972), 39.

32. For a description of the development of embalming in America, see Robert W. Habenstein and William M. Lamers, *The History of American Funeral Directing* (Milwaukee, 1955).

33. Thomas Lechford, *Plain Dealing; or, News from New England,* ed. J. Hammond Trumbull (Boston, 1867), 87–88.

34. For a description of the extravagant expenditures on early funerals, see Alice Morse Earle, *Customs and Fashions in Old New England* (New York, 1894).

35. Though Jessica Mitford argues that the excesses in funeral expenditures are only a recent phenomena, there is ample evidence that often the colonists also spent large sums on their funerals. Jessica Mitford, *The American Way of Death* (New York, 1963).

36. On the evolution of Puritan attitudes and practices at funerals, see Geddes, *Welcome Joy;* Shively, "History of the Conception of Death"; Laurel Thatcher Ulrich, "Vertuous Women Found: New England Ministerial Literature, 1668–1735," in *Women in American Religion,* ed. Janet Wilson James (Philadelphia, 1978), 67–87.

37. Harriette Merrifield Forbes, *Gravestones of Early New England and the Men Who Made Them, 1653–1800* (New York, 1927); Allan I. Ludwig, *Graven Images: New England Stonecarving and Its Symbols, 1650–1815* (Middletown, Conn., 1966); Dickran Tashjian and Ann Tashjian, *Memorials for Children of Change: The Art of Early New England Stonecarving* (Middletown, Conn., 1974).

38. On cemeteries in America, see David Charles Sloane, *The Last Great Necessity: Cemeteries in American History* (Baltimore, 1991).

39. Habenstein and Lamers, *History of American Funeral Directing,* 91–191. On burial practices in England, see also Clare Gittings, *Death, Burial and the Individual in Early Modern England* (London, 1984); John Morley, *Death, Heaven and the Victorians* (Pittsburgh, 1971).

40. On the extent of illiteracy in early New England, see Kenneth A. Lockridge, *Literacy in Colonial New England* (New York, 1974); see also chapter 4.

41. Dickran Tashjian, "Puritan Attitudes toward Iconoclasm," *Annual Proceedings of the Dublin Seminar for New England Folklife (1978): Puritan Gravestone Art,* 2:37–45.

42. Ludwig, *Graven Images;* Tashjian, *Memorials for Children.* See also chapter 1 for a discussion of changing interpretations of colonial gravestones.

43. On the importance of religion during this period, see John Higham, "Hanging Together: Divergent Unities in American History," *Journal of American History* 61 (1974): 5–29. For a useful analysis of the role of liberal clergymen in emphasizing death in the mid nineteenth century,

see Ann Douglass, "Heaven Our Home: Consolation Literature in the Northern United States, 1830–1880," *American Quarterly* 26 (1974): 496–515.

44. Cotton Mather, *A Christian Funeral* (Boston, 1713), 27.

45. Cotton Mather, *Death Made Easie & Happy* (London, 1701), 94.

46. Quoted in Geddes, *Welcome Joy,* 54. The actual extent of maternal mortality appears to have been exaggerated by contemporaries. For a discussion of the dangers of early childbirth, see Judith W. Leavitt, *Brought to Bed: Childbearing in America, 1750–1950* (New York, 1986); Catherine M. Scholten, *Childbearing in American Society, 1650–1850* (New York, 1985); Laurel Thatcher Ulrich, " 'The Living Mother of a Living Child': Midwifery and Mortality in Post-Revolutionary New England," *William and Mary Quarterly,* 3d ser., 46 (1989): 27–48.

47. Solomon Stoddard, *The Efficacy of the Fear of Hell to Restrain Men from Sin* (Boston, 1713), 10.

48. The best account of death and young children in early American society is by David E. Stannard, "Death and the Puritan Child," *American Quarterly* 26 (1974): 456–76.

49. Quoted in Shively, "History of the Conception of Death," 52.

50. Paul L. Ford, ed., *The New England Primer* (New York, 1962), 11.

51. Ford, *New England Primer,* 22.

52. Quoted in Geddes, *Welcome Joy,* 66.

Bibliography

Achenbaum, W. Andrew. *Old Age in the New Land: The American Experience since 1790.* Baltimore, 1978.

Albro, John A., ed. *The Works of Thomas Shepard.* 3 vols. New York, 1967.

Alexander, J. K. *Render Them Submissive: Responses to Poverty in Philadelphia, 1760–1800.* Amherst, Mass., 1980.

Allmendinger, David. *Paupers and Scholars: The Transformation of Student Life in Nineteenth-Century New England.* New York, 1975.

Anderson, Fred. *A People's Army: Massachusetts Soldiers and Society in the Seven Years' War.* New York, 1984.

Anderson, James D. *The Education of Blacks in the South, 1860–1935.* Chapel Hill, N.C., 1988.

Anderson, Michael. "The Emergence of the Modern Life Cycle in Britain." *Social History* 10 (1985): 69–87.

Andrews, Charles M. *The Colonial Period of American History.* New Haven, Conn., 1936.

Andrews, William D. "The Printed Funeral Sermons of Cotton Mather." *Early American Literature* 5 (1970): 22–44.

Angus, David, Jeffrey Mirel, and Maris A. Vinovskis. "Historical Development of Age-Stratification in Schooling." *Teacher's College Record* 90 (1988): 211–36.

Anthony, Sylvia. *The Discovery of Death in Childhood and After.* New York, 1972.

Ariès, Phillipe. *Centuries of Childhood: A Social History of Family Life.* Translated by Robert Baldick. New York, 1962.

———. *The Hour of Our Death.* Translated by Helen Weaver. New York, 1981.

———. *Western Attitudes toward Death: From the Middle Ages to the Present.* Translated by Patricia Ranum. Baltimore, 1974.

Ashby, LeRoy. *Saving the Waifs: Reformers and Dependent Children, 1890–1917.* Philadelphia, 1984.

Ashton, Robert, ed. *The Works of John Robinson.* 3 vols. London, 1851.

Austin, J. M. *A Voice to Youth Addressed to Young Men and Young Women.* New York, 1854.

Auwers, Linda. "History from the Mean—Up, Down, and Around: A Review Essay." *Historical Methods* 12 (1979): 39–45.

———. "Reading the Marks of the Past: Exploring Female Literacy in Colonial Windsor, Connecticut." *Historical Methods* 4 (1980): 204–14.

Axtell, James. *The School upon a Hill: Education and Society in Colonial New England.* New Haven, Conn., 1974.

Bailyn, Bernard. *Education in the Forming of American Society: Needs and Opportunities for Study.* Chapel Hill, N.C., 1960.

———. *The New England Merchants in the Seventeenth Century.* Cambridge, Mass., 1955.

Baker, Faye Joanne. "Toward Memory and Mourning: A Study of Changing Attitudes toward Death between 1750 and 1850 as Revealed by Gravestones of the New Hampshire Merrimack River Valley Mourning Pictures, and Representative Writings." Ph.D. diss., George Washington University, 1977.

Bates, Alan C., ed. *Records of the Congregational Church in Canterbury, Connecticut, 1711–1844.* Hartford, Conn., 1932.

Beales, Ross W., Jr. "Cares for the Rising Generation: Youth and Religion in Colonial New England." Ph.D. diss., University of California, Davis, 1971.

———. "The Half-Way Covenant and Religious Scrupulosity: The First Church of Dorchester, Massachusetts, as a Test Case." *William and Mary Quarterly,* 3d ser., 31 (1974): 465–80.

———. "In Search of the Historical Child: Miniature Adulthood and Youth in Colonial New England." *American Quarterly* 27 (1975): 379–98.

———. "Studying Literacy at the Community Level: A Research Note." *Journal of Interdisciplinary History* 9 (1978): 93–102.

Beier, A. L. *Masterless Men: The Vagrancy Problem in England.* London, 1985.

Belcher, Joseph. *Duty of Parents, and Early Seeking of Christ.* Boston, 1710.

Benes, Peter. *The Masks of Orthodoxy: Folk Gravestone Carving in Plymouth County, Massachusetts, 1689–1805.* Amherst, Mass., 1977.

Bercovitch, Sacvan. *The Puritan Origins of the American Self.* New Haven, Conn., 1975.

Berger, Peter L., and Thomas Luckmann. *The Social Construction of Reality: A Treatise in the Sociology of Knowledge.* New York, 1966.

Bissell, Linda Auwers. "From One Generation to Another: Mobility in Seventeenth-Century Windsor, Connecticut." *William and Mary Quarterly,* 3d ser., 31 (1974): 79–110.

Blake, John B. *Public Health in the Town of Boston, 1630–1882.* Cambridge, Mass., 1952.

Boase, T. S. R. *Death in the Middle Ages: Mortality, Judgment, and Remembrance.* New York, 1972.

Bonomi, Patricia U. *Under the Cope of Heaven: Religion, Society, and Politics in Colonial America.* New York, 1986.

Bonomi, Patricia U., and Peter R. Reisenstadt. "Church Adherence in the Eighteenth-Century British American Colonies." *William and Mary Quarterly,* 3d ser., 39 (1982): 245–86.

Bossy, John. "Blood and Baptism: Kinship, Community, and Christianity in Western Europe from the Fourteenth to the Seventeenth Centuries." *Studies in Church History* 10 (1973): 130–31.

Bowlby, John. *Loss: Sadness and Depression.* New York, 1980.

Boyer, Paul. *Urban Masses and Moral Order in America, 1820–1920.* Cambridge, Mass., 1978.

Boyer, Paul, and Stephen Nissenbaum. *Salem Possessed: The Social Origins of Witchcraft.* Cambridge, Mass., 1974.

Boylan, Anne M. *Sunday School: The Formation of an American Institution, 1790–1880.* New Haven, Conn., 1988.

Bozeman, Theodore Dwight. *To Live Ancient Lives: The Primitivist Dimension in Puritanism.* Chapel Hill, N.C., 1988.

Brace, Charles Loring. *The Dangerous Classes of New York and Twenty Years' Work among Them.* New York, 1872.

Bradford, William. *Of Plymouth Plantation.* Edited by Harvey Wish. New York, 1962.

Breen, T. H. *Puritans and Adventurers: Change and Persistence in Early America.* New York, 1980.

Bremner, Robert H., John Barnard, Tamara K. Hareven, and Robert M. Mennel, eds. *Children and Youth in America: A Documentary History.* 2 vols. Cambridge, Mass., 1971.

Brenzel, Barbara M. *Daughters of the State: A Social Portrait of the First Reform School for Girls in North America, 1856–1905.* Cambridge, Mass., 1983.

Brigden, S. "Youth and the English Reformation." *Past and Present* 95 (1982): 37–67.

Brigham, Amariah. *Remarks on the Influence of Mental Cultivation and Mental Excitement upon Health.* 2d ed. Boston, 1833.

Brooke, John. "The Earth and the Water: Human Geography, Ritual Practice, and Personal Life Cycle in Orthodox and Dissenting Communities on the Near Frontier." Paper presented at the 41st Conference in Early American History, Millersville, Pa., May 1981.

Bulkeley, Peter. *The Gospel-Covenant; or, the Covenant of Grace Opened.* 2d ed. London, 1651.

Bumsted, J. M. "Religion, Finance, and Democracy in Massachusetts: The Town of Norton as a Case Study." *Journal of American History* 57 (1971): 817–31.

Bumsted, J. M., and John E. Van de Wetering. *What Must I Do To Be Saved? The Great Awakening in Colonial America.* Hinsdale, Ill., 1976.

Butler, Jon. *Awash in a Sea of Faith: Christianizing the American People.* Cambridge, Mass., 1990.

————. "Enthusiasm Described and Decried: The Great Awakening as Interpretative Fiction." *Journal of American History* 69 (1982): 302–25.

————. "Magic, Astrology, and the Early American Religious Heritage, 1600–1760." *American Historical Review* 84 (1979): 317–46.

————. "The People's Faith, in Europe and America: Four Centuries in Review." *Journal of Social History* 12 (1978): 159–67.

Calder, Isabel MacBeath. *The New Haven Colony.* New Haven, Conn., 1934.

————, ed. *Letters of John Davenport: Puritan Divine.* New Haven, Conn., 1937.

Caldwell, Patricia. *The Puritan Conversion Narrative: The Beginnings of American Expression.* New York, 1983.

Calhoun, Arthur W. *A Social History of the American Family from Colonial Times to the Present.* 3 vols. Cleveland, Ohio, 1917–19.

Calhoun, Daniel H. *Professional Lives in America: Structure and Aspiration, 1750–1850.* Cambridge, Mass., 1965.

Carr, Lois Green, Philip D. Morgan, and Jean B. Russo. *Colonial Chesapeake Society.* Chapel Hill, N.C., 1988.

Carr, Lois Green, and Lorena S. Walsh. "The Planter's Wife: The Experience of White Women in Seventeenth-Century Maryland." In *The American Family in Social-Historical Perspective,* edited by Michael Gordon, 321–46. 3d ed. New York, 1983.

Caulfield, Ernest. "A History of the Terrible Epidemic, Vulgarly Called the Throat Distemper, as It Occurred in His Majesty's New England Colonies between 1735 and 1740." *Yale Journal of Biology and Medicine* 11 (1938–39): 219–72, 277–335.

Chauncy, Charles. *Early Piety Recommended and Exemplified.* Boston, 1732.

Christian, William A. *Person and God in a Spanish Valley.* New York, 1972.

Chudacoff, Howard P. *How Old Are You? Age Consciousness in American Culture.* Princeton, N.J., 1989.

Clark, Charles E. *The Eastern Frontier: The Settlement of Northern New England, 1610–1763.* New York, 1970.

Cohen, Charles Lloyd. *God's Caress: The Psychology of Puritan Religious Experience.* New York, 1986.

Collinson, Patrick. *The Elizabethan Puritan Movement.* Berkeley, 1967.

————. *The Religion of Protestants: The Church in English Society, 1559–1625.* Oxford, Eng., 1982.

Colman, Benjamin. *A Discourse of Seeking God Early.* Boston, 1713.

————. *The Duty and Honour of Aged Women, Deliver'd . . . after the Funeral of the Excellent Mrs. Abigail Foster.* Boston, 1711.

————. *The Warnings of God unto Young People.* Boston, 1716.

Comb, Diana Williams. *Early Gravestone Art in Georgia and South Carolina.* Athens, Ga., 1986.

Cooper, William. *How and Why Young People Should Cleanse Their Way, in Two Sermons.* Boston, 1716.

————. *Serious Exhortations Addressed to Young Men: A Sermon Preached May 14, 1732.* Boston, 1732.

————. *The Service of God Recommended to the Choice of Young People.* Boston, 1726.

Cott, Nancy F. *The Bonds of Womanhood: "Woman's Sphere" in New England, 1780–1865.* New Haven, Conn., 1977.

Cowing, Cedric. "Sex and Preaching in the Great Awakening." *American Quarterly* 20 (1968): 624–44

Cremin, Lawrence A. *American Education: The Colonial Experience, 1607–1783.* New York, 1970.

Cressy, David. *Literacy and the Social Order: Reading and Writing in Tudor and Stuart England.* New York, 1980.

Daniels, Bruce C. *The Connecticut Town: Growth and Development, 1635–1790.* Middletown, Conn., 1979.

Davis, Natalie Zemon. "Ghosts, Kin, and Progeny: Some Features of Family Life in Early Modern France." *Daedalus* 106 (1977): 87–114.

Dawson, George E. "A Study in Youthful Degeneracy." *Pedagogical Seminary* 4 (1896): 224–56.

Degler, Carl N. *At Odds: Women and the Family in America from the Revolution to the Present.* New York, 1980.

————. *In Search of Human Nature: The Decline and Revival of Darwinism in American Social Thought.* New York, 1991.

Demos, John. "The American Family in Past Time." *American Scholar* 43 (1974): 422–46.

————. *A Little Commonwealth: Family Life in Plymouth Colony.* New York, 1970.

————. "Old Age in Early New England." In *Turning Points: Historical and Sociological Essays on the Family,* edited by John Demos and Sarane Spence Boocock, S248–S287. Chicago, 1978.

————. *Past, Present, and Personal: The Family and the Life Course in American History.* New York, 1986.

Demos, John, and Virginia Demos. "Adolescence in Historical Perspective."
  Journal of Marriage and the Family 31 (1969): 632–38.

Dethlefsen, Edwin S., and James Deetz. "Death's Heads, Cherubs, and Willow Trees: Experimental Archaeology in Colonial Cemeteries." *American Antiquity* 31 (1966): 502–10.

Dexter, Franklin Bowditch, comp. *Historical Catalogue of the Members of the First Church of Christ in New Haven, Connecticut (Center Church) A.D., 1639–1914* New Haven, Conn., 1914.

Douglas, Ann. *The Feminization of American Culture.* New York, 1977.

————. "Heaven Our Home: Consolation Literature in the Northern United States, 1830–1880." *American Quarterly* 26 (1974): 496–515.

Dublin, Louis I., Alfred J. Lotka, and Mortimer Spiegelman. *Length of Life: A Study of the Life Table.* New York, 1949.

Duffy, John. *Epidemics in Colonial America.* Baton Rouge, La., 1953.

Dugdale, Richard L. *"The Jukes": A Study in Crime, Pauperism, Disease and Heredity.* New York, 1877.

Dumont, Richard G., and Dennis C. Foss. *The American View of Death: Acceptance or Denial?* Cambridge, Mass., 1972.

Dunn, Mary Maples. "Saints and Sisters: Congregational and Quaker Women in the Early Colonial Period." In *Women in American Religion,* edited by Janet Wilson James, 27–46. Philadelphia, 1980.

Earle, Alice Morse. *Child Life in Colonial Days.* New York, 1899.

————. *Customs and Fashions in Old New England.* New York, 1894.

————. *Home Life in Colonial Days.* New York, 1898.

Earle, Carville V. "Environment, Disease, and Mortality in Early Virginia." In *The Chesapeake in the Seventeenth Century: Essays on Anglo-American Society,* edited by Thad W. Tate and David L. Ammerman, 96–125. Chapel Hill, N.C., 1979.

Easterlin, Richard A. "Population Issues in American Economic History: A Survey and Critique." In *Research in Economic History, Supplement 1 (1977),* edited by Robert E. Gallman, 131–58. Greenwich, Conn., 1977.

Eisenstadt, S. N. *From Generation to Generation.* New York, 1956.

Ekrich, A. Roger. *Bound for America: The Transportation of British Convicts to the Colonies, 1718–1775.* Oxford, 1987.

Elder, Glen H., Jr. "Family History and the Life Course." In *Transitions: The Family and the Life Course in Historical Perspective,* edited by Tamara K. Hareven, 17–64. New York, 1978.

Elliott, Emory. *Power and the Pulpit in Puritan New England.* Princeton, N.J., 1975.

Ellis, John Harvard, ed. *Works of Anne Bradstreet in Prose and Verse.* Charlestown, Mass., 1867.

Elton, G. R. "Introduction: Crime and the Historian." In *Crime in England, 1550–1800*, edited by J. S. Cockburn. London, 1977.

Evans, Charles. *American Bibliography: A Chronological Dictionary of All Books, Pamphlets, and Periodical Publications in the U.S.A., 1639–1820.* New York, 1941.

Fales, Martha F. "The Early American Way of Death." *Essex Institute Historical Collections* 100 (1964): 75–84.

Farrell, James J. *Inventing the American Way of Death, 1830–1920.* Philadelphia, 1980.

Federal Writers Project. *History of Milford, Connecticut, 1639–1939.* Bridgeport, Conn., 1939.

Ferris, David. *Memoirs of the Life of David Ferris, an Approved Minister of the Society of Friends . . . Written by Himself.* 1825. Reprint. Philadelphia, 1855.

Fiering, Norman. *Jonathan Edwards's Thought and its British Context.* Chapel Hill, N.C., 1981.

Fischer, David Hackett. *Growing Old in America.* Expanded ed. New York, 1978.

Flaherty, David H. *Privacy in Colonial New England.* Charlottesville, Va., 1972.

Fleming, Stanford. *Children and Puritanism: The Place of Children in the Life and Thought of the New England Churches, 1620–1847.* New Haven, Conn., 1933.

Fletcher, Anthony, and John Stevenson. *Order and Disorder in Early Modern England.* Cambridge, 1985.

Fliegelman, Jay. *Prodigals and Pilgrims: The American Revolution against Patriarchal Authority, 1750–1800.* Cambridge, 1982.

Forbes, Harriette Merrifield. *Gravestones of Early New England and the Men Who Made Them, 1653–1800.* Boston, 1927.

Forbes, Susan S. "Quaker Tribalism." In *Friends and Neighbors: Group Life in America's First Plural Society,* edited by Michael Zuckerman, 145–73. Philadelphia, 1982.

Ford, Paul L., ed. *The New England Primer.* New York, 1962.

Foxcroft, Thomas. *Clearing Our Way in Youth.* Boston, 1719.

Frankel, Gusti Wiesenfeld. "Between Parent and Child in Colonial New England: An Analysis of the Religious Child-oriented Literature and Selected Children's Work." Ph.D. diss., University of Minnesota, 1976.

Freedman, Estelle B. *Their Sisters' Keepers: Women's Prison Reform in America, 1830–1930.* Ann Arbor, Mich., 1981.

French, Stanley. "The Cemetery as Cultural Institution: The Establishment of Mount Auburn and the 'Rural Cemetery' Movement." In *Death in America,* edited by David E. Stannard, 69–91. Philadelphia, 1975.

Friedman, Lawrence M., and Robert V. Percival. *The Roots of Justice: Crime and Punishment in Alameda County, California, 1870–1910.* Chapel Hill, N.C., 1981.

Frost, J. William. *The Quaker Family in Colonial America: A Portrait of the Society of Friends.* New York, 1973.

Fuller, Wayne E. *The Old Country School.* Chicago, 1982.

Fulton, Robert L. "Death and the Self." *Journal of Religion and Health* 3 (1964): 359–68.

Furman, Erna. *A Child's Parent Dies: Studies in Childhood Bereavement.* New Haven, 1974.

Furman, Robert A. "The Child's Reaction to Death in the Family." In *Loss and Grief: Psychological Management in Medical Practice,* edited by Bernard Schoenberg et al., 70–86. New York, 1970.

Galenson, David. *White Servitude in Colonial America: An Economic Analysis.* Cambridge, 1981.

Gawalt, Gerald W. *The Promise of Power: The Emergence of the Legal Profession in Massachusetts, 1760–1840.* Westport, Conn., 1979.

Geddes, Gordon E. *Welcome Joy: Death in Puritan New England, 1630–1730.* Ann Arbor, Mich., 1981.

George, Charles H., and Katherine George. *The Protestant Mind of the English Reformation, 1570–1640.* Princeton, N.J., 1961.

Gibney, Harriet H. "What Death Means to Children." *Parents Magazine and Better Homemaking* 40 (March 1965): 64–65, 136–42.

Gilmore, William J. "Elementary Literacy on the Eve of the Industrial Revolution: Trends in Rural New England, 1760–1830." *Proceedings of the American Antiquarian Society* 92, pt. 1 (1982): 87–177.

———. *Reading Becomes a Necessity of Life.* Knoxville, Tenn., 1989.

Gittings, Clare. *Death, Burial and the Individual in Early Modern England.* London, 1984.

Glenn, Charles L., Jr. *The Myth of the Common School.* Amherst, Mass., 1988.

Goen, C. C. *Revivalism and Separatism in New England, 1740–1800.* New Haven, Conn., 1962.

Gollin, Gillian L. *Moravians in Two Worlds: A Study of Changing Communities.* New York, 1967.

Goffman, Erving. *The Presentation of Self in Everyday Life.* Edinburgh, 1956.

Goodfriend, Joyce D. "The Social Dimensions of Congregational Life in New York City." *William and Mary Quarterly,* 3d ser., 46 (1989): 252–78.

Gorer, Geoffrey. *Death, Grief, and Mourning.* Garden City, N.Y., 1965.

Gouge, William. *Of Domesticall Duties.* London, 1622.

Graff, Harvey J., ed. *Growing Up in America: Historical Experiences.* Detroit, 1987.

Gragg, Larry. *A Quest for Security: The Life of Samuel Parris, 1653–1720.* Westport, Conn., 1990.

Grant, Leonard T. "Puritan Catechizing." *Journal of Presbyterian History* 46 (1968): 107–27.

Greene, Jack P. "Autonomy and Stability: New England and the British Colonial Experience in Early Modern America." *Journal of Social History* 7 (1974): 171–93.

———, ed. *Settlements to Society, 1607–1763: A Documentary History of Colonial America.* New York, 1975.

Greven, Philip J., Jr. *Four Generations: Population, Land, and Family in Colonial Andover, Massachusetts.* Ithaca, N.Y., 1970.

———. *The Protestant Temperament: Patterns of Child-Rearing, Religious Experience, and the Self in Early America.* New York, 1977.

———. *Spare the Child: The Religious Roots of Punishment and the Psychological Impact of Physical Abuse.* New York, 1991.

———. "Youth, Maturity, and Religious Conversion: A Note on the Ages of Converts in Andover, Massachusetts, 1711–1749." *Essex Institute Historical Collections* 108 (1972): 119–34.

Grossbart, Stephen R. "Seeking the Divine Favor: Conversion and Church Admission in Eastern Connecticut, 1711–1832." *William and Mary Quarterly,* 3d ser., 46 (1989): 696–740.

Grubb, Farley. "Colonial Immigrant Literacy: An Economic Analysis of Pennsylvania-German Evidence." *Explorations in Economic History* 24 (1987): 63–76.

———. "Growth of Literacy in Colonial America: Longitudinal Patterns, Economic Models, and the Direction of Future Research." *Social Science History* 14 (1990): 451–82.

Habenstein, Robert W., and William M. Lamers. *The History of American Funeral Directing.* Rev. ed. Milwaukee, 1962.

Haber, Carole R. *Beyond Sixty-Five: The Dilemma of Old Age in America's Past.* New York, 1983.

Hall, Brooks B., and Gerald F. Moran. "A Preliminary Time Series Analysis of Church Activity in Colonial Woodbury, Connecticut." *Journal of the Scientific Study of Religion* 28 (1989): 478–92.

Hall, David D. *The Faithful Shepherd: A History of the New England Ministry in the Seventeenth Century.* Chapel Hill, N.C., 1972.

———. "The Gravestone Image as a Puritan Cultural Code." *Annual Proceedings of the Dublin Seminar for New England Folklife (1976): Puritan Gravestone Art,* 1:23–32.

———. "On Common Ground: The Coherence of American Puritan Studies." *William and Mary Quarterly,* 3d ser., 44 (1987): 193–229.

———. "Toward a History of Popular Religion in Early New England." *William and Mary Quarterly,* 3d. ser., 41 (1984): 49–55.

————. *Worlds of Wonder, Days of Judgment: Popular Religious Belief in Early New England*. New York, 1989.

————, ed. *The Antinomian Controversy, 1636–1638: A Document History*. Middletown, Conn., 1968.

Hall, G. Stanley. *Adolescence: Its Psychology and Its Relations to Psychology, Anthropology, Sociology, Sex, Crime, Religion, and Education*. 2 vols. New York, 1904.

Hall, Michael G., ed. "The Autobiography of Increase Mather." American Antiquarian Society *Proceedings* 71 (1961): 271–360.

Hambrick-Stowe, Charles E. *The Practice of Piety: Puritan Devotional Disciplines in Seventeenth-Century New England*. Chapel Hill, N.C., 1982.

Hanawalt, Barbara A. *The Ties That Bound: Peasant Families in Medieval England*. New York, 1986.

Handlin, Oscar. "The Significance of the Seventeenth Century." In *Seventeenth-Century America: Essays in Colonial History*, edited by James Morton Smith, 3–12. Chapel Hill, N.C., 1959.

Handlin, Oscar, and Mary Flug Handlin. *Facing Life: Youth and the Family in American History*. Boston, 1971.

Hareven, Tamara K. "Cycles, Courses and Cohorts: Reflections on Theoretical and Methodological Approaches to the Historical Study of Family Development." *Journal of Social History* 12 (1978): 97–109.

————. "Family Time and Historical Time." *Daedalus* 106 (1977): 57–70.

————. "The History of the Family and the Complexity of Social Change." *American Historical Review* 96 (1991): 95–124.

————. "The History of the Family as an Interdisciplinary Field." *Journal of Interdisciplinary History* 2 (1971): 412–13.

Harris, P. M. G. "The Social Origins of American Leaders: The Demographic Foundations." *Perspectives in American History* 3 (1969): 159–344.

Hart, N. C. *Documents Relative to the House of Refuge Instituted by the Society for the Reformation of Juvenile Delinquents in the City of New York in 1824*. New York, 1832.

Hawes, Joseph M. *Children in Urban Society: Juvenile Delinquency in Nineteenth-Century America*. New York, 1971.

Hawes, Joseph M., and N. Ray Hiner, eds. *American Childhood: A Research Guide and Historical Handbook*. Westport, Conn., 1985.

Hecht, Irene. "The Virginia Muster of 1624–25 as a Source for Demographic History." *William and Mary Quarterly*, 3d ser., 30 (1973): 65–92.

Henretta, James A. "Families and Farms: *Mentalité* in Pre-Industrial America." *William and Mary Quarterly*, 3d ser., 35 (1978): 3–32.

————. "The Morphology of New England Society in the Colonial Period." *Journal of Interdisciplinary History* 1 (1971): 379–98.

Heyrman, Christine Leigh. *Commerce and Culture: The Maritime Communities of Colonial Massachusetts, 1690–1750.* New York, 1984.

Higham, John. "Hanging Together: Divergent Unities in American History." *Journal of American History* 61 (1974): 5–29.

Hill, Christopher. *Society and Puritanism in Pre-Revolutionary England.* New York, 1964.

Hill, Don Gleason, ed. *The Record of Baptisms, Marriages and Deaths, and Admissions to the Church . . . in the Town of Dedham, Massachusetts: 1638–1845.* Dedham, Mass., 1888.

Hindus, Michael S. *Prison and Plantation: Crime, Justice, and Authority in Massachusetts and South Carolina, 1767–1878.* Chapel Hill, N.C., 1980.

Hiner, N. Ray. "Adolescence in Eighteenth-Century America." *History of Childood Quarterly* 3 (1975): 253–80.

Hoadley, Charles J., ed. *Records of the Colony or Jurisdiction of New Haven, from May, 1658, to the Union.* Hartford, Conn., 1858.

Hobson, Barbara M. *Uneasy Virtue: The Politics of Prostitution and the American Reform Tradition.* New York, 1987.

Hoffer, Peter C., and N. E. H. Hull. *Murdering Mothers: Infanticide in England and New England, 1558–1803.* New York, 1981.

Hogan, David J. *Class and Reform: School and Society in Chicago, 1880–1930.* Philadelphia, 1985.

Holifield, E. Brooks. *The Covenant Sealed: The Development of Puritan Sacramental Theology in Old and New England, 1570–1720.* New Haven, Conn., 1974.

Holloran, Peter C. *Boston's Wayward Children: Social Services for Homeless Children, 1830–1930.* Rutherford, N.J., 1989.

Hooker, Thomas. *The Application of Redemption by the Effectual Work of the Word and Spirit of Christ.* London, 1656.

———. *The Soules Implantation.* London, 1637.

———. *The Unbeleevers Preparing for Christ.* London, 1638.

Huizinga, Johan. *The Waning of the Middle Ages.* New York, 1964.

Humphrey, H. *Domestic Education.* Amherst, Mass., 1840.

Jedrey, Christopher M. *The World of John Cleaveland: Family and Community in Eighteenth-Century New England.* New York, 1979.

Jones, Alice Hanson. *American Colonial Wealth: Documents and Methods.* 2d ed. New York, 1977.

———. *Wealth of a Nation to Be: The American Colonies on the Eve of the Revolution.* New York, 1980.

Jones, James W. *The Shattered Synthesis: New England Puritanism before the Great Awakening.* New Haven, Conn., 1973.

Juster, Sue. "In a Different Voice: Male and Female Narratives of Religious

Conversion in Post-Revolutionary America." *American Quarterly* 41 (1989): 34–62.

Juster, Sue, and Maris A. Vinovskis. "Adolescence in Nineteenth-Century America." In *Encyclopedia of Adolescence,* edited by Richard M. Lerner, Anne C. Petersen, and Jeanne Brooks-Gunn, 2:698–707. New York, 1991.

Kaestle, Carl F. *The Evolution of an Urban School System: New York City, 1750–1850.* Cambridge, Mass., 1973.

———. *Pillars of the Republic: Common Schools and American Society, 1780–1860.* New York, 1983.

Kaestle, Carl F., and Maris A. Vinovskis. *Education and Social Change in Nineteenth-Century Massachusetts.* New York, 1980.

———. "From Apron Strings to ABCs: Parents, Children, and Schooling in Nineteenth-Century Massachusetts." In *Turning Points: Historical and Sociological Essays on the Family,* edited by John Demos and Sarane Spence Boocock, S539–S580. Chicago, 1978.

Kamerman, Jack B. *Death in the Midst of Life: Social and Cultural Influences on Death, Grief, and Mourning.* Englewood Cliffs, N.J., 1988.

Karlsen, Carol F. *The Devil in the Shape of a Woman: Witchcraft in Colonial New England.* New York, 1987.

Katz, Michael B. *In the Shadow of the Poorhouse: A Social History of Welfare in America.* New York, 1986.

Kett, Joseph F. "Curing the Disease of Precocity." In *Turning Points: Historical and Sociological Essays on the Family,* edited by John Demos and Sarane Spence Boocock, S183–S211. Chicago, 1978.

———. *The Formation of the American Medical Profession.* New Haven, Conn., 1968.

———. *Rites of Passage: Adolescence in America, 1790 to the Present.* New York, 1977.

Keyssar, Alexander. "Widowhood in Eighteenth-Century Massachusetts: A Problem in the History of the Family." *Perspectives in American History* 8 (1974): 83–119.

Kobrin, David. "The Expansion of the Visible Church in New England: 1629–1650." *Church History* 36 (1967): 189–209.

Kübler-Ross, Elisabeth. *On Death and Dying.* New York, 1969.

Kuhn, Anne L. *The Mother's Role in Childhood Education.* New Haven, Conn., 1947.

Kulikoff, Allan. *Tobacco and Slaves: The Development of Southern Cultures in the Chesapeake, 1680–1800.* Chapel Hill, N.C., 1986.

Lane, Roger. *Violent Death in the City: Suicide, Accident and Murder in Nineteeth-Century Philadelphia.* Cambridge, Mass., 1979.

Langdon, George D., Jr. *Pilgrim Colony: A History of New Plymouth, 1620–1691.* New Haven, Conn., 1966.

Langsam, Miriam Z. *Children West: A History of the Placing-out System of the New York Children's Aid Society, 1853–1890.* Madison, Wis., 1964.

Leach, Douglas E. *Flintlock and Tomahawk: New England in King Philip's War.* New York, 1958.

Leavitt, Judith W. *Brought to Bed: Childbearing in America, 1750–1950.* New York, 1986.

Lechford, Thomas. *Plain Dealing; or, News from New England.* Edited by J. Hammond Trumbull. Boston, 1867.

Levin, David. *Cotton Mather: The Young Life of the Lord's Remembrancer, 1663–1703.* Cambridge, Mass., 1978.

Levy, Barry. *Quakers and the American Family: British Settlement in the Delaware Valley.* New York, 1988.

Lewis, Jan. *The Pursuit of Happiness: Family and Values in Jefferson's Virginia.* New York, 1983.

Linden-Ward, Blanche. *Silent City on a Hill: Landscapes of Memory and Boston's Mount Auburn Cemetery.* Columbus, Ohio, 1989.

Link, William A. *A Hard Country and a Lonely Place: Schooling, Society, and Reform in Rural Virginia, 1870–1920.* Chapel Hill, N.C., 1986.

Locke, John. *Some Thoughts concerning Education.* Edited by F. W. Garforth. Abr. ed. Woodbury, N.Y., 1964.

Lockridge, Kenneth A. *The Diary, and Life, of William Byrd II, 1674–1744.* Chapel Hill, N.C., 1987.

———. "The History of a Puritan Church, 1637–1736." *New England Quarterly* 40 (Winter 1967): 399–424.

———. *Literacy in Colonial New England: An Inquiry into the Social Context of Literacy in the Early Modern West.* New York, 1974.

———. "Literacy in Early America, 1650–1800." In *Literacy and Social Development in the West: A Reader,* edited by Harvey J. Graff, 183–200. New York, 1981.

———. *A New England Town, The First Hundred Years: Dedham, Massachusetts, 1636–1736.* New York, 1970.

———. "The Population of Dedham, Massachusetts, 1636–1736." *Economic History Review,* 2d ser., 19 (1966): 318–44.

Lovelace, Richard F. *The American Pietism of Cotton Mather: Origins of American Evangelicalism.* Grand Rapids, Mich., 1979.

Lucas, Paul R. *Valley of Discord: Church and Society along the Connecticut River, 1636–1725.* Hanover, N.H., 1976.

Ludwig, Allan I. *Graven Images: New England Stonecarving and Its Symbols, 1650–1815.* Middletown, Conn., 1966.

Ludwig, Allan I., and David D. Hall. "Aspects of Music, Poetry, Stonecarving, and Death in Early New England." *Annual Proceedings of the Dublin Seminar for New England Folklife (1978): Puritan Gravestone Art*, 2:18–24. Boston, 1979.

MacDonald, Arthur. *A Plan for the Study of Man*. Washington, D.C., 1902.

Macfarlane, Alan. *The Family Life of Ralph Josselin: A Seventeenth-Century Clergyman*. Cambridge, Eng., 1970.

Main, Gloria L. "An Inquiry into When and Why Women Learned to Write in Colonial New England." *Journal of Social History* 24 (1991): 579–89.

Malinowski, Bronislaw. *Magic, Science and Religion, and Other Essays*. Garden City, N.Y., 1948.

Malmsheimer, Linda M. "New England Funeral Sermons and Changing Attitudes toward Women, 1672–1792." Ph.D. diss., University of Minnesota, 1973.

Manning, M. L. "Three Myths concerning Adolescence." *Adolescence* 18 (1983): 823–29.

Masson, Margaret W. "The Typology of the Female as a Model for the Regenerate: Puritan Preaching, 1690–1730." *Signs: Journal of Women in Culture and Society* 2 (1976): 304–15.

Mather, Cotton. *A Christian Funeral*. Boston, 1713.

———. *Death Made Easie & Happy*. London, 1701.

———. *Early Piety Urged*. Boston, 1694.

———. *A Glorious Espousal: A Brief Essay to Illustrate and Prosecute the Marriage, Wherein Our Great Savior Offers to Espouse unto Himself the Children of Men*. Boston, 1719.

———. *Magnalia Christi Americana*. Hartford, Conn., 1820.

———. *Ornaments for the Daughters of Zion; or, the Character and Happiness of a Vertuous Woman*. Cambridge, Mass., 1692.

———. *The Pure Nazarite*. Boston, 1723.

Mather, Increase. *A Call from Heaven*. Boston, 1679.

———. *The First Principles of New England concerning the Subject of Baptisme and Communion of Churches*. Cambridge, Mass., 1675.

———. *A Sermon Occasioned by the Execution of a Man Found Guilty of Murder . . . Especially to Young Men. To be Aware of Those Sins Which Brought Him to His Miserable End*. Boston, 1686.

Mathews, Donald G. *Religion in the Old South*. Chicago, 1977.

———. "The Second Great Awakening as an Organizing Process, 1780–1830: An Hypothesis." *American Quarterly* 21 (1969): 23–43.

Matter, R. M. "The Historical Emergence of Adolescence: Perspectives from Developmental Psychology and Adolescent Literature." *Adolescence* 19 (1984): 131–42.

May, Dean, and Maris A. Vinovskis. "A Ray of Millennial Light: Early Education and Social Reform in the Infant School Movement in Massachusetts, 1826–1840." In *Family and Kin in Urban Communities, 1700–1930*, edited by Tamara K. Hareven, 62–99. New York, 1977.

Mayer, Lance R. "An Alternative to Panofskyism: New England Grave Stones and the European Folk Art Tradition." *Annual Proceedings of the Dublin Seminar for New England Folklife (1978): Puritan Gravestone Art*, 2:5–17. Boston, 1979.

McCusker, John J., and Russell R. Menard. *The Economy of British America, 1607–1789*. Chapel Hill, N.C., 1985.

McGiffert, Michael. "American Puritan Studies in the 1960s." *William and Mary Quarterly*, 3d ser., 27 (1970): 36–67.

McManis, Douglas R. *Colonial New England: A Historical Geography*. New York, 1975.

Mennel, Robert M. *Thorns and Thistles: Juvenile Delinquents in the United States, 1825–1940*. Hanover, N.H., 1973.

Middlekauff, Robert. *The Mathers: Three Generations of Puritan Intellectuals, 1596–1728*. New York, 1971.

Miller, Jill Barbara Menes. "Reactions to the Death of a Parent: A Review of the Psychoanalytic Literature." *Journal of the American Psychoanalytic Association* 19 (1971): 697–719.

Minkema, Kenneth P., ed. "The East Windsor Conversion Relations, 1700–1724." Connecticut Historical Society, *Bulletin* 51 (1986): 25–50.

Mitford, Jessica. *The American Way of Death*. New York, 1963.

Modell, John, and Madeline Goodman. "Historical Perspectives." In *At the Threshold: The Developing Adolescent*, edited by S. Shirley Feldman and Glen R. Elliott, 93–122. Cambridge, Mass., 1990.

Modell, John, et al. "Social Change and Transitions to Adulthood in Historical Perspective." In *The American Family in Social-Historical Perspective*, edited by Michael Gordon, 2d ed., 192–219. New York, 1978.

Monkkonen, Eric H. *America Becomes Urban: The Development of U.S. Cities and Towns, 1780–1980*. Berkeley, Calif., 1988.

———. *The Dangerous Class: Crime and Poverty in Columbus, Ohio, 1860–1885*. Cambridge, Mass., 1975.

Moody, Samuel. *The Vain Youth Summoned to Appear before Christ's Bar*. Boston, 1707.

Moran, Gerald F. "Adolescence in Colonial America." In *Encyclopedia of Adolescence*, edited by Richard M. Lerner, Anne C. Petersen, and Jeanne Brooks-Gunn, 1:157–71. New York, 1991.

———. "Christian Revivalism and Culture in Early America." In *Modern Christian Revivals*, edited by Randall Balmer. Urbana, Ill., forthcoming.

————. "Conditions of Religious Conversion in the First Society of Norwich, Connecticut, 1718–1744." *Journal of Social History* 5 (1972): 331–43.

————. "'The Hidden Ones': Women and Religion in Puritan New England." In *Triumph over Silence: Women in Protestant History,* edited by Richard L. Greaves, 125–49. Westport, Conn., 1985.

————. "The Puritan Saint: Religious Experience, Church Membership, and Piety in Connecticut, 1636–1776." Ph.D. diss., Rutgers University, 1974.

————. "Religious Renewal, Puritan Tribalism, and the Family in Seventeenth-Century Milford, Connecticut." *William and Mary Quarterly,* 3d ser., 36 (1979): 236–54.

————. "'Sinners Are Turned into Saints in Numbers': Puritanism and Revivalism in Colonial Connecticut." In *Belief and Behavior: The New Religious History,* edited by Phil VanderMeer and Robert Swierenga, 38–62. New Brunswick, N.J., 1991.

Morgan, Edmund S. *American Slavery, American Freedom.* New York, 1975.

————. "New England Puritanism: Another Approach." *William and Mary Quarterly,* 3d ser., 18 (1961): 236–42.

————. *The Puritan Family: Religion and Domestic Relations in Seventeenth-Century New England.* Rev. ed. New York, 1966.

————. *Virginians at Home: Family Life in the Eighteenth Century.* Williamsburg, Va., 1952.

————. *Visible Saints: The History of a Puritan Idea.* New York, 1963.

Morley, John. *Death, Heaven and the Victorians.* Pittsburgh, Pa., 1971.

Morrison, W. Douglas. *Juvenile Offenders.* New York, 1897.

Murphy, Geraldine J. "Massachusetts Bay Colony: The Role of Government in Education." Ph.D. diss., Radcliffe College, 1960.

Murphy, T. R. "'Woful Childe of Parents Rage': Suicide of Children and Adolescents in Early Modern England, 1507–1710." *Sixteenth-Century Journal* 17 (1986): 259–70.

Murrin, John. "Review Essay." *History and Theory* 11 (1972): 226–75.

Nagera, Humberto. "Children's Reactions to the Death of Important Objects: A Developmental Approach." *Psychoanalytic Study of the Child* 25 (1970): 360–400.

Nash, Gary B. *The Urban Crucible: Social Change, Political Consciousness, and the Origins of the American Revolution.* Cambridge, Mass., 1979.

Needham, A. C. "Random Notes on Funeral Rings." *Old Time New England* 39 (1949): 93–97.

Niebuhr, H. Richard. *The Social Sources of Denominationalism.* 1929. Reprint. New York, 1968.

Norton, Susan L. "Population Growth in Colonial America: A Study of Ipswich, Massachusetts." *Population Studies* 25 (1971): 433–52.

O'Connor, Mary Catharine. *The Art of Dying Well: The Development of the Ars Moriendi.* New York, 1942.

Onuf, Peter S. "New Lights in New London: A Group Portrait of the Separatists." *William and Mary Quarterly,* 3d ser., 37 (1980): 627–43.

Osterweis, Marian, Frederic Solomon, and Morris Green, eds. *Bereavement: Reactions, Consequences, and Care.* Washington, D.C., 1984.

Parker, Edwin P. *History of the Second Church of Christ in Hartford.* Hartford, Conn., 1892.

Pease, Zepharriah, ed. *The Diary of Samuel Rodman: A New Bedford Chronicle of Thirty-Seven Years: 1821–1859.* New Bedford, Mass., 1927.

Perlmann, Joel, and Dennis Shirley. "When Did New England Women Acquire Literacy?" *William and Mary Quarterly,* 3d ser., 48 (1991): 50–67.

Philips, Samuel. *Advice to a Child: Or, Young People Solemnly Warn'd Both against Enticing and Consenting When Enticed to Sin.* Boston, 1729.

Pickett, Robert S. *House of Refuge: Origins of Juvenile Reform in New York State, 1815–1857.* Syracuse, N.Y., 1969.

Pierce, Richard D., ed. "Records of the First Church in Boston, 1630–1868." Colonial Society of Massachusetts, *Publications* 39 (1961): 13–98.

———, ed. *Records of the First Church in Salem, Massachusetts, 1629–1736.* Salem, Mass., 1974.

Platt, Anthony M. *The Child Savers: The Invention of Delinquency.* 2d ed. Chicago, 1977.

Pomfret, John E. *Founding the American Colonies, 1583–1660.* New York, 1970.

Pope, Charles, ed. *Records of the First Church at Dorchester in New England, 1636–1734.* Boston, 1891.

Pope, Robert G. *The Half-Way Covenant: Church Membership in Puritan New England.* Princeton, N.J., 1969.

———. "New England versus the New England Mind: The Myth of Declension." *Journal of Social History* 3 (1969): 95–99.

Proefrock, D. W. "Adolescence: Social Fact and Psychological Concept." *Adolescence* 16 (1981): 851–58.

Prudden, Lillian E. *Peter Prudden: A Story of His Life at New Haven and Milford, Connecticut.* New Haven, Conn., 1901.

Ramsbottom, Mary MacManus. "Religious Society and the Family in Charlestown, Massachusetts, 1630–1740." Ph.D. diss., Yale University, 1987.

Range, Jane, and Maris A. Vinovskis. "Images of the Elderly in Popular Literature: A Content Analysis of Littell's Living Age, 1845–1880." *Social Science History* 5 (1981): 123–70.

Rennie, Y. *The Search for Criminal Man: A Conceptual History of the Dangerous Offender.* Lexington, Mass., 1978.

Richardson, R. C. *Puritanism in North-west England: A Regional Study of the Diocese of Chester to 1642.* Manchester, Eng., 1972.

Rorabaugh, W. J. *The Craft Apprentice: From Franklin to the Machine Age in America.* New York, 1986.

Rose, Anne C. "Social Sources of Denominationalism Reconsidered: Post-Revolutionary Boston as a Case Study." *American Quarterly* 38 (1986): 243–64.

Rosenberg, Charles E. *No Other Gods: On Science and American Social Thought.* Baltimore, 1976.

Rosenkrantz, Barbara G., and Maris A. Vinovskis. "The Invisible Lunatics: Old Age and Insanity in Mid Nineteenth-Century Massachusetts." In *Aging and the Elderly: Humanistic Perspectives in Gerontology,* edited by S. F. Spicker et al., 95–125. Atlantic Highlands, N.J., 1978.

———. "'Sustaining the Flickering Flame of Life': Accountability and Culpability for Death in Ante-Bellum Massachusetts Asylums." In *Health Care in America: Essays in Social History,* edited by Susan Reverby and David Rosner, 155–82. Philadelphia, 1979.

Ross, Dorothy. *G. Stanley Hall: The Psychologist as Prophet.* Chicago, 1972.

Royster, Charles. *A Revolutionary People at War: The Continental Army and American Character, 1775–1783.* Chapel Hill, N.C., 1979.

Rush, Benjamin. *Thoughts upon the Mode of Education Proper in a Republic.* In *Essays on Education in the Early Republic,* edited by Frederick Rudolph. Cambridge, Mass., 1965.

Rutman, Darrett B. *American Puritanism.* New York, 1970.

———. "Community Study." *Historical Methods* 13 (1980): 29–41.

———. "God's Bridge Falling Down: 'Another Approach' to New England Puritanism Assayed." *William and Mary Quarterly,* 3d ser., 19 (1962): 408–21.

Rutman, Darrett B., and Anita H. Rutman. "Of Agues and Fevers: Malaria in the Early Chesapeake." *William and Mary Quarterly,* 3d ser., 33 (1976): 31–60.

———. "'Now-Wives and Sons-in-Law': Parental Death in a Seventeenth-Century Virginia County." In *The Chesapeake in the Seventeenth Century: Essays on Anglo-American Society,* edited by Thad W. Tate and David L. Ammerman, 153–82. Chapel Hill, N.C., 1979.

———. *A Place in Time: Middlesex County, Virginia: 1650–1750.* New York, 1984.

Ryan, Mary P. *Cradle of the Middle Class: The Family in Oneida County, New York, 1790–1865.* New York, 1981.

Sanders, W. B., ed. *Juvenile Offenders for a Thousand Years: Selected Readings from Anglo-Saxon Times to 1900.* Chapel Hill, N.C., 1970.

Saum, Lewis O. "Death in the Popular Mind of Pre–Civil War America." *American Quarterly* 26 (1974): 477–95.

Schlossman, Steven L. *Love and the American Delinquent: The Theory and Practice of "Progressive" Juvenile Justice, 1825–1920.* Chicago, 1977.

Schmotter, James W. "Ministerial Careers in Eighteenth-Century New England: The Social Context, 1700–1760." *Journal of Social History* 9 (1975): 249–67.

———. "Provincial Professionalism: The New England Ministry, 1692–1745." Ph.D. diss., Northwestern University, 1973.

Scholten, Catherine M. *Childbearing in American Society, 1650–1850.* New York, 1985.

Schultz, Ronald. "Printers' Devils: The Decline of Apprenticeship in America." *Reviews in American History* 15 (1987): 226–31.

Schultz, Stanley K. *The Culture Factory: Boston Public Schools, 1789–1860.* New York, 1973.

Scott, Donald M. *From Office to Profession: The New England Ministry, 1750–1850.* Philadelphia, 1978.

Selement, George. *Keepers of the Vineyard: The Puritan Ministry and Collective Culture in Colonial New England.* Lanham, Md., 1984.

Sharpe, J. A. *Crime in Early Modern England, 1550–1750.* London, 1984.

Shaw, William H. *History of Essex and Hudson Counties, New Jersey.* Philadelphia, 1884.

Sheils, Richard D. "The Feminization of American Congregationalism, 1730–1835." *American Quarterly* 33 (1981): 46–62.

Shepherd, James F. *The Economic Rise of Early America.* New York, 1979.

Shipton, C. K. "The New England Clergy of the 'Glacial Age.'" *Colonial Society of Massachusetts, Publications* 32 (1933): 24–54.

Shipton, C. K., and J. L. Sibley. *Sibley's Harvard Graduates.* 16 vols. Cambridge, Mass., 1873–1972.

Shively, Charles Allen. "A History of the Conception of Death in America, 1650–1860." Ph.D. diss., Harvard University, 1969.

Shuffelton, Frank. *Thomas Hooker, 1586–1647.* Princeton, N.J., 1977.

Sigourney, Lydia H. *Letters to Mothers.* Hartford, Conn., 1838.

Slack, Paul. *Poverty and Policy in Tudor and Stuart England.* London, 1988.

Slater, Peter Gregg. *Children in the New England Mind: In Death and in Life.* Hamden, Conn., 1977.

Sloane, David Charles. *The Last Great Necessity: Cemeteries in American History.* Baltimore, 1991.

Smith, Daniel Blake. *Inside the Great House: Planter Family Life in Eighteenth-Century Chesapeake Society.* Ithaca, N.Y., 1980.

————. "The Study of the Family in Early America: Trends, Problems, and Prospects." *William and Mary Quarterly*, 3d ser., 39 (1982): 3–28.

Smith, Daniel Scott. "The Demographic History of Colonial New England." Reprinted in *Studies in American Historical Demography*, edited by Maris A. Vinovskis, 27–45. New York, 1972.

————. "Old Age and the 'Great Transformation': A New England Case Study." In *Aging and the Elderly: Humanistic Perspectives in Gerontology*, edited by S. F. Spicker et al., 285–302. Atlantic Highlands, N.J., 1978.

————. "Parental Power and Marriage Patterns: An Analysis of Historical Trends in Hingham, Massachusetts." *Journal of Marriage and the Family* 35 (1973): 422–24.

Smith, Daniel Scott, and Michael S. Hindus. "Premarital Pregnancy in America, 1640–1971: An Overview and Interpretation." *Journal of Interdisciplinary History* 5 (1975): 537–70.

Smith, Steven R. "The London Apprentices as Seventeenth-Century Adolescents." *Past and Present* 61 (1973): 149–61.

————. "Religion and the Conception of Youth in Seventeenth-Century England." *History of Childhood Quarterly* 2 (1974): 493–516.

Smith, Timothy L. "Congregation, State, and Denomination: The Forming of American Religious Structure." *William and Mary Quarterly*, 3d ser., 25 (1968): 155–76.

————. "Religion and Ethnicity in America." *American Historical Review* 83 (1978): 1155–85.

Smith, Wilson, ed. *Theories of Education in Early America, 1655–1819*. Indianapolis, 1973.

Smith-Rosenberg, Carroll. *Disorderly Conduct: Visions of Gender in Victorian America*. New York, 1985.

Soltow, Lee, and Edward Stevens. *The Rise of Literacy and the Common School in the United States: A Socioeconomic Analysis to 1870*. Chicago, 1981.

Sommerville, C. John. *The Rise and Fall of Childhood*. Beverly Hills, Calif., 1982.

Spufford, Margaret. "First Steps in Literacy: The Reading and Writing Experiences of the Humblest Seventeenth-Century Spiritual Autobiographers." *Social History* 4 (1979): 407–35.

Stannard, David E. "Death and Dying in Puritan New England." *American Historical Review* 78 (1973): 1305–30.

————. "Death and the Puritan Child." In *Death in America*, edited by Stannard, 9–29. Philadelphia, 1975.

————. *The Puritan Way of Death: A Study in Religion, Culture, and Social Change*. New York, 1977.

Stewart, G. *A History of Religious Education to the Middle of the Nineteenth Century*. New Haven, Conn., 1924.

Stiles, Henry. *The History and Genealogies of Ancient Windsor, Connecticut.* 2 vols. New York, 1859.

Stockwell, Edward G. *Population and People.* Chicago, 1968.

Stoddard, Solomon. *The Efficacy of the Fear of Hell to Restrain Men from Sin.* Boston, 1713.

Stone, Lawrence. *The Crisis of the Aristocracy, 1558–1641.* Abr. ed. New York, 1967.

———. *The Family, Sex, and Marriage in England, 1500–1800.* New York, 1977.

———. *The Past and the Present.* London, 1981.

Stott, Richard B. *Workers in the Metropolis: Class, Ethnicity, and Youth in Antebellum New York City.* Ithaca, N.Y., 1990.

Stout, Harry S. "The Great Awakening in New England Reconsidered: The New England Clergy as a Case Study." *Journal of Social History* 8 (1974): 21–47.

———. *The New England Soul: Preaching and Religious Culture in Colonial New England.* New York, 1986.

———. "University Men in New England, 1620–1660: A Demographic Analysis." *Journal of Interdisciplinary History* 4 (1974): 375–400.

Tashjian, Dickran. "Puritan Attitudes toward Iconoclasm." *Annual Proceedings of the Dublin Seminar for New England Folklife (1978): Puritan Gravestone Art,* 2:37–45. Boston, 1979.

Tashjian, Dickran, and Ann Tashjian. *Memorials for Children of Change: The Art of Early New England Stonecarving.* Middletown, Conn., 1974.

Teeter, R. "The Travails of Nineteenth-Century Urban Youth as a Precondition to the Invention of Modern Adolescence." *Adolescence* 23 (1988): 15–18.

Thompson, Roger. *Sex in Middlesex: Popular Mores in a Massachusetts County, 1649–1699.* Amherst, Mass., 1986.

———. *Women in Stuart England and America: A Comparative Study.* Boston, 1974.

Thompson, Warren S., and P. K. Whelpton. *Population Trends in the United States.* New York, 1933.

Todd, Margo. "Humanists, Puritans, and the Spiritualized Household." *Church History* 49 (1980): 18–34.

Tolles, Frederick B. *Meeting House and Counting House: The Quaker Merchants of Colonial Philadelphia, 1682–1763.* Chapel Hill, N.C., 1948.

Tracy, Patricia J. *Jonathan Edwards, Pastor: Religion and Society in Eighteenth-Century Northampton.* New York, 1980.

Trattner, Walter I. *From Poor Law to Welfare State: A History of Social Welfare in America.* 4th ed. New York, 1989.

Travis, Thomas. *The Young Malefactor.* New York, 1908.

Trousdale, David Mark. "Society and Culture, Order and Change in Early America: The Sociology of Edmund S. Morgan." Ph.D. diss., Case Western Reserve, 1976.

Trumbull, J. H., and C. J. Hoadly, eds. *The Public Records of the Colony of Connecticut.* 15 vols. Hartford, 1850–90.

Uhlenberg, Peter. "Changing Configurations of the Life Course." In *Transitions: The Family and the Life Course in Historical Perspective,* edited by Tamara K. Hareven, 65–97. New York, 1978.

Ulrich, Laurel Thatcher. *Good Wives: Image and Reality in the Lives of Women in Northern New England, 1650–1750.* New York, 1982.

———. " 'The Living Mother of a Living Child': Midwifery and Mortality in Post-Revolutionary New England." *William and Mary Quarterly,* 3d ser., 46 (1989): 27–48.

———. "Vertuous Women Found: New England Ministerial Literature, 1668–1735." *American Quarterly* 28 (1976): 20–40.

Vann, Richard T. *The Social Development of English Quakerism, 1655–1755.* Cambridge, Mass., 1969.

———. "The Youth of Centuries of Childhood." *History and Theory* 21 (1982): 279–97.

Vaughan, Alden T. *New England Frontier: Puritans and Indians, 1620–1675.* Boston, 1965.

Vernon, Glen M. *Sociology of Death: An Analysis of Death-related Behavior.* New York, 1970.

Vinovskis, Maris A. "Aging and the Transition from Permanency to Transiency among New Hampshire Congregational and Presbyterian Ministers, 1633–1849." In *Historical Demography of Aging,* edited by David Kertzer. Forthcoming.

———. "American Historical Demography: A Review Essay." *Historical Methods Newsletter* 4 (1971): 141–48.

———. "Death and Family Life in the Past." *Human Nature* 1 (1990): 109–22.

———. *An "Epidemic" of Adolescent Pregnancy? Some Historical and Policy Perspectives.* New York, 1988.

———. "Estimating the Wealth of Americans on the Eve of the Revolution." *Journal of Economic History* 41 (1981): 415–20.

———. "From Household Size to the Life Course: Some Observations on Recent Trends in Family History." *American Behavioral Scientist* 21 (1977): 263–87.

———. "Kübler-Ross and the Five Stages of Dying: Some Methodological and Conceptual Reservations." *Proceedings of the World Conference on Records* 3 (1981), ser. 328: 1–20.

———. "Mortality Rates and Trends in Massachusetts before 1860." *Journal of Economic History* 32 (1972): 184–213.

————. "A Multivariate Regression Analysis of Fertility Differentials among Massachusetts Towns and Regions in 1860." In *Historical Studies of Changing Fertility*, edited by Charles Tilly, 225–56. Princeton, N.J., 1978.

————. "Recent Trends in American Historical Demography: Some Methodological and Conceptual Considerations." *Annual Review of Sociology* 4 (1978): 603–27.

————. Review of *The Hour of Our Death*, by Phillipe Ariès. In *Journal of Social History* 16 (1982–83): 129–31.

————. "The 1789 Life Table of Edward Wigglesworth." *Journal of Economic History* 31 (1971): 570–90.

————, ed. *Studies in American Historical Demography.* New York, 1979.

Wadsworth, Benjamin. *A Course of Sermons on Early Piety.* Boston, 1721.

————. *The Well-Ordered Family.* Boston, 1712.

Walker, Williston. *The Creeds and Platforms of Congregatinalism.* 2d ed. 1893. Reprint. Boston, 1969.

Walsh, James. "The Great Awakening in the First Congregational Church of Woodbury, Connecticut." *William and Mary Quarterly,* 3d ser., 28 (1971): 543–62.

Walsh, Lorena S. "'Till Death Us Do Part': Marriage and Family in Seventeenth-Century Maryland." In *The Chesapeake in the Seventeenth Century: Essays on Anglo-American Society,* edited by Thad W. Tate and David L. Ammerman, 126–52. Chapel Hill, N.C., 1979.

Walsh, Lorena S., and Russell R. Menard. "Death in the Chesapeake: Two Life Tables for Men in Early Colonial Maryland." *Maryland Historical Magazine* 69 (1974): 211–27.

Walton, Gary M., and James F. Shepherd. *The Economic Rise of Early America.* Cambridge, 1979.

Webb, John. *The Young Man's Duty Explained and Pressed upon Him.* Boston, 1718.

Webber, Thomas L. *Deep Like the Rivers: Education in the Slave Quarter Community, 1831–1865.* New York, 1978.

Weber, Max. *The Sociology of Religion,* edited by Talcott Parsons. Boston, 1963.

Welch, Richard. "Colonial and Federal New York and New Jersey Gravestones." *Journal of Long Island History* 17 (1981): 23–34.

Wells, Robert V. "Illegitimacy and Bridal Pregnancy in Colonial America." In *Bastardy and Its Comparative History,* edited by Peter Laslett et al., 349–61. Cambridge, Mass., 1980.

————. *Revolution in Americans' Lives: A Demographic Perspective on the History of Americans, Their Families, and Their Society.* Westport, Conn., 1982.

Welter, Barbara. "The Cult of True Womanhood: 1820–1860." *American Quarterly* 18 (1966): 151–74.

―――. "The Feminization of American Religion, 1800–1860." In *Dimity Convictions,* edited by Welter, 83–102. Athens, Ga., 1976.

White, Elizabeth. *The Experiences of God's Gracious Dealings with Mrs. Elizabeth White. As they were written under her own Hand, and found in her Closet after her Decease, December 5, 1669.* Boston, 1741.

Wigglesworth, Edward. "A Table Shewing the Probability of the Duration, the Decrement, and the Expectation of Life, in the States of Massachusetts and New Hampshire, formed from sixty two Bills of Mortality on the files of the American Academy of Arts and Sciences, in the Year 1789." *Memoirs of the American Academy of Arts and Sciences,* vol. 2, pt. 1 (1793): 131–35.

Willard, Samuel. *A Complete Body of Divinity on Two Hundred and Fifty Expository Lectures on the Assembly's Shorter Catechism.* Boston, 1726.

Willingham, William F. "Religious Conversion in the Second Society of Windham, Connecticut, 1723–1743: A Case Study." *Societas* 6 (1976): 109–19.

Winslow, Ola L. *Meetinghouse Hill, 1630–1783.* New York, 1952.

Withey, L. *Urban Growth in Colonial Rhode Island: Newport and Providence in the Eighteenth Century.* Albany, N.Y., 1984.

Wohl, R. Richard. "The 'Country Boy' Myth and Its Place in America Urban Culture: The Nineteeth-Century Contribution." *Perspectives in American History* 3 (1969): 77–156.

Wolfenstein, Martha. "How Is Mourning Possible?" *Psychoanalytic Study of the Child* 21 (1966): 93–123.

Wrigley, E. A. *Population and History.* New York, 1969.

Wrigley, E. A., and R. S. Schofield. *The Population History of England, 1541–1871: A Reconstruction.* Cambridge, Mass., 1981.

Yarborough, Anne. "Apprentices as Adolescents in Sixteenth Century Bristol." *Journal of Social History* 13 (1979): 67–81.

Yasuba, Yasukichi. *Birth Rates of the White Population in the United States, 1800–1860: An Economic Study.* Baltimore, 1962.

Yazawa, Melvin. *From Colonies to Commonwealth: Familial Ideology and the Beginnings of the American Republic.* Baltimore, 1985.

Youings, Joyce. *Sixteenth-Century England.* New York, 1984.

Youngs, J. William T., Jr. *God's Messengers: Religious Leadership in Colonial New England, 1700–1750.* Baltimore, 1976.

Zuckerman, Michael. *Peaceable Kingdoms: New England Towns in the Eighteenth Century.* New York, 1970.

―――. "Rejoinder." *William and Mary Quarterly,* 3d ser., 29 (1972): 467–68.

Index

257